23 November 2005

The Death and Resurrection of Jefferson Davis

The Death and Resurrection of Jefferson Davis

Donald E. Collins

ROWMAN & LITTLEFIELD PUBLISHERS, INC.
Lanham • Boulder • New York • Toronto • Oxford

ROWMAN & LITTLEFIELD PUBLISHERS, INC.

Published in the United States of America
by Rowman & Littlefield Publishers, Inc.
A wholly owned subsidiary of The Rowman & Littlefield Publishing Group, Inc.
4501 Forbes Boulevard, Suite 200, Lanham, Maryland 20706
www.rowmanlittlefield.com

PO Box 317
Oxford
OX2 9RU, UK

Distributed by National Book Network

British Library Cataloguing in Publication Information Available

Library of Congress Cataloging-in-Publication Data

Collins, Donald E.
   The death and resurrection of Jefferson Davis / Donald E. Collins.
      p. cm.
   Includes bibliographical references and index.
   ISBN 0-7425-4304-8 (alk. paper)
   1. Davis, Jefferson, 1808–1889—Travel—Southern States. 2. Davis, Jefferson,
1808–1889—death and burial. 3. Davis, Jefferson, 1808–1889—Monuments. 4.
Presidents—Confederate States of America—Biography. 5. Statesmen—United States—
Biography. I. Title.
   E467.1.D26C65 2005
   973.7'13'092—dc22

                                                2004022267

Printed in the United States of America

♾️™ The paper used in this publication meets the minimum requirements of
American National Standard for Information Sciences—Permanence of Paper
for Printed Library Materials, ANSI/NISO Z39.48-1992.

Dedicated to my wife Fay
and children, Sean, Charles, and Frances,
and to my brother Gene and
sisters Evelyn, Eileen, Dorothy, and Helen

Contents

Foreword

$\mathcal{J}$efferson Davis's life reads like a roller coaster. Starting at the bottom as the son of a moderately successful planter in Kentucky, he rose steadily via a career in the army and Congress to a national reputation that brought him intersectional support for the presidency of the United States. The roller coaster moved downward as he assumed the impossible role of president of the Confederate States of America and reached its lowest point at the Civil War's conclusion, with him in shackles and chains, imprisoned in Fort Monroe. From there his roller-coaster life began a slow but steady rise, reaching a pinnacle shortly before his death, in which he was recognized by his fellow white southerners as one of the three most important leading men of the southern states.

This book began more than a decade ago on the chance discovery of several May 1893 issues of the *Wilmington (N.C.) Messenger* that told in great detail of the procession of Jefferson Davis's remains across the South, their lying in state in southern capitals, and their eventual reinterment in Richmond, Virginia, the former capital of the Confederacy. This serendipitous find resulted in the writing of an unpublished paper titled "The Second Funeral of Jefferson Davis." Its delivery at the Citadel Conference on the South on April 6, 2000, in Charleston, South Carolina, led to an interest in further research to place into perspective the reburial of the Confederate president more than three years after his death. The result is this book.

The real interest in the death, burial, and reburial of Jefferson Davis lies less in the story of those events themselves and more in how the people of the United States—northerners, southerners, blacks, and whites—viewed the man himself. The real intent of this work is to tell the story of the resurrection of Davis in the eyes of his fellow southerners following his fall from grace and how he was viewed in the eyes of his fellow countrymen. This aspect of the Civil War leader has until now never been told in book form and, in essence, completes those earlier biographies that assumed that his biography ended with his death.

I would like to recognize the help and encouragement of four persons for the help and encouragement they gave to me that ultimately brought this work to completion: Matt Hershey of Scholarly Resources, who suggested that an essay be turned into book form; Steven Woodworth, for his encouragement and patience; my wife, Fay, for putting up with the long months spent in research and writing; and, last but not least, Wade Dudley of East Carolina University, who read every word and helped make this book better than it otherwise would have been.

Jefferson Davis: American, Confederate, and Man without a Country

$\mathcal{B}$iographies normally end with a person's death. This rule is as true for Confederate President Jefferson Davis as for any other important figure in American history. Yet it may be argued that biographies of Davis come up short. While it is true that he died on December 6, 1889, his body remained aboveground for three and a half years in a temporary vault in Metairie Cemetery near New Orleans, Louisiana, awaiting a decision by his wife, Varina Howell Davis, on the location of a final resting site. The continuing presence of his unburied body had an enormous impact on the South and the nation at large. Davis's body may have been lifeless, but he remained the subject of continuous discourse and debate, pro and con, until his remains were placed in their permanent grave in the old Confederate capital of Richmond, Virginia, in May 1893.

Davis in death was still a person to be reckoned with. In the South, he received a resurrection in public feeling that rose to the stage of near adulation during the final three years of his life and would grow during the three years following his death to place him in the ranks of such Confederate icons as the beloved military heroes Robert E. Lee and Stonewall Jackson. This book, in effect, brings the incomplete biographies of Jefferson Davis to a final and logical conclusion.

The question is, How did Jefferson Davis attain such an exalted status in death? Just twenty-four years earlier, he had been a defeated man, imprisoned in Fort Monroe, Virginia, shackled and cut off from all contact with friends, wife, and children, awaiting trial for treason and complicity in the assassination of President Abraham Lincoln. There seemed to be no hope of redemption. For the remainder of his life, he was destined to be a man without a country, deprived of civil and political rights by the government he had fought against.

1

Davis's downfall came with his decision in 1861 to accept the presidency of the newly formed Confederate States of America. In accepting the position, he gave up a career in national politics in which even the presidency of the United States was potentially in sight. Prior to 1861, he had been a spokesman for his native South, a slaveholder, and an outspoken proponent of states' rights although still a nationalist opposed to secession unless as a last resort. As secretary of state, he improved and modernized the army that he would soon fight against. Popular in both North and South, his name had been placed in nomination for president at the Democratic National Convention in Baltimore by none other than Massachusetts senator and soon-to-be Union general Benjamin Butler. His was a career with promise that was crushed by the Civil War.

In looking at Jefferson Davis's rise to the presidency of the southern Confederacy, it is convenient to briefly examine those things that brought him to that position. For this purpose, his life may be examined in three easily definable parts: planter/slaveholder, soldier, and politician. One final element should also be considered for its role in Davis's ability to function as politician and president of the Confederacy. It is arguable that much of the criticism placed on Davis by contemporary critics and postwar historians could be attributed, at least in part, to his personality, which was affected to some extent by the lifelong bouts of ill health that incapacitated him and brought him near death on several occasions. That Davis suffered extreme stress from physical problems undoubtedly affected his actions as president of the Confederacy.

JEFFERSON DAVIS, PLANTER AND SLAVE OWNER

Jefferson Davis's views on slavery and race differed significantly from customary practice in the slaveholding states. These two aspects of his life are seldom isolated for comparison and are generally buried within book-length biographies. Yet it was his publicly expounded views on these subjects that allowed him to rise in the Senate as a spokesman for states' rights and slavery and that ultimately led him to be chosen for the presidency of the revolutionary republic devoted to the continuation of slavery and white supremacy. Even while preaching the rightness of slavery and the superiority of whites over blacks and fighting a war to ensure their preservation, he had a more humane or enlightened side that allowed him to treat some blacks as friends and, in 1863, to become the adoptive father of a homeless free black boy, Jim Limber, who was taken into the Davis family and Confederate White House on an equal footing with his own children.[1]

Davis believed firmly in slavery and the inferiority of African Americans. He remained consistent in these views throughout his life. Concerning the latter, his opinion was commonly shared by white Americans, North and South. Exceptions were relatively rare. In this respect, he differed little from his Civil War adversary and fellow Kentuckian Abraham Lincoln. Yet when the issue went beyond racial superiority to slavery, the two men were diametrically opposed. On a personal level, Davis's relationship with African Americans was often intimate, fair, and friendly. Little is known of Lincoln's personal contacts with the opposite race. Where Lincoln wished to abolish slavery, Davis "defended slavery as moral and as a social good, and fought a great war to maintain it."[2] But his views on black bondage were not considered radical for his time and section. While publicly espousing support for slavery and white supremacy, Davis built a reputation as a moderate nationalist with intersectional support that would end only with actual warfare between North and South in 1861.

Acceptance of the rightness and morality of slavery came naturally to Davis, who was born into a slaveholding family. His father, Samuel Davis, a native of Georgia, held a small number of slaves, working alongside them on his small Kentucky farm. Following his marriage in 1835 to Sarah Knox Taylor, daughter of future president Zachary Taylor, Jefferson Davis moved to Mississippi to live the life of a southern planter. Although these plans were interrupted by the untimely death of his wife after only three months of marriage and a recuperating stay in Cuba for his health, he created a plantation amid the briers on Davis Bend, a small peninsula formed by the Mississippi River, appropriately named Brierfield. This was adjacent to the larger Hurricane plantation of his older brother and surrogate father, Joseph.

Until he became a planter, Davis had only one slave, James Pemberton, whom he inherited from his father and who remained with him until Pemberton's death. Pemberton, when given an opportunity for freedom should his master die before him, chose to remain in the service of Davis's widow and only then take freedom. Their relationship was a close one of mutual respect and even friendship.[3] By 1836, Jefferson owned twenty-three slaves, with that number eventually increasing to forty or more. Pemberton became his trusted overseer and plantation manager.

It is difficult to separate for discussion the plantations of Jefferson and Joseph Davis because of the close personal and family relationship of the brothers and the geographic proximity of their plantations, Joseph often looking out for the interests of the former during his frequent, often lengthy absences. It is said that the elder Davis brother held a utopian view of slavery in which slaves received far more humane treatment and greater freedom than on the great majority of plantations. Neighbors were said to have joked about "Mr. [Joseph]

Davis' free Negroes" and how he would have to have the cotton rows widened to accommodate the pickers' hoopskirts.[4] While more is known about Joseph's system of slavery, it is evident that Jefferson Davis followed his brother's line of reasoning.

Thus, while holding views on race and slavery that were consistent with most in the slaveholding southern states, the brothers ran plantations in which slaves were treated as humanely as possible while still not being free. Some level of literacy was accepted, with both plantations being administered by trusted, literate slaves—Pemberton on Brierfield and Benjamin Montgomery on Hurricane. Slaves, at least in particular cases, were treated with dignity. This is particularly true with Pemberton, whom he considered a friend, and Montgomery, with whom he corresponded when he, Davis, was in Washington. Slaves had better and larger houses than normal, a hospital was built and doctors looked after their health, and they were given garden plots and allowed to raise vegetables and chickens that they could sell for their own profit. A church was constructed for religious needs, with Baptists and Methodists rotating on a two-week schedule. A court system was established in which slaves acted as judges and juries. When penalties were too harsh, they were sometimes ameliorated by the Davises. The brothers referred to their bondsmen not as slaves but as "our people," a term that was certain to ease their own minds if not those of their slaves.[5] Years later, after Davis's death, one of his slaves was asked how he felt about his old master. "That I loved him," he said, "and I can say that every colored man he ever owned loved him."[6]

This apparent dichotomy of views and practices on slavery and race would affect public opinion on Jefferson Davis throughout his life and follow him even after death. As he moved from planter to politician, his advocacy of slavery played well with the white South. But with the end of slavery following the Civil War, Davis the man would retain the love, affection, and even fierce loyalty of at least some of the family slaves up to and after his death, while Davis the proslavery senator and Confederate president engendered great hostility among most freedmen and many northern whites.

JEFFERSON DAVIS, SOLDIER

While it was life on family plantations and personal ownership of slaves that helped shape the political and social views that propelled Jefferson Davis to the political heights, it was success as an officer in the Mexican War of 1846–1848 that enabled his rise in politics. His early military experiences made him an unlikely candidate for a military career of any substance. He only reluctantly entered the U.S. Military Academy at West Point, New York, in 1824 at the age of sixteen to please his brother Joseph, at that time a wealthy lawyer and planter of substance in Mississippi. His four years at the academy were less than spectacular. His grades were low, his demerits were many, and he clearly made little effort to abide by the rules governing the conduct of the cadet corps. On three occasions, his escapades threatened his dismissal from West Point, although only one resulted in court-martial charges being brought. He graduated in 1828, ranked twenty-third out of a class of thirty-three. On the positive side, he made friends on whom he would rely when the Civil War came.[7]

Jefferson Davis spent the following six and a half years after graduating from West Point in the army, rising only to the rank of first lieutenant. The army was small, with a force of less than six thousand men, most of whom were assigned to isolated frontier outposts to protect settlers from the Indians. Davis spent the years in what are now the states of Missouri, Iowa, Illinois, Michigan, Wisconsin, and Arkansas, where he proved his courage and ability to calm tense situations between Indians and settlers. In 1829, he spent three days without food and much of the time without water while traversing the wilderness of frontier Illinois to the small settlement of Chicago.[8] In 1831, he used personality and persuasion to prevent hostility between miners and Indians near what would become Dubuque, Iowa. Whether Davis actually saw combat during this period is open to question. Home on leave during most of the Black Hawk War of 1832, he returned to duty in time for the Battle of Bad Axe. Despite the lack of historical evidence of his participation in the battle, there is little reason to doubt Davis's claim of involvement.[9]

Regardless of the question relating to the previously mentioned battle, Davis concluded the war with a singularly significant role. The young first lieutenant was assigned to lead a detachment to take the defeated Chief Black Hawk and one hundred other captives to Jefferson Barracks, Missouri. Davis admired the Indian chief and saw to it that he arrived at his destination without being made a public spectacle. Black Hawk reciprocated his captor's kindness in his autobiography, recalling the "good and brave young chief" who recognized "what his own feelings would have been if he had been placed in a similar situation, that we did not want to have a gaping crowd around us."[10] Davis would experience Black Hawk's predicament thirty-three years later, but with less kindness, following the Civil War as the captive of Union soldiers being transported to prison at Fort Monroe, Virginia.

Davis, who had been considering leaving the army for some time, handed in his resignation effective June 30, 1835. For the following ten years, he lived the life of a planter, during which time he married first Sarah Knox Taylor and, following her death, Varina Howell. On November 4, 1845, he was elected to the U.S. House of Representatives. He strongly favored the concept of Manifest

Destiny, and six months after entering Congress, he supported President James K. Polk's campaign to extend the country's borders by voting to declare war on Mexico on the pretext that blood had been shed on American soil by Mexican troops.

From Washington, Davis successfully campaigned to be "elected" commander of the First Mississippi Rifles, the only regiment authorized from that state by the secretary of war. In Mexico, he joined the command of his former father-in-law, General Zachary Taylor, with whom he developed a warm and close relationship. Davis proved to be a courageous leader, well liked and respected by his men. At the battles of Monterey and Buena Vista, he was fearless and aggressive in leading his men under heavy fire in nearly hopeless and dangerous situations. In the latter battle, the Mississippi Rifles suffered the heaviest casualties of any unit. In his official report, Taylor noted that

> the Mississippi riflemen, under Colonel Davis, were highly conspicuous for their gallantry and steadiness, and sustained throughout the engagement the reputation of veteran troops. Brought into action against an immensely superior force, they maintained themselves for a long time unsupported, and with heavy loss, and held an important part of the field until reinforced. Colonel Davis, though severely wounded, remained in the saddle until the close of the action. His distinguished coolness and gallantry at the head of his regiment on this day, entitle him to the particular notice of the government.[11]

Davis returned from the war enormously popular, with a national reputation as a war hero. His fame resulted in promotion to the rank of brigadier general in the U.S. Army on February 23, 1847, although he turned it down on principle, arguing it a violation of states' rights for an official in the national government to appoint officers in a state regiment. Because the Mississippi Rifles were state troops, he reasoned, they had a right to be under state, not national, officers. If he accepted the rank, his regiment would lose its "distinctive character [as] State troops." This was, according to Davis's wife Varina, "his first sacrifice to State rights."[12] Regardless of this decision, his newly won reputation made him the obvious choice to fill the senate seat vacated by the death of Mississippi Senator Jesse Speight. The following year, the Mississippi legislature confirmed the appointment by electing him to a full seven-year term.

NATIONALIST: SENATOR AND SECRETARY OF WAR

Jefferson Davis entered the U.S. Senate in January 1848 on the basis of the military reputation he gained in the war with Mexico. With the exception of an eighteen-month period from September 1851 into March 1853 during which he returned to Mississippi to conduct an unsuccessful campaign for governor, he was a rising star on the national scene, serving alternately as secretary of war and U.S. senator. Even the presidency of the United States was potentially within his grasp until his world began to spiral downward with the secession of Mississippi, which he felt bound to follow into the southern Confederacy.

The decade of the 1850s was a trying time for the United States and Davis. His reentry into national politics coincided with the reawakening of the slavery controversy that had enjoyed an unsettled calm following the Missouri Compromise of 1820. How he reacted to the issue would shape his political destiny. Should he join the radical southern fire-eaters who favored secession? Or should he take a moderate position, in defense of slavery and southern interests yet opposing secession and in favor of maintaining a united nation? Davis chose the latter, becoming a leader of the southern moderates.

As a states' rights Democrat, he made clear his belief that there was a constitutional right of secession. It should be used, however, only as a last resort. As with many southerners prior to the Civil War, his first loyalty was to his state—Mississippi, then to the remaining southern states that shared its culture and politics, and finally to the national government—but to the latter only so far as it did not deprive the slave states of their equality within the union.[13] Given his belief in the right of secession, Davis was still a nationalist, devoting his energies to protecting states' rights and the southern states and to keeping the nation from breaking apart.

The same year Davis entered the Senate, his friend and former father-in-law, Zachary Taylor, was elected president. The two men had been and were personally close, Taylor even advising him to choose the Senate over continuing in the army as a general. Davis's loyalty to the Democratic Party, however, would not permit him to support Taylor, a Whig, and during the presidential campaign of 1848, he worked to elect Lewis Cass in his stead. Nevertheless, with the election over, Davis became the loyal friend and confidant but still the political opponent of his friend.

One of Taylor's first actions was to recommend that California, which had been acquired only a year earlier from Mexico, should bypass the territorial stage and apply for admission as a state—a free state. With tempers rising between North and South and with threats of secession by some southern politicians, Henry Clay introduced a solution, popularly known as the Compromise of 1850. Davis became a leader in opposition, speaking against it on the day it was introduced into the Senate. The entry of California would take away the balance in the Senate between free and slave states that had existed since 1820 and would not only threaten Davis's belief in the constitutionality of slavery but also put the South and all southern issues in a minority position in the national legislature. Davis never reconciled himself to the Compromise, which he believed weakened the position of the slaveholding South in the Union.

In 1851, Davis visited Mississippi, where he became embroiled in the state's gubernatorial race. At first intending only to campaign for John A. Quitman, the party's nominee against Whig Henry Foote, he became the Democratic Party candidate when Quitman withdrew from the race. Feeling that he had to support his party, he resigned from the U.S. Senate on September 23 to devote himself to campaigning.[14] Davis lost the election, partly because of the ill health that plagued him all his life and kept him from campaigning to the fullest.

Although out of office, he remained active in state and national politics. At the Democratic National Convention of 1852, Franklin Pierce of New Hampshire and William King of Alabama were selected as the party's nominees. Although Davis did not seek or win the nomination, the Mississippi delegation put his name forward for the vice presidency. He had sufficient popularity outside the South to win votes from Illinois and New York.[15] Davis campaigned actively in Mississippi for Pierce, who won the election.

With the election over, Pierce sought Davis's advice on building a cabinet. The two men had a close relationship, with Davis advising the president throughout his four-year term. Pierce wanted a politically and geographically balanced cabinet and selected Jefferson Davis as secretary of war to represent the southern states' rights interests. The Mississippian's West Point education and regular army and Mexican War experience made him ideally suited for the post.[16]

Davis proved to be an excellent secretary of war. During his four-year administration, he took a department and military that had languished under largely do-nothing or caretaker secretaries and improved it in every respect. Characteristically, he micromanaged the department, giving careful attention to every detail. The army, with only 10,417 men, was stretched too thin to adequately perform its major mission of protecting settlers on the constantly westward-moving frontier. Inadequate transportation made it difficult to move troops in case of a military emergency and to supply isolated frontier posts. Davis saw the creation of transcontinental railroads as the solution to both problems. Survey teams were sent out to find the best routes west. In the process of facilitating the southern route that he preferred, he brought about the Gadsden Purchase, which rounded out the borders of the forty-eight contiguous states as we know them today. Intersectional rivalry in Congress prevented Davis's planned western railroad before the coming of war in 1861. A related proposal that is often looked on as a humorous curiosity was his short-lived introduction of camels for transportation in the West.

Other innovations included sending army officers to Europe to study warfare among some of the best armies in the world, adding a year onto the curriculum of the military academy at West Point, the creation of a military training manual, and technological improvements in weapons and bringing the army under civilian control. The latter brought Davis into an unseemly dispute with General Winfield Scott, who insisted that his orders came only from the president, not from the secretary of war.[17]

As secretary of war, Davis promoted his own political fortunes. He strengthened himself at home by dispensing political patronage. During a northern trip with President Pierce in 1853, he won over northern audiences in Delaware, Pennsylvania, New Jersey, and New York with politically adept speeches that flattered their home states and at the same time expounded on his constant theme of states' rights and a strict construction of the Constitution.[18]

As President Pierce's closest adviser in the cabinet, Davis became involved in major policy decisions that went beyond the scope of the War Department. The most serious of these, and the one that most affected his own destiny and that of the United States, was helping bring about passage of the Kansas–Nebraska Bill in 1854. The primary purpose of this legislation, which was introduced by Senator Stephen A. Douglas of Illinois, was to facilitate westward expansion, but it had the potential to reawaken intersectional hostilities over slavery, as it in effect abolished the now-sacred Missouri Compromise, which had kept slavery out of the northern territories. Davis, who believed the Missouri Compromise to be unconstitutional and who also favored westward expansion, used his personal influence to facilitate a meeting between the president and proponents of the legislation. In this meeting, Pierce gave the personal approval that won passage of the bill in the closely divided House of Representatives.[19] This act began the chain of events that led to the Civil War as pro- and antislavery settlers rushed into the Kansas Territory to claim it for their respective sides.

Davis's heart was in returning to the Senate. With Mississippi safely under Democratic Party control and himself as the acknowledged party leader, the legislature returned him to the seat he had vacated to enter the governor's race in 1851, his new term beginning in March 1857. On the morning of March 4, 1857, he handed in his resignation as secretary of war and immediately went down Pennsylvania Avenue to the Capitol, where he assumed his preferred position as senator from Mississippi.

Davis faced three trying years, during which he defended both the South and the nation, which were rapidly growing apart. Kansas was in turmoil over slavery, the Supreme Court's *Dred Scott* decision made slavery legal in all states and territories and inflamed the North, and John Brown's raid on Harper's Ferry in a failed attempt to create a slave insurrection infuriated southerners. On his return home prior to the opening of Congress, Davis spoke to his fellow Mississippians of the coming dangers. He pictured the Republican Party as a threat to the South and slavery and warned that 1860 would bring "the monster crisis," "the ordeal of fire."[20]

When the new congressional session convened, Davis was a consequential state, sectional, and national leader. As in the administrations of Zachary Taylor and Franklin Pierce, he was a friend and confidant of the new president, James Buchanan. Davis's picture appeared on the front page of *Harper's Weekly*, a nationally circulated New York publication, with the reporter describing him as the last person in Congress a visitor would pick out as a fire-eater.[21]

Throughout his life, Davis suffered from health problems that incapacitated him and on several occasions nearly took his life. A recurring eye disease caused him to be confined to a darkened room for months at a time, as even the slightest exposure to light caused severe pain. Davis suffered such an attack in 1858 and remained ill at home from February 11 through May 9. When he returned to the Senate, he was weak and unable to see well enough to write. On the advice of his doctor, he and his family spent the summer in Maine for his health.

The northern trip gave Davis an unplanned opportunity to gain stature as a moderate nationalist politician. He was given an honorary doctor of law degree at Bowdoin College in Maine and was called on to make speeches on at least eight occasions, including at Faneuil Hall in Boston and in New York City. On the Fourth of July, he touched on the shared legacy of all Americans and denounced those who would divide the country. He branded as "traitors" those who wanted to do away with the constitutional Union. At the same time, Davis spoke in favor of states' rights when he said that local matters should remain local concerns. And he did not hesitate to defend slavery in Boston, the heart of abolitionist country, claiming that slavery had helped blacks more than anything else by Christianizing and civilizing them. Such remarks, however, earned him vilification from fire-eaters in the South who denounced him.[22]

The coming election of 1860 presented Davis with a dilemma. He truly wanted to save the Union from secession, which he called "the grandest achievement of uninspired human intellect to be found in the records of time." He had long considered the new and growing Republican Party as a threat to the South, one that might reach the lengths that justified separation from the Union that he cherished. He worried that the Republicans, if victorious, might destroy the Union as he knew it. On the one hand, he would, if an abolitionist were elected president, "rather appeal to the God of Battles at once than attempt to live longer in such a Union." But at the same time, he argued for moderation, saying that he was equally opposed to "slavish submission" and to "the brainless intemperance of those who desired a dissolution of the Union." Yet Davis did not forget that his first loyalty, as with many southerners of the time, was to his state. Whichever way Mississippi went on the issue of secession, he would follow.[23]

Davis, like most southerners, believed the presidential election of 1860 would be critical. As the convention neared, there was support for nominating Davis in the South as well as in some northern states, including New Hampshire and Massachusetts. Surprisingly, he had the support of Benjamin S. Butler, later a Union general known after secession as "Beast Butler" for his order to treat the women of New Orleans as prostitutes. Butler believed that Davis was the strongest candidate and that, if nominated, he would defeat the Republican nominee. As a result, the forty-nine-member Massachusetts delegation voted for the Mississippian on fifty-seven consecutive ballots.[24] It was essential to avoid dissention within the Democratic Party if it were to defeat the Republicans. Davis worked against the nomination of Stephen A. Douglas, who would surely split the party, possibly giving the nomination to the Republican candidate. Davis favored former president Franklin Pierce.

When the Democratic National Convention met in Charleston, it failed to make a nomination. Meeting again in Baltimore, it selected Douglas, and southern delegates withdrew and nominated Vice President John C. Breckenridge, a moderate from Kentucky, as their candidate. Davis tried to heal the division with a published plea for the two sides to reunite under one platform and one candidate.[25]

By the time the election was held in November, there were four candidates: Abraham Lincoln for the Republican Party; Douglas, representing the northern faction of the Democratic Party; Breckenridge, the nominee of southern Democrats; and John Bell of Tennessee, representing the Constitutional Union Party, a third party created for this election. The division within the Democratic Party was sufficient to enable a victory by the Republicans. Southerners had warned that if Lincoln were elected, they would secede, and in December 1860 the movement began, with South Carolina leading the way. For Jefferson Davis, the moderate states' rights Democrat with nationalist leanings, this was the end of a promising career in a U.S. government that, until now, he had steadily defended. His fate was now tied with that of Mississippi and the South.

Mississippi seceded on January 9, 1861. Twelve days later, Jefferson Davis followed four other departing southern senators in delivering his farewell address to a crowded U.S. Senate chamber. Ill and suffering from a severe headache, he spoke for six minutes. Keeping his remarks brief because of his illness, he reiterated his long-held belief that secession was a constitutional right. The national government formed by the Constitution was, as he had long maintained, formed to act as the agent for the states that formed it and was not superior to them. Before now, he believed that conditions had not reached the point at which secession was justified. But now the time had come. Mississippi and other southern states were "about to be deprived of the rights our fathers bequeathed us." "Senators, . . . we recur to the principles upon which our Government was founded; and when you deny them, and when you deny to us the right to withdraw from a Government which thus perverted threatens to be destructive of our rights, we but tread in the path of our fathers when we proclaim our independence, and take the hazard."[26]

JEFFERSON DAVIS, CONFEDERATE

By February 1, 1861, five other states followed South Carolina and Mississippi out of the Union. Three days later, representatives from those states met in Montgomery, Alabama, to unite into the Confederate States of America. If Davis were given his choice, he would have chosen to command troops in the field as he had done in the Mexican War. On return to his home state, the governor gave him his wish, appointing him to the rank of major general with command of the Army of Mississippi. However, that service was not to be, as the delegates in Montgomery elected him to serve as the president of the new Confederacy. He accepted reluctantly—bound by duty to serve in the position he did not seek or want.

For Davis personally, the acceptance of the Confederate presidency was a mistake. The intersectional support and potential for higher office that he had enjoyed in the U.S. government now began a downward spiral that ended with his capture and imprisonment in shackles and chains. He would rise once more, but only in the South and never again to such heights. As his wife prophetically commented at the time of his inauguration, "Thus has my husband entered his martyrdom."[27]

His national prestige was such that his selection as Confederate president brought initial expressions of cautious optimism from the northern press. His reputation as a nationalist Democrat allowed many northerners to view him as a moderate who would oppose the radical fire-eaters in the South. The response of the *Philadelphia Inquirer* was typical: "He [Davis] is an able, pure and just man; and we feel confident he will exert himself to prevent a collision of arms . . . by repressing the madness of the mob which is now ruling . . . all [the seceded states]."[28] Southerners also looked for good things under Davis. Crowds gathered everywhere to see and hear him as he made his way from Brierfield to Montgomery for the inauguration, which took place on February 18, 1861.

However, Davis, the moderate nationalist who had resisted dividing the Union, was now an avowed secessionist. On his arrival at the train depot in the temporary Confederate capital, he told the crowd, "No compromise; no reconstruction can be entertained." Two days later, in his inaugural address, he restated this proposition: "We have entered upon the career of independence and it must be inflexibly pursued."[29] Davis never wavered in his new loyalty. He remained committed to the Confederacy, states' rights (in theory, and only when it did not conflict with the war effort), and the constitutionality of secession until his dying day. Once his opinions became known, and particularly after the commencement of warfare at Fort Sumter, favorable comment in northern newspapers ceased, and their editors united against him.[30] It would be nearly thirty years before Davis would regain even a grudging respect beyond the South's borders.

There was reason for optimism in Jefferson Davis's leadership. As a graduate of West Point, as a hero of the Mexican War, and as a superior secretary of war, he had earned the experience needed to conduct the war he knew was coming. As a close adviser to three presidents, as a cabinet head, and as a U.S. senator, his administrative abilities seemed beyond question. He brought to the presidency assets that appeared to ensure success. He had a masterful military knowledge, personal courage, honesty, gentlemanly conduct, and willpower in the face of debilitating illness.[31] The people of the Confederacy seemed to have a competent leader. And under normal conditions, Davis would probably have proven both competent and successful.

Yet many of his positive assets were undermined by other factors, some of which were under his control and others beyond it. Whether fairly or unfairly, Davis's reputation was bound to suffer from any number of these. From a material standpoint, he was faced with governing a new nation that was outmatched in almost every category that was needed to conduct a successful war. The twenty-three Union states had a population of twenty-two million versus eleven states with nine million, a third of whom were slaves. The North also had superiority in factories, wealth, and railroad mileage. Further, it had an army, a navy, and an established government, whereas the South had to create the same. As a result, the Confederacy could not afford to fight an offensive war but had to rely primarily on a defensive strategy, taking the offensive only when it seemed to have the advantage. Basically, it had to outlast the North; it had to win by not losing. Under such circumstances, a successful presidency was unlikely regardless of the man who held the office.

Beyond the material and technological mismatch, there were personal and physical factors that weighed against Davis. His health, never good, would negatively impact his administration of the new country. As he entered into the presidency, British journalist William H. Russell described him as being nearly blind "owing to excruciating attacks of neuralgia" and having a "very haggard, care-worn and pain drawn look" despite displaying the "utmost confidence" in his conversation.[32] Eye and other health problems caused Davis to be confined to a darkened room for many weeks during his administration. According to medical historian Harris Riley Jr., "There can be little doubt that impairment in health influenced in part his personality, especially his aversion to social intercourse, perceived deficiency in tact, ill-tempered stubbornness, and difficulty in relating to others, and thus his performance as chief executive of the Confederacy. . . ."[33]

Whether or not his personality problems were results of his poor health or were merely psychosomatic, Davis was roundly criticized throughout the war by politicians, military officers, governors, the press, and the public at large. Points of conflict included a penchant for micromanagement that extended to interference in the duties of cabinet officers, a personal attention to even insignificant detail, excessive loyalty to friends and political allies that alienated individuals important to the war effort, poor "people skills" that interfered in communicating, inflexible convictions and an unwillingness to compromise principle, and a quick but controlled temper. Recurring conflicts injured Confederate chances for success and negatively impacted Davis's reputation as a leader and statesman. As a result, both civilian and military morale were reduced.[34] In addition, Davis expected the same commitment to the Confederacy that he had. When sacred political concepts and social and economic practices, including slavery, got in the way, he did not hesitate to at least temporarily abandon them even at the risk of his own popularity. Thus, an administration that began with widespread support among radical secessionists, moderates, the southern population at large, and the guarded optimism of some northerners began a slow but steady spiral downward.

Historians continue to debate Davis's abilities and effectiveness as president of the Confederacy. Yet this book is concerned solely with how his contemporaries, not persons living in the present, viewed him, and although many learned to dislike and even hate him, his leadership of the government was never seriously challenged during the Confederacy's brief four years of existence. Historically, people either praise or blame their country's leader for the successes or failures of their government, and Davis was no exception. Jefferson Davis (and a very few others) understood that the single most important goal of the war was independence and that, without independence, slavery would be lost and states' rights would be subordinate to those of the national government in Washington, D.C. It was his stubborn attempt to do anything for independence that made him willing to take such unpopular actions as centralization of authority in Richmond with the consequent loss of support by the southern people.

Everything hinged on the success or failure of the military. In 1861, Davis was overwhelmingly popular, but as the fortunes of the Confederate armies began to fade, he found fewer and fewer supporters, until in 1865 his popularity among southerners reached its nadir. There had been reason for optimism through mid-1863, with major victories at Manassas, Fredericksburg, and Chancellorsville, although the Confederacy also suffered from the naval blockade of its coasts, the capture of New Orleans, the loss of Kentucky and much of the North Carolina coast, and Union gunboats dominating many of the South's waterways. However, growing disillusionment began to set in as the Confederacy grew geographically smaller following its losses at Vicksburg and Gettysburg in July 1863, the loss of Atlanta in 1864, the movement of General William T. Sherman's army through Georgia and the Carolinas, and General Ulysses S. Grant's steady offensive against Robert E. Lee in Virginia.

The defeat of southern armies was not the only thing that worked against Jefferson Davis's support and popularity among the southern people. He violated the two sacred southern doctrines that were regarded as the very foundation stones of the Confederacy: states' rights and slavery. Early in the war, he became convinced that the South could not win the war and thus achieve independence unless primary authority rested in the central government in Richmond. Men were needed for the army, and thus the Confederate Congress, with the president's encouragement, passed the first conscription act in American history. The act itself was opposed by southern governors, and its unfair application in favor of the wealthy led to protests among the people that it was a "rich man's war but a poor man's fight." The need for military supplies led to passage of the unpopular Impressment Act, which allowed agents to scour the countryside looking for goods for the army. While Davis justified these pieces of legislation out of wartime necessity, many could not accept either.

These and other violations of states' rights made enemies for the president in the Confederate legislature and among state governors and other political leaders. Then, in the final months of the war, Davis attacked the southern icon of slavery when he proposed and won from a reluctant Congress the recruitment of slaves as soldiers, a measure that, if carried out, could have led to eventual emancipation and the loss of the South's major source of labor. When he came to this conclusion is unclear, but he probably supported it as early as 1864, when it was originally proposed by Major General Patrick Cleburne of the Army of Tennessee. At the time, however, he felt it necessary to repress even knowledge of the proposal because of negative political repercussions.[35] Despite the necessity, Davis's willingness to forgo states' rights, at least temporarily during wartime, and his support for strengthening the army with black recruits won him many enemies.

Davis similarly suffered the loss of support from several influential southern newspapers. While virtually all supported the war effort, there were those, particularly former Whig papers, that fostered disunity of public sentiment by attacks on the policies of the Davis administration and on the president himself. This was especially true in the case of the *Charleston (S.C.) Mercury* and the *Richmond Examiner*, the latter of which was widely read throughout the Confederacy. Edward Pollard of the *Examiner*, although a strong supporter of the war effort, viewed Davis as the supreme enemy, accusing him of disloyalty to the cause and of being too conceited and provincial to lead the South to victory.[36] Southern newspaper critics accused Davis of disregarding public opinion, deplored his lack of aggressiveness in the war, denounced the quality of his appointments (both civil and military), held him personally responsible for military defeats and even the sufferings of the soldiers, and circulated the impression that he no longer possessed the confidence of the public. Their strident criticism continued throughout the war. In their efforts to belittle his administration, they undermined Davis with the Confederate public and negatively affected southern morale.[37]

It must be said, however, that the Confederate president himself was partially to blame for negative reactions that he and his administration received in some segments of the southern press. He had little understanding of or appreciation for newspapers as a medium for the formulation of public opinion and did little to cultivate cordial relations. Whereas Abraham Lincoln often confided in correspondents such as Noah Brooks and Henry Villard, apparently none of their counterparts in the South enjoyed confidential relations with Davis, who made no attempt to placate hostile editors or establish relations with the press.[38] As the war continued, Davis's popularity increasingly declined among the civilian population. Military defeats, conscription of husbands and sons, forced impressments of livestock and crops, widespread shortages, and a growing inflation rate that made Confederate currency virtually worthless were frequently blamed on the president regardless of his responsibility for them. After the losses at Vicksburg and Gettysburg, peace movements began to be held, particularly in North Carolina, where W. W. Holden, the editor of the *Raleigh Standard*, demanded a general convention to bring about peace and reunification of the states.[39]

Not everyone had the unending commitment to the Confederacy that Davis did. As the emotional and physical suffering escalated among the population, his ideology of sacrifice began to lose its meaning. Hardship and loss became causes for grievance. By 1863, dissatisfaction had erupted into bread riots in communities across the South. In Savannah, Mobile, High Point, and Richmond, crowds of women banded together to seize bread and other provisions they believed they needed.[40] In the capital, Davis's words were insufficient, and he forced their dispersal at the point of soldiers' guns.

As the war entered its final months, many if not most southerners believed the war was lost. Someone had to be at fault, and many settled on the president. The people were unwilling to believe their generals had failed, so they blamed the expected defeat on Davis and his government. The disarray he found himself in made him seem weak. According to one Richmond resident, the president was "in a sea of trouble. . . . It is the old story of the sick lion whom even the jackass can kick without fear."[41]

By the spring of 1865, few persons other than Davis believed that the tide could turn into victory. General Sherman's army was in North Carolina after having cut a swath of destruction through Georgia and South Carolina. On April 2, Grant's forces had pierced Lee's lines at Petersburg, forcing the evacuation of Richmond. On April 4, from his new but temporary capital in Danville, Virginia, he unrealistically told the southern people that the war had entered a "new phase." Now that there was no need to defend cities, he reasoned, the army could move about freely to strike the enemy. "Nothing is now needed to render our triumph certain, but the exhibition of our own unquenchable resolve. Let us but will it, and we are free."[42]

With news of Lee's surrender at Appomattox, Davis and his shrinking government abandoned Danville for Greensboro, North Carolina. There he met with generals Johnston and Beauregard, with both of whom he had feuded during much of the war, to discuss plans for rejuvenating the army with conscripts and deserters. The former bluntly informed Davis that "it would be the greatest of human crimes for us to attempt to continue the war."[43] Until then, he had seemed confident. Now, according to Robert E. Lee Jr., who was present, he seemed "broken." While Johnston met with Sherman for the surrender of his troops, Davis made his way south into Georgia. A new element of danger should he be captured resulted from the assassination of Abraham Lincoln. On May 2, the new president, Andrew Johnson, proclaimed that Lincoln's death was "incited, concerted, and procured by . . . Jefferson Davis." $100,000 was offered as a reward for his capture. To Davis the reward meant that "these people [might be] willing to assassinate me here."[44]

Federal cavalry caught up with Davis and his entourage in the early morning hours of May 10 near Irwinville, Georgia. Varina quickly threw a shawl over his head, and he threw a raglan over his shoulders in an unsuccessful attempt to avoid detection by the soldiers. For a few days after his capture, he was treated well by his captors, although he and his family were subject to the taunts of jubilant soldiers. It was not long before the country took up the ridicule through the circulation of the untrue story of his capture in women's clothing. Cartoons of Davis in a dress appeared in newspapers throughout the northern states. When Secretary of War Edwin Stanton obtained the actual clothing in question, he locked it away in a safe in order to embarrass Davis and perpetuate a myth that has endured to the present day.[45]

A MAN WITHOUT A COUNTRY

The Davis family continued to be treated well during the voyage to Fort Monroe, Virginia, where the former Confederate president would spend the following two years in confinement. Aboard the steamer, he, his family, and other high-ranking Confederate prisoners were given the freedom to walk the deck, mingle, and converse freely. Once Davis was removed from the ship at the fort, Varina Davis and his children were returned to Savannah, Georgia. For three months, he would be deprived of contact in any form with the outside world. Even letters between Davis and his family were forbidden.

For the victorious federal government, the manner of Davis's confinement proved to be a mistake, as it created in Davis a martyr who was seen as suffering for the defeated South. The harsh treatment inflicted on the defeated Confederate leader by post commander General Nelson A. Miles resurrected him in the eyes of a southern public that had become disillusioned with him as the war neared its end. Southern editorial attacks against Davis had expanded dramatically as the war neared its end. Suspension of habeas corpus, preferential treatment in governmental appointments, and increased centralization of government were only some of the issues that had added to his unpopularity.[46] The arrest and trial of the former president might have been acceptable to the defeated southern people. But persecution and humiliation were not. Even Davis's nemesis Alfred Pollard, who had spent the war years attempting to tear Davis down in the press and would continue doing so following the war, argued with some truth that had the federal authorities turned him loose or refrained from treating him with the exceptional harshness they imposed on him, "he would have remained . . . the most unpopular man in the South."[47] Similar sentiments had even been expressed earlier by Abraham Lincoln and Ulysses Grant, who agreed that it would be better for everyone if he escaped.[48]

Fortunately for Davis, both northerners and southerners became concerned and sympathetic when they read articles such as the one that appeared in the *New York Times* on May 27, 1865: "I learn from a well-informed gentleman who left Fortress Monroe yesterday that Jeff. Davis has manacles on both ankles with a chain connecting about three feet long. . . . Rather than submit, he wanted the guards to shoot him. It became necessary to throw him on his back and hold him until the irons were clinched."[49] As a result of protests from both North and South, the shackles were removed after five days. Reports on his suffering would continue and win additional sympathy until his release two years later.

Nelson Miles, commander of the fort and as such the southern leader's jailer, had some reason to maintain tight security. Davis had led a bloody four-year rebellion; he had been captured in an attempt to locate Confederates who had not yet surrendered in an effort to continue the war; Lincoln recently had been assassinated, and the country was still tense; and public outrage demanded stern measures.[50] As the challenge to the Union abated, conditions improved but still remained unnecessarily stringent. In the beginning, the small casement cell and isolation inflicted on the prisoner made him so ill that prison doctor John Craven, who befriended Davis, feared for his life. The casement cell was damp, and the constant day and night tramp of guards made it hard to sleep, as did the candle that burned all night long. A guard kept Davis in constant view, which allowed him no privacy when bathing or using the portable toilet that was brought in. He slept on a thin mattress and a pillow stuffed with hair that caused skin chafing. Food was coarse and of poor quality, and bread was shredded to inspect it for weapons. Visitors were forbidden, and access to books other than the Bible was cut off. This environment resulted in a series of medical problems including boils, carbuncles, swellings, and nervous disorders. He had lost one eye to glaucoma, and there was concern that he might lose the other.[51]

For three months, from May 22 until August 21, he had not been allowed to correspond with his wife. When he was finally permitted to write, letters had to be forwarded through the War Department. On May 3, 1866, after nearly a year's separation, President Andrew Johnston gave Varina permission to visit her husband. She was shocked by his emaciated figure. Miles had forbidden any luxuries, saying, after a group of ladies sent a dressing robe, "This fort shall not be made a depot for luxuries. . . . I shall have to open your packages and see that this is not done."[52]

Conditions improved significantly during the fall of 1866, when Miles was replaced as fort commander by General Henry S. Burton, who administered Davis's imprisonment with a much gentler hand. Mrs. Davis, their daughter, and two servants were permitted to join the prisoner in Carroll Hall, the officers' family quarters, where a four-room suite was set aside for their use. He was finally permitted to receive gifts, including bottles of chartreuse from the bishop of Montreal.

Varina Davis had worked for his release from the beginning. In this fight, she won the aid of Joseph Pulitzer, the newspaper editor; Cornelius Vanderbilt, the railroad and shipping magnate; Gerrit Smith, former New York congressman and abolitionist, who provided a $100,000 bond; and New York lawyer Charles O'Connor, who pushed for Davis's trial. Finally, on May 4, 1867, after two years of imprisonment, Jefferson Davis was released. Although he heartily desired a trial that he hoped to use as a platform to vindicate the rightness of the path he had chosen in 1861—states' rights, the right of secession, and the Confederacy—it never came. The indictment against him was dismissed on December 5, 1868. He was now a free man.

Although still widely unpopular in the North, opinion of Davis in that region grew slowly more favorable as the war years dimmed into the past. Yet a great deal of hostility remained. For many northerners, he would remain the quintessential wrongdoer—what later Americans would think of as a native Adolf Hitler. Just after the war, citizens of Sacramento, California, hanged him in effigy. In 1880, a man was shot in Madison, Indiana, because he cheered for Jefferson Davis. In 1887, future president Theodore Roosevelt and Harvard University professor Albert T. Perkins viewed him as being "among the arch-traitors" of the United States. Even some whose views were beginning to ameliorate denounced him for needlessly prolonging the war when most of his generals believed that continuing it was useless. The thing that most northerners found particularly intolerable about Davis was his refusal to admit any guilt or to apologize for his actions and the cause he had led. Another thing that caused many in the North to continue hostility toward Davis was his advocacy, as he told members of the Southern Historical Society in 1882, of history written by and for southerners. That kind of history was unacceptable.[53]

For Davis personally, the remaining years of his life would seldom be happy ones. Death hit too frequently: his brother Joseph, who had doubled as his surrogate father in earlier years, died on September 18, 1870; his ten-year-old son William Howell Davis on October 16, 1872; and son Jefferson Davis Jr. at age twenty-one, on October 16, 1878. His home life was unsettled, as he needed to move his residence from city to city and to travel for health and financial reasons to Cuba, Canada, England, and France. His family life suffered for a time when Varina, in a prolonged fit of jealousy, refused to live with him. He needed money, and financial problems were a constant worry. He resented having to accept the charity of friends. With a family to provide for, he continuously sought employment. The few jobs he accepted proved to be failures. A stubborn man, he refused to accept anything that he regarded as below the status of a former U.S. senator and Confederate president. Some jobs he turned down for fear that his reputation would harm the institution that offered him positions.[54] A life insurance venture in which he was company president and a major stockholder collapsed, leaving him in worse financial condition than before. A mining venture; a colonization effort; writing projects; and continual attempts to farm the family plantation, Brierfield—all failed to improve his financial position.[55]

Beyond keeping his family sheltered, clothed, fed, and educated, Davis devoted the last twenty-two years of his life to the defense of states' rights, the constitutionality of secession, and a justification of the Confederacy and its fighting men. Characteristically, he stubbornly refused to admit that he or the Confederacy was wrong. Although during his imprisonment, President Andrew Johnson had strongly hinted of his willingness to pardon him, he never seriously considered accepting. This would be tantamount to an admission that

Davis, secession, and the Confederacy were wrong. He would not do that. Regardless, Congress removed that option for him, and he spent his last days truly being a "man without a country."

Although Davis spoke little in public during most of the last quarter century of his life, it was those few occasions that brightened his existence. He returned to the public platform on November 3, 1870, to deliver a eulogy on the occasion of the death of Robert E. Lee. The ice was broken, and he received a flood of invitations for further speeches and appearances. He declined to accept another until July 1871, when he served as commencement speaker at the University of the South. Two years later, he addressed a meeting of the Virginia Historical Society at White Sulphur Springs, where he proclaimed that southerners had been "cheated, not conquered," and would never have surrendered had they foreseen Reconstruction. His remarks created a furor in the northern press, whose editors blamed Davis for the existence and pervasiveness of similar feeling among southerners.[56]

During the summer of 1875, Davis received seventeen invitations to speak at agricultural fairs in the Midwest. Although originally not inclined to accept, he agreed to speak at Rockford, Illinois, and Columbus, Indiana, but withdrew after bitter criticism from the *Chicago Tribune* and threats to his life in Indiana. He found southern audiences receptive, speaking to a crowd of fifteen thousand in Kansas City, Missouri, in the fall of 1875 and in Fairview, Kentucky, where he was well received.

Davis spoke only once during the following two years, appearing at a meeting of veterans of the Mexican War. His next two appearances, both in 1878, were again before former soldiers, this time Confederate veterans of the Army of Tennessee in Mississippi City and the Louisiana Division of the Army of Northern Virginia Association. Although he defended the right of secession and attacked Reconstruction in the first speech, he clearly promoted reconciliation in the second, saying that "we are now at peace . . . [and] the vast body of people at the North are our brethren still."[57]

Jefferson Davis was certainly comforted by these appearances. However, it is doubtful that he could have known the extent of his return to the hearts of southerners until the so-called Southern Tour of 1886, and the Macon, Georgia, visit of 1887 left no doubts concerning his place in the affections of the people of the former Confederacy.

NOTES

1. Peggy Robbins, "Jim Limber and the Davises," *Civil War Times Illustrated* 17 (1978): 22–27.

2. William J. Cooper, *Jefferson Davis, American* (New York: Knopf, 2000), xiv.

3. Cooper, *Jefferson Davis, American*, 49–50.

4. Felicity Allen, *Jefferson Davis, Unconquerable Heart* (Columbia: University of Missouri Press, 1999), 103.

5. Cooper, *Jefferson Davis, American*, 233–34; Lynda Lasswell Crist, "Jefferson Davis," in *Encyclopedia of the American Civil War: A Political, Social, and Military History*, ed. David S. Heidler, Jeanne T. Heidler, David J. Coles, and James M. McPherson, 5 vols. (Santa Barbara, Calif.: W. W. Norton, 2000), 2:565.

6. Mark Grimsley, "'We Will Vindicate the Right': An Account of the Life of Jefferson Davis," *Civil War Times Illustrated* 30 (1991): 35.

7. Allen, *Jefferson Davis, Unconquerable Heart*, 59–66.

8. Cooper, *Jefferson Davis, American*, 45–46.

9. Cooper, *Jefferson Davis, American*, 53–55.

10. Cooper, *Jefferson Davis, American*, 54–55.

11. Allen, *Jefferson Davis, Unconquerable Heart*, 156.

12. Allen, *Jefferson Davis, Unconquerable Heart*, 156.

13. Allen, *Jefferson Davis, Unconquerable Heart*, 185–86.

14. Hudson Strode, *Jefferson Davis, American Patriot, 1808–1861* (New York: Harcourt, 1955), 233–35.

15. Allen, *Jefferson Davis, Unconquerable Heart*, 194.

16. Cooper, *Jefferson Davis, American*, 243.

17. Cooper, *Jefferson Davis, American*, 245–56, 249–59.

18. Cooper, *Jefferson Davis, American*, 264.

19. Cooper, *Jefferson Davis, American*, 265–68.

20. Cooper, *Jefferson Davis, American*, 278.

21. "Hon. Jefferson Davis," *Harper's Weekly* 2 (1858): 17.

22. Cooper, *Jefferson Davis, American*, 290–93.

23. Cooper, *Jefferson Davis, American*, 301–2.

24. Strode, *Jefferson Davis, American Patriot*, 351.

25. Address to the National Democracy, Washington, D.C., May 7, 1860, *Papers of Jefferson Davis*, 10 vols. (Baton Rouge: Louisiana State University Press, 1971–1999), 6:289–93.

26. Farewell Address to the U.S. Senate, January 21, 1861, *Papers of Jefferson Davis*, 10 vols. (Baton Rouge: Louisiana State University Press, 1971–1999), 7:18–29.

27. Strode, *Jefferson Davis, Confederate President* (New York: Harcourt, 1959), 203.

28. Michael B. Ballard, "Yankee Editors on Jefferson Davis," *Journal of Mississippi History*, 43 (1981): 317–18.

29. Ballard, "Yankee Editors on Jefferson Davis," 319–20; Paul D. Escott, *Abraham Lincoln, Jefferson Davis, and America's Racial Future* (Greenville: East Carolina University, Department of History, 2001), 11–12.

30. Ballard, "Yankee Editors on Jefferson Davis," 320.

31. Crist, "Jefferson Davis," 569.

32. Harris D. Riley Jr., "Jefferson Davis and His Health, Part II: January 1861–December, 1889," *Journal of Mississippi History* 49 (1987): 266.

33. Harris D. Riley Jr., "Jefferson Davis and His Health, Part I: June 1808–December, 1860," *Journal of Mississippi History* 49 (1987): 286.

34. Crist, "Jefferson Davis," 569.

35. Terry Jones, *Historical Dictionary of the American Civil War*, 2 vols. (Lanham, Md.: Rowman & Littlefield, 2002), 1:23–24.

36. Jon L. Wakelyn, "Edward Pollard," in *Leaders of the American Civil War: A Biographical and Historiographical Dictionary*, ed. Charles F. Ritter and Jon L. Wakelyn (Westport, Conn.: Greenwood, 1998), 318–19.

37. Harrison A. Trexler, "The Davis Administration and the Richmond Press," *Journal of Southern History* 16 (1950): 194–95; Lawrence Henry Gipson, "The Collapse of the Confederacy," *Mississippi Valley Historical Review* 4 (1918): 454.

38. J. Cutler Andrews, "The Confederate Press and Public Morale," *Journal of Southern History* 32 (1966): 453–55, 465; Bell Wiley, "Jefferson Davis," *Civil War Times Illustrated* 6 (1967): 46.

39. Charles F. Howlett, "Peace Movements," in *Encyclopedia of the American Civil War*, 3:1470–71.

40. Drew Gilpin Faust, "Altars of Sacrifice: Confederate Women and the Narratives of War," *Journal of American History* 76 (1990): 225.

41. Herman Hattaway and Richard E. Beringer, *Jefferson Davis, Confederate President* (Lawrence: University Press of Kansas, 2002), 385, 432.

42. Grimsley, "'We Will Vindicate the Right,'" 70.

43. Grimsley, "'We Will Vindicate the Right,'" 70.

44. Benjamin Sacks, "Varina Howell Davis: A Wife's Vigil," *Journal of Mississippi History* 56 (1994): 109, 123.

45. Robert McElroy, *Jefferson Davis: The Unreal and the Real* (1937; reprint, New York: Smithmark Publishers, 1996), 516–17.

46. Ballard, "Yankee Editors," 328.

47. Edward A. Pollard, *Life of Jefferson Davis with a Secret History of the Southern Confederacy, Gathered behind the Scenes in Richmond* (1869; reprint, Salem, N.H.: Ayer Co, Publishers, 1969), 525.

48. Cooper, *Jefferson Davis, American*, 653.

49. Sacks, "Varina Howell Davis," 112.

50. Sacks, "Varina Howell Davis," 127.

51. Sacks, "Varina Howell Davis," 115–16.

52. Sacks, "Varina Howell Davis," 117.

53. Grady McWhiney, "Jefferson Davis—The Unforgiven," *Journal of Mississippi History* 42 (1980): 113–23.

54. Clement Eaton, *Jefferson Davis, Sphinx of the Confederacy* (New York: Free Press, 1977), 263; Cooper, *Jefferson Davis, American*, 662.

55. W. Stuart Towns, "'To Preserve the Traditions of Our Fathers': The Post-War Speaking Career of Jefferson Davis," *Journal of Mississippi History* 52 (1990): 111.

56. Towns, "'To Preserve the Traditions of Our Fathers,'" 111–13.

57. Towns, "'To Preserve the Traditions of Our Fathers,'" 114–15.

· 2 ·

The First Resurrection:
Davis's Southern Tour of 1886–1887

This outcast . . . is the uncrowned king of our people. . . . The resurrection of these memories that for twenty years have been buried in our hearts, have given us the best Easter we have seen since Christ was risen from the dead.

—Henry Grady, in reference to Jefferson Davis at dedication of
the monument to Ben Hill in Atlanta, Georgia, 1886
(Felicity Allen, *Jefferson Davis, Unconquerable Heart*, 551–52)

A RELUCTANT TOURIST

In 1886, Jefferson Davis was seventy-nine years of age. He had four years remaining to live. After a quarter of a century of financial struggle, shunned by the U.S. government as a man without a country, and still widely hated outside the South, he was nonetheless now a man at peace. He had a good life in retirement at Beauvoir, thanks to the benevolence of Sarah Dorsey, who tried at first to give him the property but settled for selling it at a modest price when, as always, he refused to accept charity. At her death, she also willed him three small plantations in Louisiana. Davis had also regained possession of his former plantation at Brierfield after a lengthy legal fight with the heirs of his brother Joseph. Now he could relax and enjoy the cool breezes from the Gulf of Mexico while sitting on his veranda, reading from his library, writing for publication, and entertaining foreign and American dignitaries and others who came to visit from throughout the United States and Europe.

These final years were perhaps the best of his life. Past receptions he had received at speaking engagements gave Davis the knowledge that he was popular with southern crowds. He could not, however, have been prepared for the wild enthusiasm he was about to experience on what popularly came to be called his "Southern Tour." It is arguable that few men in the history of the republic have been accorded receptions similar to those received by Davis as he traveled through Georgia and Alabama in 1886 and 1887.

Davis did not intend for such a tour to take place. Aged and content to remain at Beauvoir, he was loathe to leave home for public appearances. Although invitations poured in from a wide range of organizations and institutions, he generally declined, citing poor health.[1] Consequently, when he was approached to appear as guest of honor and to lay a cornerstone for a monument to the Confederate dead of Alabama, he replied in the negative. But W. S. Reese, mayor of Montgomery and head of the monument committee, was determined. After the initial rejection, he tried unsuccessfully to persuade Davis's friends to intercede for him. Failing that, he learned through Varina Davis that her husband doted on their daughter Winnie. Having thus found the weak link in Davis's armor, he informed him that, if he passed away without giving Alabama and the South the opportunity to publicly show their love for him, his daughter would never know how dear he was to the southern people. Davis thought for a moment, then said, "I'll go; I'll go."[2] On March 28, Mayor Reese informed the committee that the former president had agreed to make a short speech on April 28 and to participate in laying the monument's cornerstone the following day. However, Davis agreed to come only if he was not required to speak, giving his advanced age as the reason. Consequently, while he would appear on the platforms, others would act as the main speakers.[3]

Davis had agreed only to participate in the ceremonies in Montgomery. However, what began as a visit to a single city soon grew into an extended tour. Atlanta and Savannah, Georgia, were soon added to the list. Perhaps unknown to Davis, the Atlanta invitation was at least partially politically motivated. Former Confederate General John B. Gordon, who was to be the primary speaker in Montgomery, was considering a campaign for the governorship of Georgia. Henry Grady, a leading proponent of the New South movement and a supporter of Gordon's candidacy, saw an opportunity to use Davis's popularity in the coming election. As a consequence, he invited the former president to the unveiling of a statue of Davis's old friend Benjamin H. Hill in Atlanta, where a Georgia audience could see Gordon and the popular wartime leader on the same platform.[4] Hill had been a good and loyal friend, and Grady's appeal made it difficult to refuse. "Nothing that you could have asked [of Hill]," he said, "would have been refused." Davis accepted, and the trip was extended to Atlanta.

Davis was next persuaded to include a visit to Savannah, where he would participate in the unveiling of a new tablet on the monument to Revolutionary War General Nathaniel Greene. His father had served under the general, and Greene was related to Davis's mother.[5] Newspapers began to speculate that the tour might be extended to Charleston, South Carolina, and Macon, Georgia, the latter city being where Davis was taken en route to imprisonment at Fort Monroe in 1865. It was believed that he might also extend the trip to Richmond, Virginia. At the same time, it was recognized that Davis's age and physical condition might prohibit such additions.[6]

MONTGOMERY: THE RECONCILIATION THEME

As the day neared for the departure for Montgomery, Davis's grandson Addison Hayes became ill. As a consequence, it was decided that his wife Varina and daughter Margaret would remain behind to care for the sick child while Davis and Winnie would go on alone. Consequently, when the special train sent by the memorial committee arrived on April 27, the father and daughter left Beauvoir together for Montgomery.

The tour attracted immediate national attention. As Davis prepared to leave for Montgomery, newspapers from throughout the country sent correspondents.[7] Prominent among these was Frank A. Burr, a veteran correspondent for the *New York World*. His reports described events with a knack for detail that gave readers a feeling of being present. Many papers that did not send reporters made arrangements with local correspondents. Others purchased copies of southern newspapers. The *Montgomery Advertiser* of May 1 reported that during Davis's visit to that city, the Associated Press sent out four or five columns of material a day, while the Western Union telegraphed an aggregate of 84,500 words over a three-day period.

Because of the extensive newspaper coverage and the special decorations that made the train easily recognizable, the Davises were greeted by crowds all along the route. As they entered each new jurisdiction, schools and businesses closed, cannons fired, bells rang, fireworks exploded, men in uniform marched and fired salutes, and women wore their Sunday-best clothing.[8]

Montgomery set the tone for the three-city tour. Davis's presence in each city evoked wild enthusiasm and nostalgia for the Confederacy. A local newspaper in the Alabama capital announced, "Now let Dixie reign."[9] But, at the same time, each city went to some lengths to stress recognition that the country was reunited and that the South's future was as a permanent part of the United States. Much of the decorations in preparation for the former Confederate president's visit to Montgomery were placed in the hands of Frank Foster, a wounded Yankee soldier who wore a badge showing his membership in the Grand Army of the Republic. Electric lighting was also in the hands of a northern man. As reported by the *New York Times*, Montgomery was awash in U.S. flags. American flags overwhelmed the few Confederate flags present. At his hotel, Davis would pass under an arch of federal flags. An adjacent business displayed a picture of two soldiers, Confederate and Union, shaking hands in friendship.[10] Speeches regularly included references to an American future and a Confederate past. According to Burr, "There seems to be an effort on the part of all to wipe out all distinctions between the sections in this final offering to Mr. Davis."[11]

While the city showed increasing acceptance of a united present and future as part of the United States, it showed at the same time defiant pride in the old. Beyond those visible at the still-to-be-constructed monument, displays of the Confederate past were minimal. Mixed with American flags hanging from every window of the city hall, however, pictures of Confederate generals were fastened to the outside walls, while the names of Confederate generals "fluttered in the breeze on streamers."[12]

Davis's first two days in Montgomery were marred by an almost constant rain. At 8:00 in the evening, when the train carrying the former president, Mayor Reese, and Alabama Governor O'Neal arrived, they were greeted by thousands of men and women, many of whom had waited for hours standing in ankle-deep mud. A regiment of state militia stood in the rain at present arms while cannons boomed. Between the precipitation and the enthusiasm of the people, Davis and General Gordon, who had met him at the station, made their way to the awaiting carriage with some difficulty.[13]

The procession to the Excelsior Hotel, where Davis had stayed during his inauguration in 1861, resembled receptions normally staged for royalty. Escorted by platoons of soldiers marching to the sounds of "Dixie" and other Civil War tunes, the carriage made its way through a damp but enthusiastic crowd of fifteen thousand persons lining the street. The scene staggered the imagination of reporter Burr of the *New York World* newspaper, who found it difficult to adequately put what he saw into words:

> The boom of artillery grew louder and the crash of small arms and fireworks mingled strongly with the cheers of the half-wild populace as the procession moved. Added to the flash of the colored fires from the curbstones was the constant discharge of Roman candles, rockets, and bombs. Then the flames of the variously colored lights and lanterns which lined the streets, and the many lighted windows and brilliant electric sparks, helped to make a perfect archway of fires more than a half mile long.[14]

American flags hung from every conceivable location along the way. The procession was slowed by the crowd that pressed toward Davis's carriage at every step. Shouts of "three cheers for Jeff Davis" were repeated through the crowd, while women waved their handkerchiefs in the rain. Davis responded by putting aside his umbrella and bowing continuously to the left and right along the route.[15]

By the time they reached the hotel, the crowd in the streets and squares around it had swelled into a sea of faces. As Davis alighted from his carriage, fireworks extending over the street were lighted, spelling in flames "Welcome, Our Hero." The design included eleven stars representing the states of the Confederacy. The word "Welcome" was twined in evergreens over the hotel's entrance. Davis was overwhelmed by the reception and continued bowing to the crowd with an evident show of emotion as he was led through the door.[16]

As he entered the building, he passed under an arch of U.S. flags. When he reached the top of the stairs, he was surrounded by women, some of whom lost their composure in the excitement and threw their arms around his neck. As he neared his room, they threw flowers in his path. On entering his apartment, he found the bed, floor, and furniture covered with roses. The scene was such that, according to Burr, "it may be truthfully said that he walked into it on a bank of flowers."[17] The bed on which he was to sleep was covered by a quilt once used by Marquis de Lafayette during a visit to Philadelphia. Its owner sent it to Montgomery for Davis's use.[18]

When Davis and General Gordon appeared on the veranda, the same one from which he had accepted the leadership of the Confederacy in 1861, he was again greeted with "unbounded enthusiasm" by the crowd below. After partial order was restored, Davis tried to speak but was interrupted by a brass band that chose that inopportune time to strike up the music to "Dixie," which drowned out his words. Before the furious crowd could be calmed, he was led back into the room.[19] If he had not realized it before, Davis was now becoming aware of his new status as the leading living symbol of the South.

The rain continued through the night and into the next morning. Davis was scheduled to speak from the capitol steps at two in the afternoon. The weather and muddy streets, as on the day before, failed to dampen the enthusiasm or size of the crowds. At noon the rain stopped temporarily, and the sun appeared. At the sound of a bugle, cavalry, infantry, and bands swung into line along the main thoroughfare. Davis emerged from the hotel to the shouts of the crowd that had waited for him to appear. As he entered the coach with Mayor Reese, the band played "Dixie." The Montgomery Greys marched in open ranks ahead of the carriages and at the capitol opened a path from the gate to the steps. A forty-member band took its place and began to play "Hail to the Chief" when Davis entered the gates. At the command, the military companies stood at present arms. As he moved toward the steps, the "excited

populace kept yelling, and Mr. Davis, with hat in hand, kept constantly bowing to their salutes."[20]

As he took his seat alongside Gordon, Reese, O'Neal, and the other dignitaries, Davis found himself surrounded by women, some of whom began to
fan him. Just before they reached the capitol steps, the rain began again but
failed to stop the program. Virginia Clay, whose husband had been imprisoned
in Fort Monroe with Davis in 1865, remembered the scene at the capitol: "I
saw women, shrouded in black fall at Mr. D's feet, to be uplifted and comforted
by kind words. Old men & young men shook with emotion beyond the power
of words on taking Mr. Davis's hand, & I feared the ordeal wd. prove the death
of the man."[21] The *Atlanta Constitution* reported, "The demeanor of the audience was notable. The people were full of enthusiasm. They would give vent
to sudden and vociferous cheers and as suddenly check them out of consideration for the honored guest."[22]

After being introduced by Mayor Reese, Davis arose to speak but the
emotional outburst of the crowd was such that "as he stood . . . , his lips moved
in words but not a syllable could be heard. A cheer long pent up since 1861
rent the air, and was taken up by the crowds on the streets, and echoed and re-
echoed over the city. . . . Ladies stood upon seats waving handkerchiefs and alternately crying and laughing." "Men were wild for him; women were in ec-
stasy for him; children caught the spirit and waved their hands in the air."[23]
Davis responded by getting up again and again to bow in acknowledgment.

Once the audience had calmed, Davis, standing on the spot where he had
been inaugurated president in 1861, spoke briefly. He reminded the people that
he had been promised when he accepted the invitation to Montgomery that
he would not be called on to make a speech. Then, after commenting briefly
on the bravery of southern soldiers in a defensive war that the Confederacy
had not sought, he took his seat and left the platform to General Gordon, the
main speaker of the day.

Gordon's speech touched on themes that were to be repeated in Atlanta
and Savannah during the southern tour: Davis's suffering for the South in Fort
Monroe, pride in the Confederacy and its soldiers, and reconciliation between
the sections. In reference to the emotional outpouring of sentiment for Davis,
he argued that critics of such scenes were "narrow in concept and prejudiced
in vision." The South accepted defeat in battle, and its adherence to "the le-
gitimate results of the war [should] be forever unquestioned."[24] The crowd
broke into cheers, the band played the "Bonnie Blue Flag," and the day's celebrations were over.

The final day of Davis's visit to the former Confederate capitol was given
over to the solemn quiet of paying honor to the Confederate dead of Alabama.
The cornerstone was to be laid and the graves of soldiers to be decorated with

flowers. The crowds were still large, soldiers marched, cavalry rode, bands played, and the dignitaries of the previous day appeared again. And, for the first time, the weather cooperated.

Just before noon, the procession arrived at the Excelsior Hotel to escort Davis and Gordon to the capitol grounds on which the Confederate monument was to be erected. On arrival, Davis made his way to the platform through a silent crowd with uncovered heads. To the side of the platform, the cornerstone lay with the words in raised letters: "Corner-Stone Laid by Jefferson Davis, Ex-President of the Confederate States."

Davis's speech covered the themes that he had repeated many times in speeches and letters since the war. He blended reconciliation between the sections with a defense of the southern past, arguing that "when passion shall have subsided and reason shall have resumed her dominion, it must be decided that the General Government had no constitutional power to coerce a State and that a State had the right to repel invasion." He went on to praise southern soldiers and women, defended states' rights, and described the war as defensive in nature. He concluded with comments on the South's roll in a reunited country: "though the memory of our glorious past must ever be dear to us, duty points to the present and future. Alabama having resumed her place in the Union, be it yours to fulfill all obligations to restore the general government to its pristine purity, or as best you may to promote the welfare and happiness of your common country."[25]

Davis and his daughter Winnie joined others in placing a Confederate flag from the war and other items in a vault to be sealed in the monument. They then adjourned to the cemetery to decorate the graves of soldiers. The day ended with a reception in the governor's mansion, after which the Davises returned to their hotel to dine and spend the evening. *New York World* correspondent Burr wondered if the success of the Montgomery trip might convince Davis to extend his tour all the way to Richmond. "All the South is aflame," he wrote, "and where this triumphant march is to stop I cannot predict."[26]

ATLANTA: A REUNION WITH LONGSTREET

Davis and his daughter left for Atlanta on the morning of April 30 to participate in the dedication of the statue to his old friend Ben Hill. They departed to the sounds of artillery, bands, and a crowd of well-wishers who came to bid them farewell. Their route, as throughout the Southern Tour, was publicized in advance, and the train was easily identifiable by watchers along the tracks. The train cars were well decorated with flowers, flags, and bunting. An enlarged portrait of the former president was attached to one side of his coach, and on the other the name "Davis" was written high in immortelles. Within the train, flowers hung in silver baskets from the ceiling.[27] As if to ensure that Davis's train would not go by unobserved, a cannon was placed on board by the *Atlanta Constitution* newspaper with the intention of firing a salute at each station as the train made its way to the Georgia capital.[28]

Not to be outdone by the treatment Davis had received in Montgomery, elaborate plans were made for his reception in the Georgia capital. Each square, from the railroad depot to the home of Ben Hill's widow, where the Davises would reside during their visit, was placed in charge of a committee. Women in every town and community in the state were urged to send flowers so that "every express car that comes into Atlanta from Thursday to Friday [will] come filled to the ceiling with flowers." In addition, the people of Atlanta were expected to supply many more. "Every yard, and every house will be stripped and the flowers sent in." The woods were to be searched for flowers, and "every merchant and every man that has a dray, or wagon, or buggy [was requested to send] it out . . . and bring it in filled with wild flowers." The flowers were to be dispersed by a line of eight thousand children provided by the schools to form a "floral carpet" to make "the path of the old man glorious."[29] It was expected that the Confederate president would literally walk on a path of flowers.

The ride to Atlanta was "one long ovation."[30] Every station was covered by bunting and flags, and towns all along the route made preparations in hopes that the train might stop. *New York World* correspondent Burr continued to be overwhelmed with the outpouring for the former southern leader:

> I could not help but note what a wealth of affection there is in this country for Mr. Davis and for the 'Lost Cause.' It can be truthfully said that he was brought from the capital of Alabama to the capital of Georgia upon a pathway of flowers. More than a car-load of floral offerings . . . were upon the train, and again the platform of the car on which he bowed his thanks to the people was covered with flowers ankle deep. Old men and women shed tears as they hung upon his words.[31]

The train made several stops along the way during which Davis made short speeches. The only planned stop was at LaGrange, the birthplace of Ben Hill, whose statue Davis was scheduled to help dedicate in Atlanta. Two hundred schoolgirls dressed in white were at the station, one of whom delivered an address of welcome. "If that does not get the old man to talk," said one person, "we'll put these girls in front of the train and keep them there until he speaks. LaGrange is going to beat them all."[32] The spirit of rivalry in showing the most feeling was, according to the *New York Times*, "manifest in the talk of all the men here who are here from the different cities."[33]

The enthusiasm of Montgomery was repeated in Atlanta. Beginning early in the day, thousands of people came into the city by railroad and other means of conveyance. There was great outpouring of townspeople, a large procession of Confederate veterans, innumerable flags, and a wilderness of bunting. Dozens of bands and militia companies paraded all morning. Crowds gathered at the train depot hours before Davis's arrival. A wide banner proclaimed "Welcome to our illustrious ex-President Jefferson Davis." At 1:30, several hundred Confederate veterans lined up in front of the depot, cheering lustily at the slightest provocation. The train arrived at 3:30 to increasingly louder and longer cheers. As Davis was recognized emerging from the depot, a deafening cry of several minutes' duration began and extended to people lined up blocks distant from the depot. As he entered the carriage, the cheers doubled in volume. Some of the veterans rushed toward Davis and had to be restrained by mounted police.[34]

The route to the Hill mansion, Davis's residence during his stay in Atlanta, was "one long ovation" from the crowd estimated at between forty and fifty thousand persons. Six thousand schoolchildren, each holding flowers, lined the road, throwing them in front of his carriage as it passed so that he literally rode on a bed of flowers. When he stepped from the carriage at the Hill home, he was greeted by deafening cheers. From the gate to the porch, a line of young girls holding flowers stood on each side of the pathway, throwing their floral offerings in his path so that he walked to the house on a floral carpet.[35]

The dedication of the Ben Hill statue was held on May Day 1886. The weather cooperated, being a little cool but bright and fair. While Davis rested, a stream of visitors continued to pour into the city. Morning trains were loaded to capacity even though the normal number of cars had been doubled. Thousands of former Confederates flocked from the surrounding country on foot, on horseback, and in every conceivable kind of vehicle. By 9:00 A.M., the route of the procession to the monument was a blaze of color. Long before Davis was scheduled to appear, a dense crowd assembled in front of the Hill home. A large squad of police, both mounted and on foot, had all they could do to keep them back, the crowd insisting on blocking the streets despite efforts to keep them in check. At length a rope was stretched along the street in front of the mansion to hold the crowd back, and the parade began to form.

Davis left the Hill mansion in the company of Henry Grady and other dignitaries to join the procession behind the Governor's Horse Guard and a company of cadets. As he entered his carriage, he found it nearly filled with flowers. He responded to loud and vociferous cheering from the crowd by lifting his hat and waving to the left and right. Near the head of the procession an estimated one thousand Confederate veterans marched, many gray haired and with empty coat sleeves from wounds received in the war.[36]

Correspondent Burr was particularly struck by the participation of African Americans in the parade. He had noticed how black farmers working in the fields had waved at the train as it passed between cities. At the stations and on the streets, he found their presence conspicuous. At Tuskeegee, a mixed-race crowd of five hundred had mingled to cheer Davis. Now, most conspicuous of all, black bands played at the head of white military companies and in other ways joined in the ceremonies.[37]

Apparently unobserved by Davis, former Confederate General James Longstreet, regarded as an outcast by many southerners because of his support for the Republican Party, was riding in the parade behind him dressed in the full uniform of a Confederate lieutenant general.[38] When the procession reached the monument, the Confederate veterans opened ranks, four deep on each side, and let the military and carriages pass through. The entrance of the former Confederate president to the platform was greeted by loud cheering and cries of "Hurrah for Jeff Davis."

Following speeches by Governor McDaniel, R. D. Spaulding, and J. C. C. Black, the primary speaker of the day, Longstreet rode up to the stand. When he reached Davis, the two embraced emotionally and sat side by side for the remainder of the ceremonies. The meeting was in all likelihood arranged by Henry Grady, who, in editorials for the *Atlanta Constitution*, had defended Longstreet against charges that he was responsible for Lee's defeat at Gettysburg. The newspaper editor also undoubtedly realized that the appearance of the two southern heroes together on the same stage would do much to boost the gubernatorial candidacy of Gordon, who shared the platform with them.[39] Within two weeks, Gordon announced his candidacy and went on to easily win the governor's race.

Davis was last on the agenda. After the formal orations, Grady introduced the former president to the audience as "the uncrowned king of our people." "The resurrection of these memories that for twenty years have been buried in our hearts, have given us the best Easter we have seen since Christ was risen from the dead."[40] Davis spoke for only a few minutes, confining his remarks to tributes to Ben Hill, the subject of the occasion. Following his speech and the closing prayer, Spaulding introduced Winnie Davis to the crowd as the "daughter of the Confederacy" since she had been born in the Confederate White House during the war.[41] Perhaps because of this introduction, she became a favorite of Confederate veterans and carried the title thus bestowed for the rest of her life.

Although Davis was clearly invigorated by the receptions he had received in Montgomery and Atlanta, the exertion was also taking a toll on him physically. Following the exercises, he retired to the Hill mansion. Those who hoped to personally meet him were excused with the explanation that he was "by no means in vigorous health, and [was] too feeble and worn out" by the day's excitement to see any visitors.[42] It was becoming clear that any hopes of extending the tour to Richmond would be disappointed. "He is," according to reporter Burr, "growing weaker . . . and is obliged now to husband his strength."[43]

SAVANNAH

The next morning at 10:00, the Davises departed for Savannah, a 296-mile journey. The train continued to be easily recognizable as it moved through the countryside. Two slogans attached to the sides reminded onlookers of his military record and martyrdom at Fort Monroe: "Buena Vista" and "He Was Manacled for Us." The decorations were so abundant on Davis's car that neither wood nor metal was visible. As happened earlier, the journey continued to a continuous ovation. The enthusiasm everywhere was unbounded.[44]

Crowds collected at every station in hopes of a brief view of the Confederate president. At Tennille, one of the many places the train passed without stopping, a thousand people waited at the station. Confederate veterans had come from twenty miles distant, women and children stood waiting with flowers, and the town's cornet band had assembled, only to face disappointment as the train sped by.[45]

The train made eight stops. A planned stopover at Macon was shortened to twenty minutes. Davis begged off giving any kind of reception of more than two minutes.[46] Nevertheless, he was met at the depot by an immense crowd that included Mrs. Howell Cobb. He kissed her as she came up on the platform, where they reminisced about how her husband had received Varina and their children in Macon during his imprisonment in Fort Monroe. Then he placed his arm around Winnie and introduced her to the people. Picking up on the title bestowed on her the previous day in Atlanta, he said, "This is my daughter, the child of the Confederacy [who] exults in the fact that she was born in the Southern Confederacy."[47]

Davis's reluctance to make speeches was changing following the emotional and uplifting experiences of Montgomery, Atlanta, and the wayside tributes he witnessed through Alabama and Georgia. Despite a precondition for accepting invitations to participate in ceremonies in those states, he now appeared almost eager to meet and speak to the crowds. "Do they want me?" he asked several times as he lay resting on the couch in his railway car and heard the rousing cheers from the shouting multitude for speeches. "All right," he would continue, "tell them I'm coming." Then, taking his cane in his hand, he would walk slowly to the platform and say a few words.[48]

Despite the late hour of Davis's arrival in Savannah, fifteen military companies and a large number of people were on hand to greet him. Their shouts "pierced the roof" and were taken up by others outside the station. Although it was dark and difficult for people to see him during the drive to the H. M. Comer residence, where he would remain as a guest while in the city, he was nonetheless recognized, and the people broke into loud cheers. As in Atlanta, flowers were rained on him, and men pushed frantically up to the carriage door to shake his hand.[49]

On arrival at the Comer house, the crowd was so dense that it was difficult for the Davises to make their way to the door. Just then, an unthinking member of their escort attempted to clear a path by pushing through the people with his horse, which began to behave badly. Women in the way became frightened, and Davis was saved from possible injury by two men who took him by the arms. At length, a passage was cleared, and he ascended the steps and stood at the door. The crowd cheered for a full ten minutes before it calmed down enough for Davis to say a few words, after which he entered the house and retired for the evening.[50]

Davis remained in Savannah for four days, during which he maintained a strenuous pace that was certain to fatigue a man of his age. While it was the rededication of the monument to Nathaniel Greene that drew him to the city, this was only one part of a week devoted to celebrating the hundredth anniversary of the Chatham Artillery, founded in 1784. This unit was the pride of the city, and plans had long been in the works to bring in other military organizations from all over the nation to participate in the celebration. A total of forty-six militia companies were camped on the outskirts of town. Savannah had the appearance of an armed camp, with infantry, artillery, and cavalry companies and uniforms everywhere. This and the presence of the former Confederate president drew enormous crowds to the city.

Davis, still tired from the earlier exertions of the trip, rested most of the first day, disappointing visiting soldiers who had expected him to join Georgia Governor McDaniel in reviewing the two-thousand-strong parade of troops that opened the week's activities. By evening, he had sufficiently recouped his strength to attend a banquet in honor of the Chatham Artillery. In response to a toast to his health given by a member of the New York Old Guard, he complimented the "citizen soldiery" of all sections. Then, seeming to apologize for the demonstrations of the past week as he traveled through Alabama and Georgia, he explained that they were for him personally and were not against the government. In the spirit of reconciliation, the band played "Hail Columbia" and the "Star-Spangled Banner" "with as much enthusiasm as if they had been entertaining an audience at Boston's Faneuil Hall. By far the loudest and most prolonged cheering, however, were reserved for Davis and "Dixie."[51]

The next day, Davis continued his grueling schedule. That morning, he attended a meeting of the state Teachers Association, after which he went to Chatham Academy, where three thousand public schoolchildren were waiting with flowers in their hands to throw in his path. Moving to the shade of a tree, he placed a chair on top of a table and, with some assistance, climbed up and sat in the chair. No speeches were planned. The children crowded around, shaking his hand, cheering, and yelling until he tired and had to be taken into the school for some rest.[52] After half an hour, he was escorted to his carriage through a large cheering crowd and driven to his host's home to recuperate.

The schedule for May 5 called for a public reception at the City Exchange (that is, city hall). Between 2:30 and 3:30 P.M., the former president sat in an easy chair in the mayor's office, meeting and shaking hands with an estimated three thousand men, women, and children who stood in line to meet him, including approximately fifty African Americans. As at a political rally, children were patted on the head, babies were kissed, and veterans told him with pride of their service in the war.[53]

After the reception, Davis was taken to Camp Washington to see the Volunteer Southrons of Vicksburg, Mississippi. He arrived too late to witness the unit in competition, but when they heard that he was present, they put their dress uniforms back on and put on an exhibition specifically for him. At the close, he complimented the company and spoke briefly to them. The day concluded with a late-night reception at the Oglethorpe Club.[54]

The event that originally drew Davis to Savannah, the dedication of the new bronze tablets on the Nathaniel Greene monument, took place the following day, May 6. The monument had been erected in 1846 without inscriptions of any kind carved on it. The Georgia Historical Society took it on itself to prepare two large bronze tablets that were to be dedicated as part of the Chatham Artillery's centennial celebration. The militia unit's first official act on its founding in 1786 was to stand guard over the funeral bier of General Greene. With military precision, at precisely 5:00, every one of the several dozen military units in the city began their march to the square in which the monument was located. The streets along the line of march as well as every open space surrounding the monument were thronged with people. Davis was joined on the speaker's platform by Governor McDaniel, General Gordon, Mayor Reese of Montgomery, and Mayor Lester of Savannah. Following the speech by C. C. Jones of Augusta, Georgia, the Chatham Artillery fired a thirteen-gun salute. When the firing stopped, the crowd called for Davis, who, in response, rose amid tremendous cheering.[55]

Up until now, Davis had avoided controversy, realizing that the widespread coverage of his southern tour in the national press had placed him under a microscope. There had been criticism in the northern press, but it had been expected and was relatively mild. But in front of the monument to Nathaniel Greene, he made an impassioned defense of state sovereignty that stirred negative responses from beyond the South:

> In 1776 the colonies acquired State sovereignty. They revolted from the mother country in a desperate struggle. That was the cause for which they fought. Is it a lost cause now? Never. Has Georgia lost the State sovereignty which . . . she won in 1776? No, a thousand times no. "Truth crushed to earth will rise again." You may hold it down for a time, but it will rise again, its might clothed in all the majesty and power that God gave it. And so the independence of these States, the Constitution, liberty, the State sovereignty, which they won in 1776 and which Nathaniel Greene, the son of Rhode Island, helped win for Georgia as well as for Rhode Island, can never die.[56]

At the close of these remarks, the stage was filled with old veterans eager to grasp the hand of their wartime leader. The rush was so great that there was danger that he would be crushed.

As northern reporters rushed to telegraph Davis's "inflammatory" remarks to their papers, friends advised him to correct the impression. The opportunity came that same evening in a brief speech given at a banquet hosted by the Savannah Guards in which he returned to the theme of intersectional reconciliation:

> If Savannah needs a guard, here it is; if the United States needs defenders, here they are. If the United States need troops for war, I don't know where they could get better, braver, or more trustworthy men than right here in Georgia. There are some who take it for granted that when I allude to State sovereignty I want to bring on another war. I am too old to fight again, and God knows I don't want you to have the necessity of fighting again.[57]

Then, as if to emphasize the point that the South's future lay as a part of the United States, he added, "The celebration today is a link in the long chain of affection that binds you and the North together. Long may it be true."[58]

Davis spent the following day at his leisure, resting for the trip home to Beauvoir. That morning he watched a cavalry demonstration at Camp Washington and during the afternoon took a short carriage ride around town with his host. The next morning he boarded a special car of the Savannah, Florida, and Western Railroad Company for the journey home, which took him through Waycross, Valdosta, and Albany, Georgia, and Montgomery, Alabama. The trip was a repetition of those taken earlier on the Southern Tour. Telegrams from towns all along the route begged that the train stop for at least a few minutes. Citizens and veterans crowded the depots, bands played, and cannons fired. The tour had been a great success. Winnie, as her father had hoped, saw the love and admiration he evoked across the South. And she herself gained the sobriquet "Daughter of the Confederacy" and thenceforth would remain a favorite of Confederate veterans. Davis returned to Beauvoir satisfied with his place in the affections of the southern people.

Beyond the South, Davis's Southern Tour generated a broad spectrum of reactions ranging from deep, long-held hostility to understanding and even near admiration. A number of newspapers attacked him "as if he had blown the roof off the house." Some resorted to preposterous slanders, one going so far as to claim that Davis said that he was ready to die now that Lincoln and Grant were dead and in hell.[59]

Despite the overwhelming display of symbols of national unity and the many statements of reconciliation made during the tour, many in the North saw the enthusiastic demonstrations for the former president of the Confederacy as reason to distrust southern loyalty to the national government. The *Cincinnati Commercial Gazette* predicted renewed danger to the Union as a result of the trip. The *New York Times* regarded Davis's defense of secession as a "melancholy exhibition of senile pedantry" and condemned him for looking back. With twenty-one years of hindsight, other papers reported on the tour in less emotional tones. The *Springfield (Mass.) Republican* wrote, "We have reached that distance when we can recognize the genuine convictions that filled the men of the South. . . . Now . . . they gather to commemorate the lost cause with no desire to recall it. . . . This is the way we read the honors to Jefferson Davis. . . . How could we respect the southern people . . . if they did not honor their leaders and their soldiers."[60] Clearly, the northern protests were an overreaction, given the efforts of Davis, Grady, Gordon, and the organizers of the celebrations in Alabama and Georgia to keep the Southern Tour from reflecting any regional disloyalty. The *New York Times* warned, "Any utterances of Jeff Davis and any momentary display of enthusiasm over the exhibition of this ancient fossil are poor material out of which to make political capital. It won't keep."[61] If anything, their protests produced a negative counterreaction by southern papers that reprinted their comments for southern audiences. The tour was in fact an early indication of a movement that would grow greatly over the next decade, with Jefferson Davis its leading symbol.

The remaining few years of Jefferson Davis's life were generally quiet ones spent at home in Beauvoir. He ventured beyond Mississippi on only two later occasions. Prior to agreeing to the Southern Tour, he had committed himself to participate in the dedication of a Baptist church built on the site of his birthplace in Fairview, Kentucky. In 1885, Kentuckians had subscribed money to purchase the Jefferson Davis birthplace in order to erect a Baptist church as a memorial to him. A deed was made out to Davis, and he in turn deeded the land to the church. He agreed to attend the dedication only on the condition that his travel route not be made known and that he would not have to make a speech. But, as usual, when pressured by his audience, he spoke briefly and shook hundreds of hands of those in attendance.[62]

MACON, GEORGIA: THE SOUTHERN TOUR RESUMED

In late October 1887, Jefferson Davis made what was to be the last extended trip of his life. Although not actually connected to the 1886 visits to Montgomery, Atlanta, and Savannah, it was, despite the yearlong intermission, in essence simply a continuation of that tour. In midsummer, committees of Confederate veterans began to plan for a grand reunion in Macon to coincide with the Georgia State Fair. Pressure was put on their wartime president to meet with the soldiers of the Confederacy "perhaps for the last time." Since his wife and daughter Margaret had not experienced the grand tour of the previous year, Davis reluctantly accepted.[63]

In agreeing to attend the fair, the seventy-nine-year-old Davis placed limits on the activities in which he would be expected to participate in order to preserve his fragile strength. During the Southern Tour of 1886, he had become extremely exhausted after attending numerous planned and unplanned meetings, shaking thousands of hands, sometimes within the span of a single hour, and being called on to speak to every group in which he came in contact. Consequently, the people of Macon were informed through that city's newspaper that "Mr. Davis is feeble. . . . He makes his last journey to meet old Confederates upon the understanding that nothing will be required of him to tax this strength. He will not be allured to make speeches, however urgent the demand upon him, nor can the people even shake his hand. . . . His spirit is willing . . . but his failing strength restrains him."[64] On the advice of his physician, he canceled a planned extension of the trip to include Athens, Georgia. Instead, his two daughters would go in his place.

The Davis family departed from Beauvoir at 11:00 on the evening of October 23 on a special train sent by the Macon committee to bring him to the city. Davis was assigned a special car in which it was intended that he could rest undisturbed throughout the trip. As on the earlier tour, the train was colorfully decorated, and the route was well publicized so that cities and towns along the route were aware of when and where the train would be at all times. This brought out crowds at every station requesting to see the former president. Cannons boomed and people cheered as the train arrived in the Alabama capital at 7:30 A.M. Winnie was introduced to great enthusiasm as the "Daughter of the Confederacy," and a profusion of flowers was placed on the train.[65]

In some respects, the ride through Georgia was an ordeal. At every stopping place, veterans and sons and daughters of veterans stormed the train and took him by assault. The enthusiasm was, according to Georgia writer Harry Stillwell Edwards, "indescribable. We seemed to be borne forward upon the crest of some mighty wave in a sea of voices. Flowers covered us, and the train ran under triumphal arches." At Montgomery, newspaper correspondents from the East and North joined the train, some representing journals that were still bitter against Davis. None were to be admitted access to Davis without his permission. Being a journalist, Edwards was appealed to by other reporters to gain entrance. In reply, Davis said, "Admit them!" Winnie greeted the reporters, pinned small Confederate flags on their lapels, and brought them under her spell.[66]

The trip was a triumphal procession. Even at stations where the train only slowed without stopping, individuals ran alongside throwing flowers. Davis soon forgot his self-imposed limitations and actively reciprocated in the enthusiasm of the crowds. At Fitzpatrick Station, Alabama, cries of "Davis! Davis!" caused him to pull up his curtain and allow people to see him reclining on a pillow. A little further down the line at Thompson, the clamor was such that he put up his window and held an informal reception. At Union Springs, he posed at his window for a photographer who, in his enthusiasm, never got the picture as the train moved away. At Midway, an enthusiastic crowd grabbed his hand and almost pulled him out through the open window. Children by the dozen were handed up for him to kiss, and he shook the hand of every child who came within reach. Davis was again in danger of having his arm wrenched off by enthusiastic veterans at Cuthbert. He was saved by his daughters, who drew his hand inside the window and substituted their own. By the time the train reached Macon, Winnie's hand was so sore to the touch that she could not put on gloves for several days.[67] At some stations, the train only slowed as it passed cheering onlookers. His daughters entertained the people at some stations while their father slept. At Americus, Georgia, as cannon boomed, the entire family was encouraged to pass under a specially built arch onto a platform next to the train, where Davis consented to speak briefly to the dense crowd.[68]

The train pulled into Macon at 5:40 P.M. to the cheers of seven thousand persons and an artillery salute of thirteen guns. An almost impenetrable crowd blocked access to the carriages waiting outside the station. As a passageway was created, the crowd continued to surge forward, with some men reaching over the heads of others to touch Davis on the shoulders and back. At length, Davis and his family reached their carriage and were taken to Hillcrest, the hillside home of Captain and Mrs. Marshall Johnston, where they would be houseguests for the week.[69] The going was difficult because of the surging pressure of the crowds that followed the carriages and lined the route.

All along the way, roman candles were fired into the air, and the streets and buildings were decorated with lights. At one point, the Davises passed under the words "Welcome Honored Chief" formed by gas jets. Other banners read "All hail to our chief" and "Long live Jefferson Davis and his vets." During the week, an estimated fifty-thousand visitors were attracted to the city to see the Davises and attend the Confederate reunion. Special trains added on by the railroad became so crowded that at times they had to leave people in some stations to await later trains.[70]

Most of the coming week was given over to mundane activities. When Davis was asked if he would like to see the animals, a parade of cows, horses, and so on was led before him. Wednesday, October 27, was Veterans' Day at the fair. The weather was inclement, but veterans from all over the South had traveled to Macon to see their wartime leader, and they were not to be deterred. In terms of emotional enthusiasm, their demonstration surpassed all Davis had experienced since the war. The city had done all in its power to guard his health. As a result, the veterans were brought to him, rather than he to them, as he remained seated comfortably on the veranda of his host's mansion.

An estimated five thousand veterans, headed by cavalry, formed a long procession and marched to the Johnston home on Hillcrest Street. As the procession neared the gateway, the Davises took their seat alongside Georgia's Senator Alfred H. Colquitt, Captain Johnson, and General Gordon, who had been elected governor of the state following his appearances alongside the former Confederate president on the Southern Tour.[71]

As the procession reached the Johnson home, the veterans in their enthusiasm got out of hand. Some jumped the iron fence in their eagerness to be near Davis. They surrounded the house. Davis, still sitting, lifted his hat repeatedly, but the veterans wanted to shake his hand. As they crowded about him, Davis leaned forward in his chair and extended his hand. The veterans also called for Varina and then the Davis daughters. For several minutes, the entire family was kept busy shaking hands. The shouts became deafening. Calls of "God bless the old man," "There's the old hero," and similar expressions were heard as the veterans reached over to shake Davis's hand. Some kissed the hands of his wife and daughters, while others lifted their sons so that they might touch the man they fought under.[72]

Davis again broke the promise he had made to himself not to talk or to allow himself to be worried. Becoming fatigued from the handshaking, he fell back into his chair and simply watched as thousands of veterans surged forward. Senator Colquitt tried to intervene, telling the crowd that Davis's health had to be respected, as "we want him to live to a green old age. He must not be expected to shake hands with every one of you. It is impossible for him to do so." The veterans, slightly calmed, began to pass slowly, although many still tried to get to him, and one climbed the veranda's railing.[73]

Davis contented himself with looking on until the battle flag of Cobb's Legion neared. Then he could not restrain himself from speaking. Rising, he leaned over the veranda rail and took hold of the flag. Then, waiting for the applause to slacken, he told the veterans, "I am like that old flag, riven and torn by storms and trials. I love it as a memento; I love it for what you and your fathers did. God bless you! I am glad to be able to see you again!" The veteran who carried the banner then placed it in Davis's hands, and, again rising from his chair, Davis waved it over the heads of the crowd to deafening shouts of the men. Before the flag was returned, Varina tore off a piece for a memento.[74]

The crowd being so dense and eager to shake hands gave rise to fears that Davis would be worn out. Efforts to induce the men to pass on to allow others to see him proved fruitless. The veterans wanted to be near him and had no thought for others. Senator Colquitt had tried and failed, and Governor Gordon then appealed to the men. When the veterans only cheered without moving, the Davises were quietly taken inside. Despite his absence, the crowd continued to grow larger, and late arrivals tried to peer through the windows for a glance at the former president.[75]

The theme of reconciliation was present in Macon as it had been during the earlier Southern Tour. Yet it was less evident given the large number of Confederate veterans present. The Stars and Bars flags proudly and visibly waved, although they were greatly outnumbered by U.S. flags and were generally placed alongside the national colors. During the evening following Davis's review of the veterans, a candlelight parade was held. Six thousand men, each carrying a torch and splitting the air with rebel yells, passed through the city. Several floats interspersed through the parade were devoted to Confederate history and heroes. One bore the wording "The Fall of Fort Sumter, April 13, 1861"; others bore portraits of Robert E. Lee, Stonewall Jackson, Jefferson Davis, and the Confederate cabinet.[76]

Inclement weather the following day forced a postponement of planned activities, giving the fatiguing Davis the opportunity to sleep late, remain indoors with family and friends, and visit a livestock show in the afternoon. He was nonetheless disappointed that the day's events had to be postponed. He had requested that the day be set aside so that he could spend it with children coming to the fair from all over Georgia. Telegrams had been sent to newspapers throughout the state advising them of the event, and railroads offered half-price fares for children.

Because of the constant rain, Children's Day was moved to Saturday, October 29, the closing day of the fair. Just after noon, Davis was driven to the fairgrounds to meet the children. A band played "Dixie," and several thousand spectators cheered as he took a seat on the bandstand. He asked to see the orphans first. As they were led forward by Sister Margaret, he embraced and kissed the nun, and Varina did the same. As each child was introduced, they in turn were affectionately embraced and kissed by both Davises. After the orphans passed, the Davises shook hands with every child present, and children who were too young to walk were taken in their arms and kissed. Following the children, the general audience came up. During the handshaking, his hand grew fatigued, and he had to rest it on a table. When the event concluded, the Davises returned to the home of their host.[77]

Davis's last few days in Macon were spent in much-needed rest. The exertions of the previous ten days had taken a toll on him physically. On November 1, Davis became critically ill. Bishop J. N. Galleher of Louisiana telegraphed, offering to come immediately to Macon. But the patient rallied and insisted that he was well enough to travel. So, on the third day of his illness, the family decided to return home to Beauvoir.

On their last full day in the city, Davis remained in his room, appearing downstairs for only a brief time when his daughters returned from Athens, where they had gone in his place. Although the people of that city were disappointed that he could not come, Winnie and Margaret were given an ovation similar to what their father had received during other parts of his Southern Tour. All along the route, people waited to see them and presented them with flowers. During a reception, over a hundred Confederate veterans answered a bugle call and lined up to shake their hands. At the conclusion of the ceremony, the Davis daughters kissed the folds of a battle flag that had been carried in the war and were presented with two stars cut from the flag.[78]

The Davises left for home on the morning of November 3. They were escorted to the depot by thirty-two men of the Macon Volunteer Regiment and the music of an African American band. The streets were lined with people who bared their heads in respect for their visitor. Out of concern for his health, they strictly adhered to the warning of the *Macon Daily Telegraph* that they should not attempt to get near him or shake his hand. At the depot, a path was created through the crowd, and the Davises entered the train through two lines of soldiers. As a surprise gift to the former president, five boxes loaded with cigars, champagne, and a variety of alcoholic beverages collected from the citizens of Macon had been placed on the train without his knowledge.[79]

The Davises arrived back at Beauvoir on the same train on which they had left, still covered with bunting and American flags. As emotionally rewarding as the Southern Tour and Confederate reunion of the past two years had been, the physical strain made such future exertions unwise. There had been concern from the beginning of the potential strain of the visit to Macon. Even before Davis left Beauvoir, he told Varina that he expected to return a corpse. But, he added, "If I am to die it would be a pleasure to die surrounded by Confederate soldiers."[80] Although he had wanted to go, his age and physical condition placed a constant strain on his health. The close confinement on the train and demonstrations along the route tired him. Even with rest, his condition was not as favorable as his family had hoped. After the emotional demonstration by the veterans, he was almost prostrate and had to be examined by a physician. He spent much of the stay in Macon in his room, with Varina attempting to limit his conversation. Although rest rejuvenated him, he continued to tire easily. Few of the many who called to see him were permitted a visit. A reporter who was ordered by his newspaper to get an interview failed in a dozen visits, despite varying his excuses to see the former president. His physician became seriously alarmed at one point, and some northern newspapers reported that he was near death.[81] On the return to Beauvoir, his Macon physician accompanied him part way.

Davis would venture forth beyond Beauvoir to speak in a public forum only one more time before his death. In March 1888, a delegation of young men who were holding a convention at Mississippi City asked him to speak one last time. On this occasion, a positive reply was easy, given that the distance he had to travel was only a six-mile buggy ride from Beauvoir. It is significant that his last speech to the men of the South was not of the Confederacy but of their role in a reunited United States:

> The past is dead; let it bury its dead, its hopes and its aspirations. Before you lies the future—a future full of golden promise; a future of expanding national glory, before which all the world shall stand amazed. Let me beseech you to lay aside all rancor, all bitter sectional feeling, and to take your places in the ranks of those who will bring about a consummation devoutly to be wished—a reunited country.[82]

According to some historians, Davis not only refused to accept national reunion but also "harshly" rejected reconciliation with his former enemies.[83] However, a closer study of Davis's last years demonstrates that although he rejected a personal pardon from the government, he accepted reconciliation not only for the people of the South but within his own family as well. That the former Confederate president was sincere in his desire for reconciliation was demonstrated shortly before his death when his daughter Winnie asked her father's permission to marry. Her proposed fiancé was not only a Yankee but also the grandson of a well-known abolitionist. Although originally declining to approve, he was eventually won over and accepted the engagement.

NOTES

1. William J. Cooper, *Jefferson Davis, American* (New York: Knopf, 2000), 647–78.

2. Hudson Strode, *Jefferson Davis, Tragic Hero, the Last Twenty-Five Years, 1864–1889* (1964; reprint, New York: Harcourt, 2000), 478.

3. *Montgomery (Ala.) Advertiser*, March 30, 1886.

4. Michael B. Ballard, "Cheers for Jefferson Davis," *American History Illustrated* 16, no. 2 (May 1981): 9; Clement Eaton, *Jefferson Davis, Sphinx of the Confederacy* (New York: Free Press, 1977), 266.

5. Strode, *Jefferson Davis, Tragic Hero*, 279.

6. *New York World*, April 30, 1886.

7. *New York World*, May 1, 1886.

8. *Atlanta Constitution*, April 27, 1886.

9. *New York World*, April 28, 1886.

10. *New York Times*, April 28, 1886.

11. *New York World*, April 28, 1886; Robert McElroy, *Jefferson Davis: The Unreal and the Real* (1937; reprint, New York: Smithmark Publishers, 1996), 674–75.

12. *New York Times*, April 29, 1886; *Atlanta Constitution*, April 29, 1886.

13. *New York World*, April 28, 1886.

14. *New York World*, April 28, 1886.

15. *New York World*, April 28, 1886; *New York Times*, April 28, 1886.

16. *New York World*, April 28, 1886.

17. *New York World*, April 28, 1886.

18. *New York Times*, April 28, 1886; McElroy, *Jefferson Davis*, 674.

19. *New York Times*, April 28, 1886; Felicity Allen, *Jefferson Davis, Unconquerable Heart* (Columbia: University of Missouri Press, 1999), 552.

20. *New York World*, April 29, 1886.

21. Cooper, *Jefferson Davis, American*, 649.

22. *Atlanta Constitution*, April 29, 1886.

23. *Atlanta Constitution*, April 29, 1886.

24. *New York World*, April 29, 1886.

25. *Atlanta Constitution*, April 30, 1886.

26. Ballard, "Cheers for Jefferson Davis," 11.

27. Strode, *Jefferson Davis, Tragic Hero*, 483.

28. *Atlanta Constitution*, April 27, 1886.

29. *Atlanta Constitution*, April 27, 1886.

30. Strode, *Jefferson Davis, Tragic Hero*, 483.

31. *New York World*, May 3, 1886.

32. *New York Times*, April 30, 1886.

33. *New York Times*, April 30, 1886.

34. *Atlanta Journal*, May 1, 1886; *The World*, May 3, 1886.

35. *Atlanta Constitution*, May 1, 1886; Ballard, "Cheers for Jefferson Davis," 11.

36. *Atlanta Constitution*, May 1, 1886.

37. *New York World*, May 3, 1886; Strode, *Jefferson Davis, Tragic Hero*, 483.

38. *Atlanta Journal*, May 1, 1886; Strode, *Jefferson Davis, Tragic Hero*, 484.

39. *New York World*, May 3, 1886; Ballard, "Cheers for Jefferson Davis," 11.

40. Allen, *Jefferson Davis, Unconquerable Heart*, 551–52.

41. *Atlanta Journal*, May 1, 1886. Winnie Davis became enormously popular with white southerners and Confederate veterans, and she was rarely mentioned in the press or in public addresses without the inclusion of her nickname as the "Daughter of the Confederacy." Most sources, including her contemporaries, credited the name to Henry Grady during the dedication of the Ben Hill monument. Historian Hudson Strode, in his *Jefferson Davis, Tragic Hero*, states, "While the echoes of applause were still reverberating, Grady led Winnie before the crowd and presented her as the Daughter of the Confederacy" (484). Because of the proximity in time and place to the actual event, this writer accepts the newspaper's report.

42. *Atlanta Journal*, May 1, 1886.

43. *New York World*, May 3, 1886.

44. Strode, *Jefferson Davis, Tragic Hero*, 485; *Savannah Morning News*, May 3, 1886.

45. *Savannah Morning News*, May 3, 1886.

46. *Atlanta Journal*, May 1, 1886.

47. *New York World*, May 3, 1886.

48. *New York Times*, May 4, 1886.

49. *New York Times*, May 3, 1886; *The World*, May 2, 1886.

50. *Savannah Morning News*, May 7, 1886; *The World*, May 2, 1886.

51. *Atlanta Constitution*, May 4, 1886; *The World*, May 4, 1886.

52. *Savannah Morning News*, May 5, 1886.

53. *Savannah Morning News*, May 6, 1886.

54. *Savannah Evening News*, May 5–6, 1886.

55. *New York World*, May 7, 1886.

56. *New York World*, May 8, 1886.

57. *New York World*, May 7, 1886.

58. *New York World*, May 7, 1886; Strode, *Jefferson Davis, Tragic Hero*, 485–86; Stuart Towns, "'To Preserve the Traditions of Our Fathers': The Post-War Speaking Career of Jefferson Davis," *Journal of Mississippi History* 52 (1990): 117.

59. Strode, *Jefferson Davis, Tragic Hero*, 487.

60. Ballard, "Cheers for Jefferson Davis," 14–15.

61. Ballard, "Cheers for Jefferson Davis," 15.

62. Strode, *Jefferson Davis, Tragic Hero*, 487–88.

63. Strode, *Jefferson Davis, Tragic Hero*, 492.

64. *Macon Telegraph*, October 24, 1887.

65. *Macon Telegraph*, October 25, 1887.

66. Strode, *Jefferson Davis, Tragic Hero*, 492–93.

67. Strode, *Jefferson Davis, Tragic Hero*, 492–93.

68. *Macon Telegraph*, October 25, 1887.

69. Strode, *Jefferson Davis, Tragic Hero*, 493.

70. *Macon Telegraph*, October 21, 1887.

71. *Macon Telegraph*, October 27, 1887.

72. *Macon Telegraph*, October 27, 1887.

73. *Macon Telegraph*, October 27, 1887.

74. *Macon Telegraph*, October 27, 1887.

75. *Macon Telegraph*, October 27, 1887.

76. *Macon Telegraph*, October 26–27, 1887.

77. *Macon Telegraph*, October 29–30, 1887.

78. *Macon Telegraph*, November 3, 1887.

79. *Macon Telegraph*, November 4, 1887.

80. *Macon Telegraph*, November 4, 1887.

81. *Macon Telegraph*, November 4, 1887; Strode, *Jefferson Davis, Tragic Hero*, 494.

82. Strode, *Jefferson Davis, Tragic Hero*, 495.

83. David W. Blight, *Race and Reunion: The Civil War in American Memory* (Cambridge, Mass.: Belknap Press, 2002), 267.

The Second Resurrection:
The Death and Funeral of Jefferson Davis

Let our flags stand at half-mast,
For a high soul has passed
....
Now he has reached, we feel,
The Court of last appeal,

Where those whose lives seemed cursed
Earth's sentence find reversed,
And oft the last stand first.

—"Lines on the Death of Jefferson Davis," *Charleston (S.C.)*
News and Courier, December 10, 1889

The reception on the Southern Tour and in Macon left Davis secure in the feeling that whatever the country thought of him, he had regained and even surpassed the affection that the South had for him in 1861. Life at Beauvoir seemed good. In 1889, the last year of his life, his daughter Margaret came for an extended visit, and Davis rejoiced in spending time with his grandchildren. Visitors continued to come to Beauvoir to pay their respects. Jubal Early, every bit as unreconstructed as Davis himself, brought him a new tailor-made suit of Confederate gray that he wore during his final months and in which he would soon be buried. The old man continued to occupy himself with his writing. In the summer of 1888, James Redpath, managing editor of the *North American Review*, a longtime political enemy who became an admirer within days of their first meeting, convinced him to write a series of articles, at $250 apiece, as well as a book to be titled *A Short History of the Confederate States*.[1]

Though Davis found satisfaction at home in Beauvoir, he was not out of the financial woods. He agreed to write the articles partly because of his concern about the family's finances. His indebtedness was widely known. Many felt that much of his debt had resulted from the "boundless hospitality" he offered to the steady stream of visitors to his home on the Gulf of Mexico. But pride would not permit him to accept charity. His normal reply to offers of financial aid was that any funds raised should go to disabled veterans or widows and orphans. As a result, aid to the former president had to be given through subterfuge. Had he know about it, he would certainly have rejected the food and delicacies left on the back veranda of Beauvoir by neighbors who visited in the dark of night. Varina, however, was more realistic and quietly accepted.[2]

A project to aid Davis and his family proposed during his lifetime was a planned "Davis Land Company" in which investors would pay $10 per share for 5,700 acres of undeveloped land that Davis owned in Arkansas. This same device would be resurrected following his death in order to care for his widow. According to the prospectus for the proposed land company, "The Hon. Jefferson Davis owes more than $40,000, and . . . his actual income . . . does not amount to $200."[3]

DEATH

Davis's concern over finances played a role in his death. In good years, his Brierfield plantation produced a good income. However, two successive floods of the Mississippi River over his land had plunged him deeply into debt to his commission merchant, J. U. Payne. Although Payne was an old friend who never pressed him for payment, the debt preyed on Davis's mind.[4] In November 1889, he made his annual visit to collect rents from his tenants. Varina normally accompanied her husband on these trips, but with guests visiting Beauvoir, he told her to remain home with them. She was nevertheless concerned, since he had been weak and unable to exercise for some time. Despite her anxiety over his health, she agreed to stay behind while he tended to business at the plantation.[5]

Davis boarded the steamboat *Laura Lee* in New Orleans during a cold rain. As he made his way up the Mississippi, he fell ill with influenza. When the boat reached the Brierfield landing, he felt too weak to disembark and decided to continue to Vicksburg, where he spent the night. The next day, although still sick, he made his way downriver to the plantation. There he lay ill for four days, refusing to send for a doctor. On November 12, he wrote his last letter, clearly revealing his physical weakness to Varina as well as the unclear state of his mind. "My deerest," he wrote, "if I can get to the landing I will go down on the heathers [a misspelling of the steamboat *Leathers*] to-morrow . . .

I have suffered much. . . . Nothing is as it should be, and I am not able to look at the place [Brierfield]."[6]

Before the letter arrived, Varina received a telegram sent secretly by one of their employees, informing her of his condition. She immediately entrained for New Orleans, where she boarded a northbound steamer. As her ship neared Davis's vessel, the captain hailed it to ask if there was any news of her husband. On hearing that he was aboard, the two steamboats drew alongside, and Varina transferred to the *Leathers* in mid-river for the journey back to New Orleans. At Bayou Sara, two physicians came aboard to examine Davis. They determined that he was suffering from acute bronchitis, complicated by a recurrence of malaria.[7]

There was a cold rain falling as the couple arrived in New Orleans. They were met by their old friend J. M. Payne, Payne's son-in-law, Justice Charles E. Fenner, the Davis's family physician and friend Stanford E. Chaille (dean of the medical faculty of Tulane University), and Edgar H. Farrar and Lucinda Stamps, a niece and nephew by marriage. As Davis was too weak for the trip to Beauvoir, Judge Fenner offered his home as a place to recuperate. Varina accepted, and an ambulance was brought from Charity Hospital to take him there. During the ride, Davis was tended to by a Catholic nun, Mother Agnes, and four medical students, all of whom were children of Confederate veterans.[8] The prognosis was grim, as he had gone for a week without the benefit of medical care.

Davis would live out the final twenty days of his life in the Fenner home, an impressive two-story brown stucco house with broad verandas, on the corner of First and Camp streets. In the yard, camellia bushes bloomed, and orange trees bore fruit. Inside, a wide hall ran through the center of the house with drawing rooms on one side and a library on the other. Davis was assigned a corner room to the rear of the house. There he lay on a large, carved oak Victorian bedstead from which he could view the outdoors through four windows decorated with lace curtains.[9]

Throughout Davis's final days, Varina remained constantly by his side. On those occasions when she had to leave the room, he asked for her and was uneasy until she returned. She was assisted in caring for him by her own "handmaiden," Betty, who had access to the room at all times, and by a hired African American nurse named Lydia. Although friends constantly sent flowers, Varina allowed them to remain in the sickroom for only a short time. She at first accepted gifts of jellies, fruits, and other delicacies, but these were soon banned completely. The patient was allowed only milk, ice, beef tea, and, on rare occasion, a pork chop. Very little talk was allowed, and newspapers, letters, and telegrams were forbidden.[10]

For the first week after his arrival, Davis remained in a dangerous condition. After that, there was hope for improvement until shortly before his death.

Dr. Chaille informed a reporter that chances were favorable for recovery, although he was not sure of it. Varina was nevertheless optimistic, feeling that his health would eventually return. It was the patient himself who insisted that his case was, if not hopeless, at least nearly so. Dr. Charles J. Bickham (vice president of the board of administrators of the charity hospital), who, with Chaille, attended him throughout his final illness, noted that the former president "seemed to foresee the end, and if asked how he felt, even when not in pain, . . . would say, 'I feel as though I were going down, down, down.'" Nonetheless, he did not fear death and did not let its prospects dampen his spirit. Although his doctors tried in vain to convince him that he was improving, he steadily insisted there was no improvement and that he was content to accept "whatever Providence had in store for him."[11] Reiterating this same sentiment to his wife, he said, "I have much to do, but if it is God's will, I must submit." "I want to tell you," he added at another time, "I am not afraid to die."[12] This state of mind, according to his physician, had considerable effect on the prognosis for recovery.[13]

Regardless of his acceptance of his own death, he chose to keep the facts of his condition from their two surviving children. In reply to Varina's plea to inform them by telegram, he told her, "Let our darlings be happy while they can; I may get well."[14] Nevertheless, Margaret, who was tending her sick husband at home in Colorado, ignored their advice not to come and boarded a train for New Orleans. Unfortunately, an accident on the train prevented her from arriving in time to see her father while he still lived. Winnie, who had gone to France for her health, was kept in ignorance of her father's true condition until his death.

Near the end, Davis's health seemed to improve despite the fact that he had begun to refuse food. On Thursday morning, the day before his death, he playfully remarked to his friend J. M. Payne, "I am afraid that I shall be compelled to agree with the doctors for once, and admit that I am a little better."[15] As favorable symptoms continued during the day, Varina sent a positive message to several friends and relatives. "He is better," she wrote, "but very low. . . . I have every hope of final recovery, though of course expecting a weary convalescence. As for me, to have even this hope and care is joy."[16] With feelings of optimism, several of Davis's relatives, anticipating no danger, attended the opera, only to be summoned home. At 6:00 P.M., Davis awoke from a sound sleep with a congestive chill that seemed to crush the vitality out of his body. When Varina tried to give him medicine, he told her, "Please excuse me, I cannot take it." These were the last words he would speak.[17]

At 7:00, Doctors Bickham and Chaille arrived to consult over their patient's condition. When they realized he was dying, they remained with him to the end. Gathered around his bed were Varina, the doctors, Payne, Judge Fenner, the judge's wife and son, Davis's grandniece Nannie Smith, and Edgar H. Farrar. Davis remained comatose, showing no signs of consciousness. Varina, dressed in a gray and black home-wrapper, remained constantly by his side with his hand in hers. Whether or not she could actually feel any movement, she believed that she could feel an occasional pressure on her hand, although he could neither speak nor make a sign.[18]

Seeing that he was breathing heavily as he lay on his back, the doctors assisted him to turn on his right side. He lay for some fifteen minutes with his cheek resting on his right hand like a sleeping infant, his left hand across his chest, breathing softly but gently. Respiration became more and more feeble until he was silent. At 12:45 A.M., Jefferson Davis was dead. The end came "gently and utterly without pain."[19] The cause of death was declared to be a combination of chronic diseases coupled with malarial fever and old age.

VARINA'S VIGIL

Varina, grief stricken and weakened from the ordeal, was taken upstairs, where friends tried to comfort her. At her request, the body remained at the Fenner home for nearly a full day, not being removed until nearly midnight. While she was resting, funeral director Frank R. Johnson was called to prepare the remains, which were straightened, bathed, and embalmed. By 5:30 A.M., the task was completed, and Davis was dressed in the same suit of Confederate gray that had been made from material given to him by his friend Jubal Early and that he had worn when he was carried from the steamboat *Leathers* to the Fenner home.[20] According to historian Charles Reagan Wilson, Johnson failed to fully embalm the body, with the result that the body began to show signs of deterioration while lying in state.[21] However, this was not evident to the several reporters who wrote that Davis appeared much as he had in life. As a final irony, or perhaps as a symbol of the reconciliation he had preached late in life, the casket and the embalming fluid for the southern leader were produced in the North.

When the funeral director left, Varina returned and took her seat beside the body. She said that she wished to remain alone with the remains for the day. Friends tried to dissuade her because of her weakened condition, but she was insistent, and they gave way. In an effort to give her privacy, the front door was locked, and callers were rigidly excluded. As a result, the large number of visitors who increasingly began to appear with flowers and offers of help at the door of the residence from an early hour in the morning were turned away.[22] A notable exception was made for Miles Cooper, a former slave of Davis's brother, Joseph.

He had moved to Florida fifteen years earlier but maintained contact with the family through gifts of fruit that he sent every year. When he read of Davis's illness, he immediately traveled to New Orleans but suffered innumerable delays, arriving too late to see him alive. Although everyone but members of the family had been denied entrance, Varina ordered that Cooper be admitted. When he entered the room, he burst into tears, fell to his knees, and prayed.[23]

At 9:00 A.M., photographer E. F. Blake appeared with his assistant to take pictures of the body in death. Varina temporarily left the room while the remains of her husband were transferred to the parlor, where six photographs, full length and half figure, were taken. When they left, Varina returned and remained the entire day, disturbed on occasion only by her maid Betty.[24]

At 4:15 P.M., two Catholic nuns from Saint Alphonsus Convent appeared at the door with a request to pray before the body of the deceased man. Varina consented and left the room while they knelt beside the casket along with a small group of female orphans who accompanied them. Several members of the household staff also remained in the room while the visitors prayed.[25]

THE DAVIS CHILDREN LEARN OF THEIR FATHER'S DEATH

The first to be notified of Davis's death were his daughters Margaret and Winnie and the governor of Mississippi, the state from which he rose to political prominence. This was done by Edgar Farrar, who appeared at the Western Union office to wire Margaret Hayes in Colorado and Winnie in Paris. The older daughter was already en route but was delayed by a missed train connection in Fort Worth, Texas. She finally arrived at 8:00 the following evening (December 7), after her father had already been removed from the Fenner mansion. Winnie, who was in Paris for her health with her friends the Pulitzers, had been led to believe by a telegram received the previous day that her father was improving. Then, at noon, she received a dispatch that told her only that her father was dead. Winnie assumed he had died of heart disease.[26] When she insisted on returning home, Joseph Pulitzer wired Varina to seek her help in dissuading her daughter from making the trip. Because of the widow's state of mind, Farrar and Joseph Davis cabled Winnie, asking her to remain in France. As a result, she did not attempt to return for her father's funeral.[27]

THE NEWS IS SPREAD

The people of New Orleans learned of Davis's death through the ringing of bells. Since his passing had been expected for some time, plans had been made to spread the news to the city's population by the tolling of fire bells. Within five minutes of his death, the news was telephoned to the central fire station, and soon the bells sounded, informing the city of his demise. People began gathering at various hotels, and by 3:00 that morning, hundreds were discussing the event.[28]

Farrar's appearance at the Western Union office was noticed by the city's press, which in turn alerted the world to the event that took place that morning in New Orleans. In a day in which public opinion polling was still in the future, newspapers were arguably the best source for revealing the perceptions of individual persons, given that people influenced and were influenced by the editorial opinion and news they read. Judging by that medium, Davis at the time of his death had attained the highest status, one generally reserved for national leaders.

In all sections of the country, Davis, his death, and his funeral were given full front-page attention. Within twenty-four hours, newspapers began to publish a virtual deluge of information on the former Confederate president. Few items were too small for coverage. For more than a week, newspapers throughout the United States informed the public of every detail of Davis's last moments, funeral preparations, and the funeral itself. Headlines reported Varina's last kiss on her husband's "Cold Dead Lips."[29] The question of where he would be buried was treated as news and even discussed editorially. Lengthy columns retraced Davis's life. His will was printed for everyone to read. Full-length letters written over a period of thirty years by and to him appeared regularly in both North and South. Stories of his capture in women's clothing were repeatedly dragged out—with both fact and fiction printed as truth. Contradictory stories about his first marriage to Knox Taylor were resurrected. Many accounts were written by participants in the know and were accurate. Others were false.

PUBLIC REACTION TO DAVIS'S DEATH:
LOVE, HATE, AND INDIFFERENCE

The southern press was universal in its praise. The *New Orleans Daily Picayune* editorialized, "The funeral should be a demonstration of respect and love that would be the grandest and most impressive that had ever been witnessed in this city, and should be conducted on such a scale as to show the world that the South, in the face of sectional abuse and criticisms, does not hesitate to honor in the profoundest manner the memory of the greatest of her sons."[30]

These sentiments seemed to speak for the white South. Davis was treated with reverence, affection, and even adoration in numerous poems, editorials, and news accounts. The most common theme pictured him as the martyr who had lived and suffered imprisonment and chains for and in place of the people of the South. Southern governors used the press to issue proclamations that declared the day of the funeral to be a holiday in which state and local governments virtually shut down across the region. Businesses were asked to and did close, and residents were asked to decorate their homes in mourning. Every town, large and small, used the press to publicize memorial services and processions to be held to coincide with the funeral in New Orleans.[31]

The nonsouthern press also treated Davis's death and funeral as major events. Newspapers in Boston, New York, Chicago, and elsewhere gave the events full, detailed treatment similar to those recorded in the South. And with some exceptions, the news was printed objectively and without evident anti-Davis bias. In some cases, the portrayals of Davis and his funeral were so even-handed and positive that a reader could not distinguish whether the newspaper was southern or northern without reading the masthead. While this was the rule, Davis was also criticized and reviled by a significant minority of the nonsouthern press.[32]

For nearly a week, reactions to Davis's death dominated the southern press. Newspapers, government officials, veterans' associations, and others in city after city pleaded for the right to bury the Confederate president in their soil. Statues and memorials were planned. Virtually every town, regardless of size, held mass meetings to plan memorial services to coincide with the funeral in New Orleans. Bells were rung; cannons boomed; private, public, and business buildings were decorated profusely in mourning colors; and speakers vied with one another to express the glories of the deceased former leader of the Confederate states.[33]

Yet lingering hatred for Davis still existed beyond the South. Again, it was the press that spread the news of his treason during the war and nonrepentance following it. On the day of his death, the *Chicago Evening News* compared him to a "wife murderer" who "did what he could to destroy the best government on earth . . . [to be replaced by] a reign of slave holders." The *Detroit Journal* predicted "posterity will gibbit him high against the horizon of history . . . for bringing misery, poverty, [and] death to millions of his fellow beings in order to preserve a barbarous and inhuman wrong."[34] The *New York Tribune* of December 7 added that "Davis let no opportunity pass to fan the dying flames of sectional hatred and disloyalty. Surely it is permitted to hope that he represented only what was worst in the southern character and that as he departs from the state, the narrow and dictatorial and vindictive spirit which he so sharply represented may also fade away." The *Hartford Courant*, while acknowledging that "the seeds of 'the irrepressible conflict' were sown before Jefferson Davis was born," nevertheless wrote that he "led the wrong side. . . . No recollection of amiable, personal qualities, no generous emotion of graveside charity, can obscure—much less obliterate—that unalterable fact."[35] And the *Cleveland Gazette* argued that Davis was "a dangerous man, because he was at heart an enemy to the Union and all that it means to the people."[36] "Nobody doubts," wrote the editorial writer for the *Dayton Journal*, "the ability, courage, or devotion of the chief organizer of the conspiracy and rebellion . . . , but all his brilliant qualities as a man make his treason the more infamous. Of course he was a brave man, so were all his victims, so are all desperadoes who engage in conspiracy and rebellion."[37]

Such hostile editorial sentiments were also reflected in scattered news reports. In Denver, Colorado, E. E. Brannon, chairman of the Republican Central Committee, became so enthusiastic over Davis's death that he raised the Stars and Stripes to full mast over his office and kept it flying all day.[38] In Allegheny, Pennsylvania, a large attentive audience listened while their pastor, A. M. Hills, excoriated Davis as a soulless traitor and an offense to god.[39]

Reaction to Davis's death on the part of African Americans was not widely reported and is more difficult to gauge. Only a small number of black newspapers from this period are currently extant, and these chose to ignore Davis and his death. It appears from the little existing evidence that African Americans who knew the former Confederate president personally were close to him and considered him to be a friend. This was the opinion of Davis's nurse Betty.[40] Miles Cooper became visibly upset at news of his death. And James Jones, a free-black servant who was with Davis during his capture in 1865 and later became active in Republican politics in Raleigh, North Carolina, addressed him as "my best friend."[41]

On the other hand, African Americans who saw him from a distance still recalled his attempt to perpetuate slavery as president of the Confederacy. In one of the few known references to black reaction to Davis's death, the *Pittsburg (Pa.) Dispatch* of December 8, 1889 reported that African American students at Shaw University in Raleigh, North Carolina, gathered on campus and boisterously sang "Hang Jeff Davis on the Sour Apple Tree" and otherwise derided the name of the deceased wartime southern leader. It is safe to say that most African Americans were either hostile or indifferent to the leader of the Civil War South.

Despite the scattered instances of hostility to Davis on hearing of his death, negative news reports and editorials were relatively few in number. Their failure to result in counterdemonstrations in either North or South reveal the extent to which public sentiment had shifted by 1889. Despite the fact that the African American demonstration in Raleigh was conducted within the view of members of the white population, the incident ended quietly. A similar nonreaction met the honoring of the deceased southern president by former Confederate members of the Southern Society who lowered a flag in New York City. Even an overt display honoring Davis near Capitol Hill in the national capital failed to surprise passersby. Mrs. Frederick Fairfax, a native of Washington and widow of an American army officer, draped her home in obvious mourning while proclaiming her admiration for Davis to visiting reporters. Although a number of African American residents gathered on the street that morning to loudly criticize the display, they went no further, and the display remained.[42]

The healing of hostilities between the North and South by 1889 was evident in a reading of newspapers in both regions. In Kansas, whose statehood Davis had opposed unless it entered the Union as a slave state, the editorial writer for the *Wichita Eagle* eschewed negative criticism, writing admiringly of Davis's refusal to admit error even though other "living statesmen of the south" had agreed that the Civil War was necessary to end slavery. He nevertheless found it admirable that "to the last he held that his course was justifiable, reasonable, and patriotic."[43] The *Boston Globe*, in a state that had led the abolitionist movement, both in its reporting and editorials wrote sympathetically of Davis.

"WE KNOW OF NO SUCH MAN": A NONPERSON IN THE NATIONAL CAPITAL

Slight notice was given by the chaplain of the House of Representatives who made note in his prayer of December 9 to members of that chamber that "millions sit cold in the atmosphere of death, mourning the departure of a man dear to their hearts, who had reached the age of four score years."[44] However, the most widely reported and visible reaction to the death of Jefferson Davis was the decision of the national government to ignore it. The former Confederate president was considered to be officially dead in Washington, D.C. The failure to take official notice was made easier by the fact that he had not been pardoned and was no longer a citizen of the United States. Unofficially, southern senators, representatives, and Justice L. Q. C. Lamar of the Supreme Court mourned his death and made laudatory statements to the press. However, the War Department, where Davis had served as secretary from 1853 to 1855, and Congress, on whose capitol dome stood the statue of liberty that had been designed with direct input from Davis as secretary of war, took no official action.

Southern attention centered particularly on the failure of the War Department to mourn its former secretary. On a personal level, Major William B.

Lee, the only remaining employee who had served there during Davis's tenure, remembered him fondly as "one of the best secretaries of war who ever served ...a kind, social man, very considerate, and pleasant to serve under."[45] But Lee's was a minority opinion within the department. Secretary of War Redfield Proctor pursued a hard line of nonrecognition. Although news of Davis's death had reached the nation's capital via the telegraph and press, the flag at the War Department was run up to full mast and remained there all day, while the portrait of the former secretary within the building remained undraped.

The question of recognizing former secretary Davis at the time of his death had been discussed informally for some time among officials of the department. The general opinion held that his condition as an "unreconstructed rebellionist" who had refused to avail himself of an opportunity to remove his own political disabilities precluded the possibility of recognition. A few believed that the office and not the man should be honored, but others continued to point to the fact that Jefferson Davis did not exist as far as the U.S. government was concerned, and this opinion prevailed when news of his death was learned through the press. When approached by a reporter on the morning of the former secretary's death, Proctor replied, "I do not see that there is anything before us in the matter. We know nothing; we know no such man. It is better to forget such things, to let them pass away from our minds."[46]

When pressed on the department's practice of half-masting the flag on the death of a former secretary and whether it would be done on the day of Davis's funeral, Proctor acknowledged that it was the custom but replied firmly that "it will be safe to say the flag will not be placed at half-mast upon that occasion."[47] The secretary's snub was without precedent since the department had followed official protocol on the death of Charles M. Conrad, Davis's immediate predecessor in the position and a former Confederate congressman from Louisiana, on his death in 1878. On that occasion, orders were issued that the department be closed, the flag lowered, and the building draped on the day of the funeral. However, the order was issued after Conrad's funeral and was therefore not carried out. Davis's exclusion was explained solely by the fact that Conrad had received a governmental pardon for his role in the Confederacy and Davis had not.[48]

On December 7, Proctor received a telegram from Mayor Joseph A. Shakespeare officially notifying him that the "one time Secretary of War of the United States" was dead. In reply, the current secretary diplomatically tried to soothe southern feelings. He telegraphed the mayor that taking no action was the "right course for one and all." Its adoption, he argued, was prompted by "a sincere wish and purpose to act in that spirit of peace and good will which should fill the hearts of all our people."[49] Proctor's snub, which was reprinted widely in the southern press, was accepted with only minor critical comment. The *New Orleans Picayune* simply noted that "the Secretary of War, so far from intending wrong, has adopted what he believed and what we believe was a wise and conservative course in the [War Department] premises."[50]

NEW ORLEANS PREPARES FOR A GRAND FUNERAL

While southerners elsewhere were experiencing the initial reaction to the news of Jefferson Davis's death, New Orleans began to prepare for his funeral. Mayor Shakespeare was among the earliest notified. Awakened from his sleep, he quickly dressed and hurriedly walked through the still-dark streets to the Fenner residence. Arriving at approximately 3:00 A.M., Farrar and Payne escorted him into the parlor, where, in consultation with members of the family, he hastily sketched a proclamation to the people of New Orleans informing them of the event and announcing a meeting of certain named citizens to be held at nine that morning in the city hall. At 4:10 A.M., it was handed to a reporter for the *New Orleans Times-Democrat*, which had held up publication of the morning edition until it received a copy.[51]

More than sixty of the city's elite, representatives of the city and state government, the judiciary, and the political, social, religious, labor, business, and military organizations met in the mayor's parlor at city hall in answer to the call. Particularly significant among these were Justice Fenner of the state supreme court, there as a representative of the Davis family; Episcopal Bishop John Galleher, who would soon be placed in charge of all religious aspects; William Preston Johnston, president of Tulane University and a son of General Albert Sydney Johnston, who was to be placed in charge of overall planning; Colonel J. B. Richardson of the Washington Artillery, who was to command the military guard surrounding Davis's bier; and the heads of the various Confederate veterans' associations, including the Army of Northern Virginia, the Army of Tennessee, the Confederate Cavalry Association, and the United Confederate Veterans, which participated in various military aspects of the lying in state and burial. Particularly notable from a symbolic sense was the inclusion of two Union army veterans, Colonel T. L. Bayne, then serving as the deputy collector for the port of New Orleans, and Captain Jacob Grey, commander of the Louisiana Department of the Grand Army of the Republic (GAR).[52]

The meeting opened with a call for suggestions. Associate Justice Fenner informed the assembly that Davis's widow recognized the right of Confederate veterans and other southerners to plan, prepare, and organize all activities related to the burial of the man they had followed during the war. She did, however, wish to keep his remains with her for the remainder of the day.[53] In response to her wishes and in order to avoid observation by crowds of curious bystanders, it was decided that Davis's body would remain in the Fenner home until "an appropriate hour of night" at which time it would be transferred to the city hall to lie in state until noon Tuesday, December 10.

Although it was still too early to discuss the location of a permanent gravesite with his widow, it was assumed that the family cemetery at Brierfield plantation in Mississippi would be the eventual resting place for the remains. This seemed logical, as that was where his beloved brother Joseph was buried. However, when it was realized that a public funeral of the size demanded for a person of Davis's stature precluded holding it at his plantation, plans were made for temporary interment in Metairie Cemetery. The mausoleums of the veterans' associations of the armies of Tennessee and Northern Virginia were located there. Both organizations desired the honor of providing the temporary resting place for the Confederate president's remains. To settle the issue, straws were reportedly drawn, with the latter organization winning the contest.[54]

Before the meeting of December 6 was over, it had also notified the governors and Confederate veterans' organizations throughout the South and elsewhere of the death and funeral plans. It had delayed the funeral date until noon December 11 once it was realized the large number of out-of-state persons who wished to attend. It arranged for the transfer of the body to the council chamber of city hall for lying in state. Finally, it had created an Executive Committee on Funeral Ceremonies whose charge it was to plan and coordinate the activities surrounding Davis's death and burial, with authority to create any necessary subcommittees.

From this point, the Executive Committee assumed all responsibility for the funeral and burial, with frequent input from Farrar, Fenner, and Shakespeare. The chairmanship was assigned to William Preston Johnston, who had served on Davis's staff during the war and was a close friend of the family. The committee was composed of seven members appointed by the mayor, with representation from all the major veterans' organizations, both Confederate and Union. Colonel J. Richardson, as commander of the Washington Artillery, which had seen combat throughout the entire Civil War, was responsible for guarding Davis's body while it lay in state, along with former soldiers from the Veterans' Home and the armies of Tennessee and Northern Virginia. Captain A. J. Lewis of the Army of Tennessee and President Fred S. Washington of the Army of Northern Virginia, played active rolls. The city council, Sons of Veterans, and the [Confederate] Veterans Cavalry Association were also represented.[55]

Clearly more important, however, from a purely symbolic perspective was the inclusion of Captain Jacob Grey. The Union veteran and GAR officer's participation was of great significance in easing the sting of expected northern criticism that would have been certain if the funeral were turned into a memorial to the Confederacy. With his help, the ceremonies could honor Davis and at the same time set a tone of national reconciliation. Grey's statement that he "would be proud, as a soldier of the United States, to honor the memory of the illustrious patriot, soldier, and statesman of the South" was widely approved. Recognizing that Jefferson Davis had been a soldier of the U.S. Army who had rendered distinguished service to the national government before the Civil War, he suggested to the committee that he be given a military funeral. "If it is agreed," he said, "that the body of the dead chieftain shall be borne into the cemetery upon the shoulders of the old veterans, I, as a representative of the Grand Army of the Republic, shall certainly demand to have the right to assist in the performance of that honorable duty."[56] Grey's proposal was accepted, and the funeral would be a military one.

Throughout the period of lying in state and burial, the prominence of the American national flag over that of the Confederacy would emphasize Davis's ties to the United States. A small American flag in mourning, with a portrait of Davis in the center, was a common decoration during the funeral.[57] Grey's proposal of a role for the GAR in the Davis funeral activities was applauded by southerners and by some northern members of the organization itself. A telegram from a GAR member in Pittsfield, Massachusetts, praised his "particip[ation] with the South in the funeral of the great chief. Your record on the field will stand it now, and time will applaud it hereafter."[58]

Grey's acceptance of a participatory role for the GAR in the Davis funeral activities did not, however, sit well with the national organization of Union veterans, which had also criticized him for his earlier participation with Jefferson Davis in the dedication of a monument to Confederate General Albert Sydney Johnston. The national office, which opposed the inclusion of African Americans as members of its organization, was further upset by Grey's role in accepting a black post in his district. According to *The Bee*, an African American newspaper in Washington, D.C., the captain chose this as a means to revenge himself on members of the GAR who questioned his loyalty for taking part in the ceremonies for Davis.[59]

The Executive Committee was the workhorse of the general committee, which did not meet again after December 6. Everything related to Davis's death and funeral was left to it. It met regularly in the city hall, and what it could not do itself it farmed to subcommittees that handled such mundane activities as finances, planning for visitors, decorations, religious services, establishing a military honor guard, selecting pallbearers, funeral trains, and numerous other things. No detail was too small to be overlooked. The time set for public viewing of the remains was ten in the morning until ten each night. Colonel Richardson informed the committee that the Washington Artillery would be sent to guard the bier, to be relieved at intervals by members of the city's other veterans' organizations. Telegrams were sent to the governor of every southern state, announcing Davis's death and the time of the funeral.

One of the first issues addressed was the nomination of a grand marshal for the funeral procession. William Preston Johnston declined the honor. But when John Gordon, head of the recently formed United Confederate Veterans organization and governor of Georgia, was proposed, one member of the committee thought it might be a slur on the Louisiana National Guard to select a person from another state. For that reason, the issue of grand marshal was moved to a subcommittee that returned with a compromise decision, naming John G. Glynn, head of the Louisiana National Guard, as grand marshal and Gordon as honorary grand marshal.[60]

THE COUNCIL CHAMBER: A SOLDIER LYING IN STATE

Once the meeting of the general committee adjourned, the council chamber was emptied, and work began in earnest to prepare the room for the reception of the body. A two-step catafalque, twelve by twelve feet in dimension, on which Davis's coffin would be placed during the lying in state, was erected in the center of the room. Black crepe was profusely draped over windows, on walls, and around columns and was strung from light fixtures. It bordered framed portraits and other pictures and was placed along the hallway of the city hall, through which visitors would pass to view the body in the council chamber. Plants and shrubbery were placed along the walls to offset the somber tones. The mayor's and city clerk's desks were hidden from view by a stand on which flowers could be placed. A portrait of Davis was placed on the wall. This was draped in black through which small incandescent lights blinked, giving the impression of stars in the night sky.

In keeping with the decision of the Executive Committee to bury Davis as a soldier of the United States rather than as the president of the Confederacy, the chamber was given a distinct military appearance. Floral swords were placed on the wall, with crossed U.S. and Confederate flags. The latter, the flag of the Fourteenth Louisiana Regiment, bore the tatters of age and bullet holes from four years of service during the Civil War. An image of the American eagle and the coat of arms of the United States stood above the flags. Stacked arms were placed around the room, and two twelve-pound bronze mountain howitzers were brought in by the Washington Artillery, one placed on each side of the catafalque on which the coffin would lie. These were supplemented by the sword carried by Davis during the Black Hawk War, which Varina ordered retrieved from Beauvoir and placed on the bier. Once the remains entered the chamber, they would be guarded by uniformed members of the Washington Artillery and veterans of the armies of Tennessee and Northern Virginia as well as a representative from the Confederate veterans' home.[61]

THE REMOVAL FROM THE FENNER HOME
TO THE CITY HALL

While workers continued to prepare the council chamber for the lying in state, undertakers Frank Johnson Jr. and R. C. Davey journeyed to the Fenner home to retrieve the body of Jefferson Davis, where it had lain since his arrival three weeks earlier during a cold rainstorm. The streets were again wet when the hearse reached the mansion at 10:55 that evening. When Varina heard the sound of the wheels on the pavement outside, she kissed her husband's lips one final time, then left the room for her own apartment.

The door had scarcely closed behind her when the undertakers entered the main hall. Johnson and Davey placed Davis's body in a coffin specially designed to permit public viewing while it lay in state. A single sheet of heavy French plate glass extended the length of the top of the coffin through which lines of mourners could view the deceased southern leader. Otherwise, it was devoid of much ornamentation. A silver plaque attached simply stated, "Jefferson Davis. At Rest," with the date of death added. The handles on both sides consisted of single square bars of silver across which there was a short bar of gold. The only other ornamentation was a cover of black plush edged with broad black braid.[62]

While the undertakers did their work, the hearse and two carriages waited at the door. First the floral offerings were placed in the coaches, and then the casket was carried to the hearse by the deceased man's friends and relatives, including E. H. Farrar, Judge C. E. Fenner, J. U. Payne, and three others. The six then entered the carriage and followed the hearse as it moved slowly under a full moon down the rain-dampened First and Saint Charles streets to the city hall. In describing the scene, a reporter for the *New Orleans Times-Democrat* noted that a "thick vale [*sic*] of misty clouds swept . . . up from the river . . . drenching the foliage of the spreading magnolias on either side of the street. Great drops of water hung like crystals from the points of the drooping leaves . . . as though the trees were shedding tears of sympathy as the . . . cortege passed."[63]

Despite the near-midnight hour (11:55 P.M.) when the carriages arrived, the city hall, lobbies, corridors, and council chamber were crowded with people. A police escort cleared a path as the same six men who had taken the coffin from the residence carried it through the broad hallway into the council chamber. There it was carried up the catafalque and placed gently on a bier that rested on top of a thick Turkish rug of black hair.

The crowd in the hall watched silently with bowed heads as the casket was placed gently in position while undertaker Johnson arranged the lid so that the remains might be viewed through the glass cover. The battle-worn flag of the Fifth Company of the Washington Artillery was thrown "with studied and effective carelessness" across the coffin, leaving Davis's head and part of the bust exposed. A four-man guard was immediately placed over the remains, one at each corner of the catafalque. Although at this time the viewing was officially closed to the public, the police and military guards allowed the crowd in the hallway to begin filing past as soon as the coffin had been placed in position. This unofficial viewing continued throughout the night.[64]

The city responded to the news of Davis's death by draping itself in mourning and lowering flags to half-mast. City and municipal buildings, private residences, the cotton and other exchanges, stores, newspaper offices, and ships and boats of all sizes on the river began to display symbols of mourning. Public schools were dismissed to reopen on "Monday next." Tulane University, Sophie Newcombe College, and a number of private schools closed, as did the cotton and other exchanges. Other agencies, public and private, including the state supreme court, announced their closure for the day of the funeral.

From the morning of December 7 through noon on December 11, the center of public interest in New Orleans was the council chamber in the back part of the city hall where Davis lay. At precisely 10:00 A.M., the doors to the chamber opened, and a steady line slowly proceeded in single file up the steps of the catafalque, past the coffin, and departed through the gateway in the iron fence that separated the council chamber from the lobby. The chamber by this time smelled of flowers from the many floral offerings placed around the room. Davis's lifelong friend, General George W. Jones of Iowa, was among the first to enter. The sight brought tears to his eyes as he said, "My dear friend," referring to the deceased man.[65]

During the first day of viewing, an estimated twenty thousand people of different ages, races, and economic status filed past the coffin at the rate of fifteen hundred per hour. As they peered at the remains, they looked on a face reportedly little different than it appeared in life. "The plentiful white hair, the full white beard, and the distinct features were just as they were often seen by the populace of New Orleans."[66] Among the viewers were a large number of

Mississippians, including a number who had been slaves of the Davis family. As reported in the *New Orleans Times-Democrat*, they

> spoke in the highest praise of their dead master. One of them wept as he looked at the face of the dead man. He gave his name as Wm. Sanford, of Vicksburg, and said that he had come to the city to pay his last tribute to his old master. "That I loved him this shows, and I can say that every colored man who he ever owned loved him. He was a good, kind master." During the day, James Lewis, a leader of the African American community of New Orleans, visited Mayor Shakespeare who assured him that the city hall was open to all and that no cards of admission were needed.[67]

When the council chamber closed for the day at ten in the evening, many persons were still in line. The room was placed under the charge of the Washington Artillery, and access was restricted only to family members and authorized individuals. At five minutes before midnight, the guards were temporarily removed, and undertaker Johnson and his assistants entered to remove the glass top from the coffin, then left the room to Davis's daughter Margaret Hayes, who entered on the arm of his nephew General Joseph R. Davis. They remained alone with the body for ten minutes.

At their departure, the sculptor Orion Frazee entered the room with Farrar and city councilman James G. Clark, a member of the Executive Committee. Frazee was there at the request of the *Atlanta Constitution*'s editor Henry Grady and Georgia Governor Gordon, who had received permission from the widow to make a death mask for use in creating a statue of the Confederate president to be erected in Atlanta. The sculptor raised Davis's head and took an impression in plaster of paris. Frazee was "much pleased with the impression of the head." "The features," he stated, "he would be able to reproduce from a photograph."[68] He had also hoped to get an impression of the right hand and foot but found it impossible because they had become shrunken. Frazee continued to work with the body until four in the morning, when he finished his labors.

On the evening of December 7, while the public filed past the coffin, the Executive Committee met to discuss and vote on issues related to the funeral procession that would follow the lying in state. There was general agreement on the format. The procession would be divided into six divisions: military escorts, the clergy, and a caisson bearing Davis's coffin; Confederate veterans followed by Union veterans; city, state, and military officials from Louisiana and elsewhere; Masonic and similar organizations; the fire department; other miscellaneous organizations; and, bringing up the rear, associations of African Americans.

While it was accepted that bells throughout the city would toll and minute guns fire as the cortege passed, there was disagreement over the manner in which Davis's remains should be transferred the estimated two and a half miles from the city hall to the cemetery. Captain J. A. Chalaron of the Confederate Veterans Association proposed that the coffin be conveyed by caisson only as far as the Confederate Half-way House out of fear that the body would be unnecessarily shaken if carried the entire route in that manner. On further discussion, however, he admitted that his primary interest was to allow Confederate veterans the opportunity to carry the body on their shoulders the remainder of the way. "Every veteran," he said, "would consider it an honor to carry the dead body of their old leader to the tomb."[69]

Captain Grey "exhibited much feeling" in supporting Chalaron's proposal. "The illustrious dead about to be buried was a gallant soldier and should be buried as a soldier." He added that every organization should walk to the cemetery and not hurry the "honored dead" to the grave. In regard to whether Davis should be carried to the cemetery by veterans as Chalaron wished, the Union veteran was adamantly in favor. Grey repeated his argument made the previous day that he, himself, was an old soldier of the United States army, and so was Jefferson Davis, and he, Grey, wanted to be represented in carrying the corpse of "a grand man, an honorable man, and above all, a dead soldier, to the grave." When questioned about the possibility of rain during the procession, Grey refused to back down: "Let us walk in the rain. We have done it before without umbrellas or overcoats, and there is not an old soldier who would not willingly walk that distance." In regard to concern that the distance was too long for aged soldiers to march, Grey replied that "six miles was nothing for an old soldier; coming back was different." The committee then voted to approve the recommended arrangement of the funeral procession but rejected Chalaron's proposal. It was agreed that Davis would be transported the entire route by caisson.[70]

The issue of whether the GAR should participate as a body in the funeral procession was also discussed. Two members of the organization were in attendance, General A. S. Badger and Captain Grey. Both men actively participated as members of committees and subcommittees in preparing for the Davis funeral. Grey felt that the GAR was represented through his presence; however, he announced that he would call its council of administration together for a decision. He believed, nevertheless, that even should the GAR decide against appearing as a group, most of the members would do so as individuals.[71] Press reports indicated that there were a significant number of Union veterans in New Orleans who, "while they cannot take any official action in regard to the death of Mr. Davis, have great respect for him as a soldier and statesman, and will attend the funeral." Those members that chose to participate did not wear the badges that would have distinguished them as GAR members.[72]

In an effort to deal with the large numbers expected to arrive in New Orleans for the funeral and/or to participate in the procession to the cemetery, the committee authorized the collection of $10,000 for expenses, part to be used for a hundred or more carriages for the funeral procession, with the remainder to be used for a monument to Davis. It was announced further that railway accommodations had been arranged to handle four thousand persons at one time. As of December 7, the Queen and Crescent, Louisville and Nashville, and Illinois Central railroad companies had announced low excursion rates and the addition of special trains to New Orleans between December 9 and 15.[73]

As the session drew to a close, chairman Johnston read a letter from the Metairie Cemetery Association requesting that Davis's body be permanently interred on its grounds: "New Orleans asks that Jefferson Davis be laid to rest within the city where he fell asleep." Toward that end, the association offered "the mound to the left of the entrance to the cemetery, and immediately opposite to and corresponding with that where rest the heroes of the Army of Tennessee." Copies were forwarded to Davis's widow and to each Confederate organization with the note that if accepted, the veterans would erect a "magnificent monument."[74]

While the Executive Committee planned from the beginning on the participation of an African American contingent in the funeral procession, the issue was far from settled. On December 7, Mayor Shakespeare received a resolution signed by sixteen local black residents that expressed solidarity with the white population in honoring "the memory of the great and good man, Jefferson Davis," but did not promise participation.[75] As events would soon demonstrate, the funeral procession proved to be an all-white affair, with no African American contingent.

On Sunday, December 8, the second day of lying in state, the number of visitors greatly increased. "A careful tally" showed that forty thousand persons, including both African Americans and whites, passed through the council chamber in which Davis lay, despite the rainy weather and muddy streets.[76] Before the doors opened, a photographer, Charles H. Adams, visited the scene in order to take pictures of the death chamber as well as the interior and exterior of the city hall for a planned book on the funeral.

The emotional attachment of many veterans who had served under Davis was evident. Colonel D. M. Hollingsworth, who had served under him in the Mexican War, began to weep when he saw his former commander lying dead. Before leaving, he tearfully placed beside the coffin a rifle that bore the inscription "Buena Vista, February 23, 1847, First Sergeant D. M. Hollingsworth,

Company A, First Mississippi Rifles, Col. Jeff. Davis."[77] Father Darious Hubert, a Jesuit priest who had served throughout the war in a Louisiana regiment, fell to his knees in prayer and wept.[78] An elderly woman, overcome at seeing Davis lying dead, lifted the flag from the coffin and held it to her lips and wept audibly as the line of mourners piled up waiting their turn to pass.[79]

While most visitors came alone or with friends and family, many came in groups from schools, orphanages, veterans' organizations, and other bodies. On December 8, pupils of the public schools, residents of the Catholic and Protestant orphan homes, and many of the local clergy visited. Some came with their teachers, while many others came alone. A number said prayers, some bending to their knees as they paused by the coffin.

Many visitors left flowers as they passed through the chamber. These ranged from small clusters to large floral arrangements. Some simply lay their flowers on the big table near the door without a word. A significant number handed beautiful bouquets of exotics to the officers standing nearby. Nearly all murmured apologies for the simplicity of their gifts. When the public school teachers came after 3:00, each one had a handful of flowers that she laid beside the bier. Some swept their flowers across the glass lid, carrying them away again as cherished souvenirs. This was particularly true beginning around noon on Tuesday, from which time one of Davis's military guards was kept constantly busy until midnight placing them in the chamber, giving the room a pleasant floral scent. A virtual wall of roses grew up on all sides of the bier.[80]

Among those who came to visit the remains of the former Confederate president were many African Americans. Some came doubtlessly out of curiosity and others as genuine mourners. On December 9, a large number whose age showed that they had lived during the time of slavery appeared in line. Very few young individuals were among them. One person, an aged black man said to be more than four score years, viewed the remains of "Marse Jeff" and commented, "I fit under him and wanted to see him once more." Others initially showed defiance. According to a reporter for the *New Orleans Times-Democrat*, some "burly Negro women with market baskets hung to their arms would march defiantly" past the dead man but, on seeing him, changed "their arrogance to humility and reverence."[81]

The streams of people filing into the council chamber remained constant throughout the period of lying in state, resulting at times in "awful jams." Estimates varied from forty thousand to sixty thousand in a single day, with inclement weather not seeming to materially affect the volume. On December 9, despite a light rain, one thousand persons were reported passing through the doorway at one time. In order to handle the large number, estimated at thirty-three hundred per hour passing the bier, the people were allowed to pass in double lines instead of the earlier single line.[82]

Tuesday, December 10, was the last full day of public viewing. By this time, the local press described the people on the street as having an "out-of-town look," as southern governors, their staffs, various dignitaries, and travelers from beyond New Orleans and Louisiana swelled the city's population. When the time arrived to admit mourners into the city hall's council chamber, the crowds were lining the sidewalks. "As the hour appointed for admitting the public struck, bayonets were lowered, and the eager visitors formed in line to enter the heavily-draped corridor." "Those in attendance had thought Sunday the great day, believing it impossible to exceed the multitude who passed. . . . That they were mistaken was clearly proven. . . . If anything, the crowds were more cosmopolitan. . . . The scene increased hourly in interest as the tide grew stronger as the day waned."[83]

Because they had to travel some distance by train to reach New Orleans, many of the out-of-state dignitaries had only Tuesday and the few hours before the funeral on Wednesday to visit the remains and see Davis's face for a last time. These included Governor Gordon and his staff, General Stephen D. Lee of Mississippi, and Francis R. Lubbock, the Civil War governor of Texas. When General Jubal Early entered the room, the honor guards presented arms and stepped aside, leaving him alone with the coffin on the platform. As Colonel John B. Richardson passed, his wife placed on the coffin a white handkerchief bearing the Confederate battle flag that her husband had carried through the war.[84]

Varina Davis visited her husband's remains for the last time at 10:50 P.M. on the day before the funeral. She was accompanied by her daughter Margaret as well as General Joseph Davis, Mrs. E. H. Farrar, and J. U. Payne. They all arrived with flowers and remained for approximately an hour before leaving. After their departure, Captain Charles H. Adams, assisted by Mr. Placide Revues of the New Orleans Camera Club, took a number of flash pictures of the council chamber where the body was exposed. The views were taken from various parts of the room so as to include all the floral offerings.[85]

On the evening of December 10, with the funeral of Jefferson Davis only hours away, the Executive Committee met to publicly announce the names of the pallbearers. It is likely that the delay was caused in part by the fact that Varina Davis, who was still grieving for her husband, took part in the process.[86] Eight southern governors were chosen to represent their states as honorary pallbearers: Francis Fleming of Florida, James P. Eagle of Arkansas, Francis T. Nicholls of Louisiana, Daniel G. Fowle of North Carolina, J. P. Richardson of South Carolina, John B. Gordon of Georgia, Robert Lowry of Mississippi, and Simon Bolivar Buckner of Mississippi. These men symbolized most of the states of the old Confederacy. In addition, forty-eight others were named active pallbearers. Among these were Charles Fenner, who had helped oversee every step of the funeral process; Davis's lifelong friend, General George W. Jones of Iowa; Thomas H. Watts, who had served in the Confederate Cabinet; General Jubal Early; Commander W. W. Hunter of Louisiana; General Stephen D. Lee of Mississippi; F. R. Lubbock, the former governor of Texas; and the two members of the GAR who had played a significant role in planning the funeral, A. S. Badger and Jacob Grey. Twelve of the pallbearers had been Confederate generals during the war. The entire list was, in fact, only ceremonial since none of the fifty-six men named would so much as touch the handles of Davis's coffin. The task of carrying Davis's coffin was assigned to soldiers of the state militia. The named pallbearers would follow the hearse in carriages.[87]

"THE CONFEDERACY IS BURIED": DECEMBER 11, 1889

At last, the day of the funeral arrived. The rain of the past week was gone, and the eighty-degree temperature and cloudless skies made it seem to one observer "as if May had spread over the year and spring had determined on being perennial." It was "bright and balmy and fragrant with the perfume of flowers" in the air. If there were a drawback, it was for the soldiers who sweltered in their heavy uniforms as they marched to the cemetery.[88]

During the previous four days, the attention of the city had focused on providing for Jefferson Davis a grand funeral the likes of which had perhaps never been witnessed in the South and which would be comparable to any ever held in the nation. On this final day, in which Davis would be committed to the ground, the city and the entire South virtually closed down for the day as schools, courts, government offices, and retail and wholesale businesses shut their doors. Throughout the morning and during the funeral itself, the air was laden with funeral dirges. The solemn requiem of bells was heard on every hand, and at regular intervals minute guns loudly thundered forth tributes to the deceased southern leader.[89]

The city was crowded with more people than normally appeared even for carnival season. Railroad companies reported that the demand for cars to handle the vast crowds entering New Orleans continued to grow during the period. Members of Congress, the U.S. Supreme Court, governors past and present, former Confederate military and political officials, veterans of the Civil War, and many thousands of people from all walks of life were in attendance. Flags on ships in the harbor, both American and foreign, flew at half-mast. Homes and buildings in the city and in distant locations were draped in mourning colors in such profusion that early reports claimed that the number of decorators available was insufficient to do the work.[90]

From early morning, large numbers of people were on the streets moving toward Lafayette Square and the funeral route to seek good viewing points. Except for the somber colors that decorated thousands of homes and buildings around the city, the crowds gave the appearance of a great celebration rather than the solemnity of a funeral. The men, women, and children appeared in holiday attire; bands with their music seemed to be at every corner; and soldiers, firemen, and various associations in their uniforms—all gave a bright and almost festive appearance to the streets. Nor was there an atmosphere of sadness. Dozens of "hawkers" went among the crowds selling Confederate badges, photographs of Davis "in every attitude," and medals of all kinds. Like an average New Orleans crowd, the people appeared to enjoy the soldiers, the music, and the pomp of the parade and pointed out General Gordon, General Jubal Early, and other distinguished men as they marched in the procession.[91]

Lafayette Square was reserved exclusively for the military that were to participate in the funeral parade. The large police detachment that attempted to enforce this injunction met with innumerable obstacles. The crowd became so unwieldy that the police force had great difficulty forcing people back from the square. Long before the ceremonies were to begin, the square and the streets leading to it were a sea of faces. From Canal Street to the Robert E. Lee monument, there were no vacant spaces. There were twenty-thousand people in the square and ten thousand in the neighboring streets. The balconies and every available place from which either an unobstructed or a partial view could be had of the portico of city hall on which the funeral would take place were crowded almost to suffocation.[92]

Noticeably missing from the crowds and the parade, however, was any significant number of African Americans. The Executive Committee had provided a place in the funeral procession for a contingent of African Americans and had even named Colonel James Lewis, a prominent black veteran of the Civil War and a former collector of the port of New Orleans, to lead them. However, the black population appeared to express their opinion of Davis by their absence. Although some had been observed passing the bier during the lying in state, few were in evidence among those who came to view the funeral procession. Miles Cooper, who obviously did not represent the majority sentiment of his race, rode with the Davis family in the funeral procession to the cemetery, while a second African American, James H. Jones, who was Davis's body servant at the time of his capture in 1865 and was now a Republican alderman in Raleigh, North Carolina, wired his regrets at being deprived of the opportunity of showing his "lasting appreciation" for his "best friend."[93]

Also noticeably absent were any significant signs and symbols of the Confederacy. Davis wore a suit of Confederate gray, and here and there among the floral offerings were the blue, white, and red colors of the Confederacy. However, these were among the few tokens that called up the late war. Although tens of thousands of houses were decorated, not one bore a Confederate flag, and the decoration most general was a small American flag in mourning, with the portrait of Davis in the center. The whole town seemed hung with the flags of the Union, and in the funeral procession there were borne but three or four Confederate banners, all of them being relics of the war.[94]

The period of lying in state was scheduled to end at 11:30, only minutes before the remains were to be moved to the front steps of the city hall for the religious funeral services. The council chamber mortuary opened at 7:00 A.M., three hours earlier than previously, for the public to have one final look at the Confederate president. Although officially closed since 10:00 P.M. the previous night, the viewing had in fact not ceased. The guards had continued to permit visitation by Confederate veterans until the general public was admitted again the next day. As described by a reporter who viewed the remains, Davis was remarkably well preserved despite the very warm and exceptionally oppressive weather of the past week. "As he reposed on his coffin this morning, he presented just such a picture as those who knew and loved him in life would like best to carry in his memory."[95]

At 10:00 A.M., city hall was closed for a final time to the general public, and everyone was excluded except members of the funeral cortege, the officiating clergy, the choir, the pallbearers, and the "distinguished ladies" who had been invited to attend. Several military organizations from elsewhere in the South that were to form part of the procession to the cemetery were among the last to pass the open casket. Several southern governors who were to act as honorary pallbearers arrived too late and were turned away.[96]

At 11:10 A.M., the coffin was closed, and it would be more than three years before anyone would look on the dead man's face again. Shortly after noon, the tolling of city bells and the firing of minute guns gave notice that the ceremonies had begun. Davis's coffin was moved from the council chamber to the front portico of the city hall with solemn pomp and ceremony. A detachment of twelve members of the Louisiana Grand Artillery carried the coffin, across which lay a silk Confederate battle flag entwined with roses and the sword that Davis had carried during the war with Mexico. The casket was accompanied by a procession that included Episcopal bishops Galleher of Louisiana and Thompson of Mississippi, both walking with open prayer books, as well as a large number of assisting clergy from various denominations, the fifty-six ceremonial pallbearers, and the mayor and city council of New Orleans. As they passed, women on both sides of the procession broke into sobs.[97]

At the front entrance, color sergeants of Mississippi, Alabama, North Carolina, Georgia, and other state troops held their colors at present arms. Davis's coffin was placed on a bier on the portico in full view of the thousands of spectators who crowded Lafayette Square. The pallbearers and honorary pallbearers stood near the clergy. The Davis family and relatives were able to watch the proceedings unobserved through a window in the mayor's office, that had been assigned to them. According to the *Chicago Tribune* of December 12, 1889, "Mrs. Davis, her daughter, Mrs. Hayes, and Mr. J. U. Payne . . . did not leave their carriage, but remained where they could hear and see the services."

The religious ceremony was brief. The services were those of the Episcopal Church, but they were made ecumenical through the participation of five officiating clergymen from the Catholic, Presbyterian, and Episcopalian churches. Bishop Galleher, in his eulogy of Davis, avoided any direct references to the Civil War or the Confederacy. But indirectly, he characterized the deceased southern leader as "a man who, in his person and history, symbolized the solemn conviction and tragic fortunes of millions of men." With his death, "a moving volume of human history has been closed and clasped." In this, he reiterated the opinions of such northern newspapers as the *Boston Globe*, which believed that Davis was the "last link that bound the South with the past" and that with his passing "the Confederacy is buried." As quoted by an individual identified only as "one of the most prominent men present at the funeral," "I will feel now that the war is over, as far as the South is concerned. We have only its memories left to us."[98]

Following Galleher's eulogy, a short prayer was delivered over Davis's body by Father Hubert, a Jesuit priest and former Confederate chaplain. A thirty-six-voice choir sang the hymn "Through the Valley of the Shadow of Death," and the funeral service concluded. Eight artillerymen then lifted Davis's coffin to their shoulders and carried it to the caisson for the three- to four-mile procession to Metairie Cemetery.

The vehicle in which Davis was carried to the cemetery was designed to show that this was the burial of an American military hero rather than simply the president of the Confederacy. A specially modified four-wheeled caisson of the Louisiana Field Artillery had been converted into a funeral car for the occasion. The coffin was placed on a platform supported by three springs. Six bronze Napoleon cannons resting upright on their muzzles and braced by crossed rifles supported an eight-foot-long, four-foot-wide canopy of heavy sable cloth decorated with a rich frieze and braid border. Furled and crossed U.S. flags were placed on each side, and a Confederate flag lay across the coffin. Cannon balls rested on each corner of the canopy, the dome of which was ornamented in bronze. Crossed sabers were placed to the front in an effort to represent as many branches of the military service as possible on the funeral car. Six black horses in artillery harness and plumes, walking two abreast and each led by a soldier in uniform, drew the caisson.[99]

The funeral car waited in front of the city hall building while General Gordon brought the various elements of the parade of ten thousand to fifteen thousand persons to order. The various battalions wheeled into line with military precision, preceded by a detachment of city police and followed in turn by the clergy, pallbearers, and so on in respective order until the mammoth procession was completely formed. First came the military contingent of thirty-five companies and about two thousand men. The New Orleans troops led, followed by visiting companies from Alabama, Mississippi, Tennessee, and other southern states. All units carried U.S. flags shrouded in crepe, and some carried faded and torn Confederate battle flags.[100]

The caisson carrying Davis's remains followed the military, and behind that came the carriages with his family and close personal friends. Varina, Margaret, Joseph Davis, and family friend J. U. Payne occupied the lead carriage, followed by others with near relatives of Mrs. Davis, the widows of Stephen R. Mallory, and General Braxton Bragg, and following them were the veterans' associations of the armies of Northern Virginia and Tennessee. A group of about fifty veterans of the Union army marched together, having discarded their GAR badges in order to avoid conflict with their national organization and thus identifying themselves only by their Union army badges.[101]

The third division followed, consisting of executive, judicial, and consular personnel in carriages. Prominent among these were the southern governors, the judges of the state supreme court, and the municipal officers of the New Orleans city government. The fourth division was composed of uniformed members of the Odd Fellow, Knights of Pythias, and the Patriotic Order of Sons of America. The fifth and sixth divisions were composed of students from Tulane University and public schools, the Catholic Knights of America, scores of benevolent and civic societies, members of some twenty other organizations, and fifteen hundred members of the New Orleans fire department in uniform.[102]

The route was a long one of approximately two miles through the center of the city, then another two over the hot, dusty Canal Street shell road to Metairie Cemetery. Both sides of the route were crowded with spectators. The length of the parade was such that it took an hour and ten minutes for the procession to pass any given point. As it moved along the streets, bells could be heard tolling from every church tower, bands played funeral dirges, and minute guns boomed. Parts of the city not located on the line of march were literally depopulated as their inhabitants gathered in large numbers along the sides of the roads and in other places where a view of the funeral parade could be had.[103]

Some of the civic organizations tired along the way and marched back to the city. The military, however, including the veterans, some of whom were minus arms and hobbling on wooden legs, continued the march despite the broiling sun. The head of the procession arrived at the canal bridge that led to the main gate of the cemetery at a few minutes after 3:00 P.M. As they entered, they passed the tomb of the Army of Tennessee, towered over by an equestrian statue of General Albert Sydney Johnston that had been covered with crepe in honor of the occasion. Several years earlier, Jefferson Davis had spoken at its dedication. Except for the luck of a draw between the two veterans' organizations, this would have been Davis's resting place.[104]

The tomb of the Army of Northern Virginia was at the extreme end of the cemetery. It consisted of subterranean grave chambers lying below a mound of earth, topped by a column bearing a statue of General Stonewall Jackson. The shaft and statue combined rose to a height of approximately fifty feet above the ground. A profusion of flowers sent from every state in the South gave the appearance that the column rose out of a floral sea. Conspicuous among them was one whose flowers formed a battle flag of the Confederacy. The mound covered an underground chamber of burial vaults, in one of which the body of Jefferson Davis would soon be encased.[105]

The cemetery was already crowded with people by the time the procession reached Metairie. Many spectators and mourners had arrived hours earlier, even before the noon funeral ceremonies began at city hall, in hopes of finding a good place from which to observe the proceedings. Several thousand walked to the cemetery because all the available trains and streetcars were jammed with several of the nonmarching divisions of the funeral pageant, leaving the nonparticipating public to fend for themselves. By late afternoon, when the burial ceremonies began, every space that had not been reserved for the funeral participants was taken, as people climbed trees, mounted tombs, and crowded the lawns and walkways from which they might see the ceremonies. As each train emptied, its passengers reformed in open order to let the veterans, soldiers, and other walking divisions, dusty and tired from the long route in the hot sun, through.[106]

At 4:00 P.M., the police and military drew up around the circle and saluted as the funeral car, followed by a long line of carriages, pulled up to the monument. The choir, which had arrived earlier, took up a position to the left of the tomb. The Episcopal clergymen and the assisting interdenominational clergy formed in lines on either side of the walk. The pallbearers and distinguished guests did the same. Bishops Galleher and Thompson moved slowly into position, followed by General Gordon, who stood quietly with his head bowed. The caisson bearing the body stopped at the base of the walk, and a detail of soldiers carried the casket to the foot of the monument. As they moved up the walk to the mound, the military stood at "rest on arms."

The veterans' associations marched into the cemetery together. When they reached the monument, they separated, one going to the left and the other to the right. When they met, they charged up the mound and formed an inner circle, the Army of Northern Virginia in front and the Army of Tennessee in the rear. Davis's family moved slowly up to the mound, Varina on the arm of family friend J. U. Payne and Margaret on the arm of General Joseph R. Davis. Then came Robert Brown, Davis's African American friend and former body servant, and others.[107] A bier had been erected on top of the mound at the sight where the burial services took place. Davis's wife and daughter sat near the bier. Beside them were the other close family connections. In open file leading down from the mound were the clergy and then the pallbearers. Crowded in and on the mound itself were the veterans of the Confederacy.[108]

There were no speeches or anything that recalled the southern Confederacy or Davis's role in it but simply the committal service of the Episcopal Church. When all were assembled, Bishop Thompson opened the ceremonies by reading the first portion of the Episcopal burial service. Then "Taps" were blown on a bugle, and Bishop Galleher read the second part of the ritual, reciting a list of the governmental and military positions Jefferson Davis had held during his life. The choir sang an anthem, "I Heard a Voice from Heaven," the Lord's Prayer was recited, the hymn "Rock of Ages" was sung, and the religious ceremonies ended.[109]

It was late in the day when the religious services concluded, and darkness was coming on when the time finally came to commit Davis to the grave. A command was given, and soldier pallbearers raised the casket from its bier and carried it down the stairway into the subterranean chamber of the tomb. Members of the family followed, and the casket was placed in the middle vault of the first perpendicular row immediately to the right of the descent into the chamber. The Confederate flag that had covered the coffin was removed, the slab was screwed tight, and Davis lay in his temporary grave to await the decision on a permanent home. An artillery detachment of the Louisiana State Guard fired three rounds, and the military stood at present arms as the family exited the tomb and descended the mound on the way to their carriages.[110]

With their departure, the governors, pallbearers, guests from other states, the Ladies' Memorial Association, and finally the public crowded down into the "still cold white-washed room below and gazed for a moment on the narrow chamber, with its sweet incense of growing flowers, wherein all that remained of the former president of the Confederacy lay."[111] Some of the old soldiers lingered for an hour or so longer, but the vast majority of the crowd soon marched back to the city. A guard of honor was placed on duty to remain day and night until a decision was made on the location of a permanent gravesite.

MOURNING IN THE SOUTH

Although the funeral and burial took place in New Orleans, the ceremonies went well beyond that city into every state of the old Confederacy and into virtually every community in those states. Within hours of his death, events were set in motion to ensure that the former Confederate states would join in memorializing their wartime leader. Governor Gordon of Georgia presented the initial push for some form of united showing among the southern states. On the morning that the Confederate president died, Gordon took the initiative by issuing a proclamation that "invit[ed] the people of the different communities of this State to assemble together at the hour of Mr. Davis's funeral at 12 P.M., Wednesday, the 11th instant, and unite in suitable and solemn memorial services."[112] He followed this by sending telegrams to his fellow southern governors suggesting that they issue similar proclamations arranging for memorial services the day and hour of the funeral. Within hours, his suggestion was followed by the governors of Florida, Louisiana, Mississippi, Alabama, Texas, and North Carolina. They were soon joined by their colleagues elsewhere.

Gordon's influence with other southern governors was reinforced by his authority as commander of the United Confederate Veterans, an association that reached into the homes of white southerners throughout the South and in communities elsewhere as well. His concern, shared by many others, was not solely with honoring Davis through joint commemorative services but with the related issue of care for the Confederate president's survivors, Varina and Winnie, who were believed to have been left in serious financial straits. (Daughter Margaret's marriage to a well-to-do banker left her financially secure.) Thus, he used his dual positions as a southern governor to suggest to colleagues that services be coordinated so as to be held on the same day and hour as the funeral in New Orleans and as commander of the United Confederate Veterans to issue an order for the associations throughout the South and elsewhere to provide for collections for the benefit of the Davis family at all of the memorial services.[113]

Given Davis's stature as the former president of the Confederate States, which alone would have produced large-scale demonstrations of mourning, along with the encouragement to memorialize the deceased man by Gordon and the governors, the turnout in the South was on a massive scale. The mood was that of the loss of a national hero. At noon on December 11, as funeral services began in New Orleans, towns large and small across the South witnessed shows of mourning that included the closing of schools, businesses, government agencies, courts of law, and so on; church bells ringing; minute guns firing; processions of civilians and military to churches, theaters, auditoriums, opera houses, and other spaces big enough to accommodate large crowds; the half-masting of flags, including those on foreign ships in the southern port cities of Charleston, Norfolk, New Orleans, and Beaufort, North Carolina; speeches made and resolutions passed eulogizing Davis; homes and buildings of all types draped in mourning colors; and other methods of commemorating the life of Jefferson Davis. The mourning was widespread and general. Union veterans reportedly joined memorial services in Atlanta, New Orleans, Chattanooga, and other towns. And although these celebrations tended to be confined largely to the white populations, scattered reports showed limited participation by African Americans. In Blackville, South Carolina, the black Baptist church joined with white churches in tolling their bells during the hours of the funeral.[114] In Raleigh, North Carolina, James Jones, Davis's wartime free-black servant sat immediately in the front row during memorial services.[115]

Although the federal government in Washington, D.C., chose to officially ignore Davis's death, the sounds of cannons and bells honoring the Confederate president could be clearly heard from across the Potomac River in Alexandria, Virginia, where, by proclamation of the mayor, fire bells tolled from noon until 1:00 P.M. and everything of a public nature ceased. Senators and congressmen crossed the river into the southern city to join former Confederate generals and cabinet members in eulogizing Davis. These included Robert E. Lee's son, William; Joseph Wheeler; Montgomery Corse; Dabney H. Maury; and John H. Reagan, the last of whom spoke of reconciliation and read Jefferson Davis's letter written on the death of Ulysses S. Grant in which he refused to criticize the leader of the northern armies but instead wished him "peace of mind and comfort of his body" in his final hours.[116]

In Atlanta, a mile-long procession led by veterans marched to ceremonies held at the state capitol. In Savannah, the military companies and veterans marched to St. John's Episcopal Church while eighty-one minute guns fired.[117] In Richmond, Virginia, the firing of cannons began at sunrise, and the streets filled with people on the way to memorial services. In Columbia, South Carolina, the legislature convened in joint session at noon to hold memorial services, while at the same hour services took place at the city hall under the auspices of the city government and Ladies Memorial Association. However, not all went smoothly in the capital city, as a cannon that had been used to celebrate the secession of the state in 1860 exploded during a salute and seriously wounded two men and slightly injured two others.[118] In

Charleston, West Virginia, a well-attended meeting listened to speeches by S. A. Miller, a former member of the Confederate Congress, and others.[119]

THE DAVIS LAND COMPANY FUND

As mentioned previously, the movement for South-wide memorial services for Jefferson Davis was seen as an opportunity to provide for his family in a manner befitting a former head of state. According to Henry Grady, managing editor of the *Atlanta Constitution*, in reply to a query from the editor of the *New York World* on the possibility of the two newspapers cooperating in such a fund,

> Three or four times in the past ten years, touched by Mr. Davis's known poverty, we have started to make a fund for him, and once had a considerable amount subscribed without his knowledge; each time he gratefully but firmly declined, saying that so many widows and orphans of our soldiers, and so many disabled veterans themselves, were poor and in need of the necessaries of life that all generous offerings had best be directed to them and to their betterments. He has grown steadily poorer, and I fear, leaves his family nothing. I am now in communication with the friends of his family, and if permitted to raise a fund the people of the South will spontaneously give all that is needed and more. But we shall advise you promptly, and any voluntary offerings from the North would honor those who gave and be accepted in the South as evidence that the hostility of the North to a man who deserved no more of censure than his associates, but who went to his grave carrying the whole burden of responsibility, is at last allayed.[120]

Varina Davis, now that her husband was gone, maintained the same position in regard to direct charity. She would, however, accept aid if it came indirectly. She let it be known that she would accept financial help through the sale of stock in the Davis Land Company. As a result, Grady and Gordon threw themselves with enthusiasm into resurrecting the Davis Land Fund, which had been proposed during Jefferson Davis's lifetime. Unfortunately, Grady contracted pneumonia and in less than three weeks was dead, leaving the leadership in the hands of Governor Gordon.[121]

The plan called for raising $100,000 to be obtained by subscriptions from private individuals, which would be used to purchase six thousand acres of land held by the Davis estate in Arkansas. The money, rather than going directly to her as a donation, could be viewed as earnings from the family-owned land. By December 10, the South-wide efforts to raise funds coalesced into a plan under the leadership of Governor Gordon, who used his name and offices to promote the plan. At his request, Louisiana Governor Nichols placed Davis's friend Charles Fenner in charge of a committee to raise and receive funds. On December 10, the committee sent out a request, under Gordon's name, to the southern colony in New York City and the governors of each southern state to lead the efforts in their own jurisdictions.[122]

The veterans were barely rested from the march to and from Metairie Cemetery to bury Davis when they were called to attend an evening meeting at the Washington Artillery Hall in New Orleans to hear appeals that "his wife and children do not suffer want." A steady stream of speakers led by Gordon and followed by the southern governors who had earlier acted as pallbearers, Mayor J. Taylor Ellyson of Richmond, and a series of former Confederate generals eulogized the deceased southern president and asked for support for the Davis Land Company Fund. Each plea and reference to Davis was greeted by enthusiastic applause from the crowded hall.[123] The Georgia governor pointed out that the city of Atlanta had already provided several thousand dollars and would pledge more. He asked that others do the same. "My brothers," he pleaded, " because of our love for him as our representative; because of our love for those who have shared his fate; because of our love for our own honor, we intend to see that his wife and children do not suffer want." Following great applause, he then urged that "this assemblage . . . disperse with the determination that not many moons shall wane until an ample fund is provided for her and her worthy daughter, because our honor and our manhood demand it."[124] General Stephen D. Lee then proposed a resolution in support of the fund that would "leave [Varina and her daughter] in comfort." It was easily passed. Within days, the press of the South began reporting similar meetings throughout the South in southern enclaves in New York and elsewhere.

Within five days of Jefferson Davis's death, southerners had come together in a common cause. Thousands had passed his bier in mourning as he lay in state. Municipalities from the smallest to the largest joined in mourning through memorial services held to coincide with the funeral in New Orleans. They were beginning to meet the longtime concern for the financial welfare of the Davis family. Yet there was one issue that was left unresolved. The chamber in the tomb of the Army of Northern Virginia that held his remains was only a temporary grave until a decision could be made on a permanent burial site. That was a question that would take years to resolve.

NOTES

1. Hudson Strode, *Jefferson Davis, Tragic Hero, the Last Twenty-Five Years, 1864–1889* (1964; reprint, New York: Harcourt, 2000), 497.

2. Strode, *Jefferson Davis, Tragic Hero*, 503–4.

3. Strode, *Jefferson Davis, Tragic Hero,* 503.

4. Varina Howell Davis, *Jefferson Davis, Ex-President of the Confederate States of America: A Memoir by His Wife,* 2 vols. (New York: Belford 1890), 2:927.

5. Eron Rowland, *Varina Howell, Wife of Jefferson Davis* (1931; reprint, New York: Pelican, 1999), 510.

6. Strode, *Jefferson Davis, Tragic Hero,* 506; Davis, *Jefferson Davis, Ex-President,* 2:927–28.

7. Strode, *Jefferson Davis, Tragic Hero,* 507; Davis, *Jefferson Davis, Ex-President,* 2:928–29.

8. Davis, *Jefferson Davis, Ex-President,* 2:929.

9. *Life and Reminiscences of Jefferson Davis, by Distinguished Men of His Time* (Baltimore, 1890), 65–66; undated article from the *New Orleans Picayune,* in J. William Jones, *Davis Memorial Volume; or Our Dead President, Jefferson Davis, and the World's Tribute to His Memory* (1890), 471–72.

10. Jones, *Davis Memorial Volume,* 472; *Life and Reminiscences of Jefferson Davis,* 66.

11. Jones, *Davis Memorial Volume,* 474.

12. Davis, *Jefferson Davis, Ex-President,* 2:931.

13. Jones, *Davis Memorial Volume,* 497.

14. Davis, *Jefferson Davis, Ex-President,* 2:930–31.

15. Jones, *Davis Memorial Volume,* 474.

16. *Cincinnati Enquirer,* December 7, 1889.

17. Davis, *Jefferson Davis, Ex-President,* 2:931–32.

18. *Washington Post,* December 7, 1889; *Life and Reminiscences of Jefferson Davis,* 68–70.

19. *Buffalo (N.Y.) Courier,* December 7, 1889; *Washington Post,* December 7, 1889; *Boston Globe,* December 6, 1889; Jones, *Davis Memorial Volume,* 496.

20. *New Orleans Times-Democrat,* December 7, 1889.

21. Charles Reagan Wilson, "The Death of Southern Heroes: Historic Funerals of the South," *Southern Cultures* 1 (1994): 6.

22. *New Orleans Times-Democrat,* December 7, 1889.

23. *New Orleans Times-Democrat,* December 7, 1889; *Reminiscences of Jefferson Davis,* 75–76.

24. *New Orleans Times-Democrat,* December 7, 1889; *Chicago Tribune,* December 7, 1889; *Cincinnati Enquirer,* December 7, 1889; Jones, *Davis Memorial Volume,* 493.

25. *Life and Reminiscences of Jefferson Davis,* 77–78.

26. *Chicago Tribune,* December 7, 1889.

27. *New Orleans Times-Democrat,* December 8, 1889.

28. *Wilmington (Del.) Every Evening,* December 6, 1889.

29. *Boston Globe,* December 7, 1889.

30. Quoted in Todd W. Van Beck, "Jefferson Davis, 1808–1889," *American Funeral Director* 122 (1999): 68.

31. Survey of newspapers.

32. Survey of newspapers in each region.

33. Survey of southern newspapers.

34. Reprinted in *Chicago Evening News,* December 11, 1889.

35. *Hartford (Conn.) Courant,* December 7, 1889.

36. *Cleveland Gazette,* December 21, 1889.

37. Reprinted in *Cleveland Gazette*, December 28, 1889.

38. *Washington Post*, December 8, 1889.

39. *Pittsburg (Pa.) Dispatch*, December 16, 1889.

40. *Life and Reminiscences of Jefferson Davis*, 76.

41. James Jones, interview published in an unidentified Washington, D.C., newspaper, circa January 1901, in Jefferson Davis Papers, P. C. 1085.1, North Carolina State Archives, Raleigh, North Carolina.

42. *Chicago Tribune*, December 8, 1889.

43. *Wichita (Kans.) Eagle*, December 13, 1889.

44. *Cincinnati Enquirer*, December 10, 1889.

45. *Chicago Daily News*, December 7, 1887.

46. *Chicago Daily News*, December 7, 1887.

47. *Chicago Daily News*, December 7, 1887.

48. *Chicago Daily News*, December 7, 1887; *Chicago Daily News*, December 7, 1998.

49. *Washington Post*, December 9, 1889.

50. *Washington Post*, December 10, 1889.

51. *New Orleans Times-Democrat*, December 7, 1889; *Boston Globe*, December 7, 1889.

52. *New Orleans Times-Democrat*, December 7, 1889.

53. *Davis Memorial Volume*, 488–89.

54. *Boston Globe*, December 7, 1889; *New Orleans Times-Democrat*, December 7, 1889.

55. *New Orleans Times-Democrat*, December 7, 1889.

56. *Washington Post*, December 10, 1889.

57. *Boston Globe*, December 12, 1889.

58. Telegram from Morris Scheff, December 9, 1889, in *Boston Globe*, December 10, 1889.

59. *The Bee*, Washington, D.C., January 11, 1889.

60. *New Orleans Times-Democrat*, December 7, 1889.

61. *New Orleans Times-Democrat*, December 7, 1889; *Chicago Tribune*, December 8, 1889; *Pittsburg (Pa.) Dispatch*, December 8, 1889.

62. *Chicago Tribune*, December 8, 1889; *Wilmington (N.C.) Messenger*, December 8, 1889.

63. *New Orleans Times-Democrat*, December 7, 1889.

64. *New Orleans Times-Democrat*, December 7, 1889; *Chicago Tribune*, December 8, 1889; *Wilmington (Del.) Messenger*, December 8, 1889.

65. *New Orleans Times-Democrat*, December 8, 1889.

66. *Chicago Tribune*, December 8, 1889.

67. *New Orleans Times-Democrat*, December 8, 1889.

68. *New Orleans Times-Democrat*, December 8, 1889.

69. *New Orleans Times-Democrat*, December 8, 1889.

70. *New Orleans Times-Democrat*, December 8, 1889.

71. *New Orleans Times-Democrat*, December 8, 1889.

72. *Cincinnati Enquirer*, December 10, 1889.

73. *New Orleans Times-Democrat*, December 8, 1889.

74. Letter, Metairie Association to Colonel William Preston Johnston, chairman of the Executive Committee, reprinted in the *New Orleans Times-Democrat*, December 8, 1889.

75. *New Orleans Times-Democrat*, December 10, 1889.

76. *Washington Post*, December 9, 1889; *Chicago Tribune*, December 9, 1889.

77. *Washington Post*, December 9, 1889.

78. *Wilmington (Del.) Every Evening*, December 9, 1889.

79. *New Orleans Times-Democrat*, December 10, 1889.

80. *New Orleans Times-Democrat*, December 10–11, 1889.

81. *New Orleans Times-Democrat*, December 12, 1889.

82. *New Orleans Times-Democrat*, December 10, 1889; *Wilmington (Del.) Every Evening*, December 9, 1889; *Cincinnati Enquirer*, December 9, 1889.

83. *New Orleans Times-Democrat*, December 11, 1889.

84. *New Orleans Times-Democrat*, December 11, 1889.

85. *New Orleans Times-Democrat*, December 11, 1889.

86. *Cincinnati Enquirer*, December 9, 1889.

87. *New Orleans Times-Democrat*, December 11, 1889.

88. *Chicago Tribune*, December 12, 1889; *Boston Globe*, December 12, 1889.

89. *Boston Globe*, December 12, 1889; *Pittsburg (Pa.) Dispatch*, December 12, 1889.

90. *Washington Post*, December 10, 1889.

91. *Boston Globe*, December 12, 1889.

92. *Pittsburg (Pa.) Dispatch*, December 12, 1889; *Cincinnati Enquirer*, December 12, 1889.

93. *Charleston (S.C.) News and Courier*, December 12, 1889; *Boston Globe,* December 12, 1889.

94. *Pittsburg (Pa.) Dispatch*, December 12, 1889.

95. *Pittsburg (Pa.) Dispatch*, December 12, 1889; *Cincinnati Enquirer*, December 12, 1889.

96. *New Orleans Times-Democrat*, December 11–12, 1889.

97. *Boston Globe*, December 12, 1889.

98. *Boston Globe*, December 12, 1889; *Pittsburg (Pa.) Dispatch*, December 12, 1889.

99. *Davis Memorial Volume*, 543; *Boston Globe*, December 12, 1889; *Chicago Tribune*, December 12, 1889; *Pittsburg (Pa.) Dispatch*, December 12, 1889.

100. *Charleston (S.C.) News and Courier*, December 12, 1889; *Boston Globe*, December 12, 1889.

101. *Chicago Tribune*, December 12, 1889; *Boston Globe*, December 12, 1889.

102. *Chicago Tribune*, December 12, 1889; *Boston Globe*, December 12, 1889.

103. *Cincinnati Enquirer*, December 12, 1889.

104. *Boston Globe*, December 12, 1889; *Chicago Tribune*, December 12, 1889.

105. *Boston Globe*, December 12, 1889; *Cincinnati Enquirer*, December 12, 1889.

106. *Cincinnati Enquirer*, December 12, 1889.

107. *Cincinnati Enquirer*, December 12, 1889.

108. *Chicago Tribune*, December 12, 1889.

109. *Cincinnati Enquirer*, December 12, 1889; *Boston Globe*, December 12, 1889.

110. *Cincinnati Enquirer*, December 12, 1889; *Wichita (Kans.) Eagle*, December 13, 1889; *Boston Globe*, December 12, 1889.

111. *Wichita (Kans.) Eagle*, December 13, 1889; *Cincinnati Enquirer*, December 12, 1889.

112. *Davis Memorial Volume*, 609.

113. *Davis Memorial Volume*, 609.

114. *Charleston (S.C.) News and Courier*, December 12, 1889.

115. *Hartford (Conn.) Courant*, December 13, 1889.

116. *Washington Post*, December 12, 1889, December 14, 1889; *Boston Globe*, December 12, 1889.

117. *Charleston (S.C.) News and Courier*, December 12, 1889.

118. *Chicago Tribune*, December 12, 1889.

119. *Cincinnati Enquirer*, December 13, 1889; *Wichita (Kans.) Eagle*, December 13, 1889.

120. *Davis Memorial Volume*, 613.

121. *Davis Memorial Volume*, 613.

122. *Washington Post*, December 10–11, 1889.

123. *New Orleans Times-Democrat*, December 12, 1889.

124. *New Orleans Times-Democrat*, December 12, 1889.

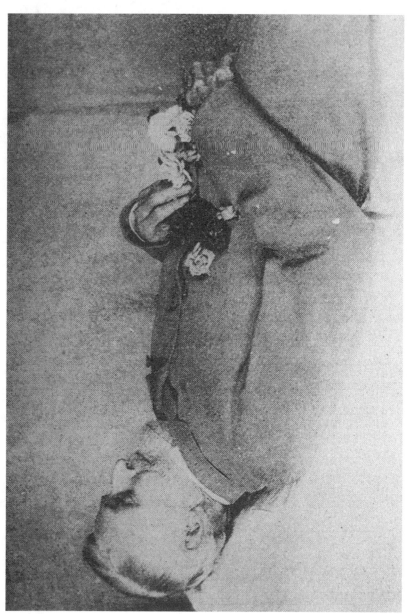

The body of Jefferson Davis, photographed the day of his death, before his removal to New Orleans city hall to lie in state.

The coffin of Jefferson Davis resting on the catafalque in the council chamber of the New Orleans city hall, during the week of December 6–11, 1889. The prominence of the United States flags illustrates his burial as an officer in the American Army prior to the Civil War, rather than as the president of the Confederacy. New Orleans Public Library

Confederate veterans and Guards of Honor await the remains of Jefferson Davis at the tomb of the Army of Northern Virginia in Metairie Cemetery. The bier upon which the coffin was placed for the burial ceremonies sits directly in front of the monument. New Orleans Public Library

Jefferson Davis's remains being carried to the funeral car in front of the New Orleans city hall, as the crowd watches. Taken at 12:30 p.m., December 11, 1889. New Orleans Public Library

The remains of Jefferson Davis lying in state below the rotunda of the state capitol building in Raleigh, North Carolina, May 30, 1893. North Carolina Office of Archives and History

THE CATAFALQUE.

The funeral carriage was a remodeled artillery caisson bearing six bronze Napoleon cannon placed upright on their barrels supported by crossed muskets. The canopy bore crossed U.S. flags, with cannon balls in the four corners. The purpose was to bury Jefferson Davis as an American military hero rather than as president of the Confederacy.

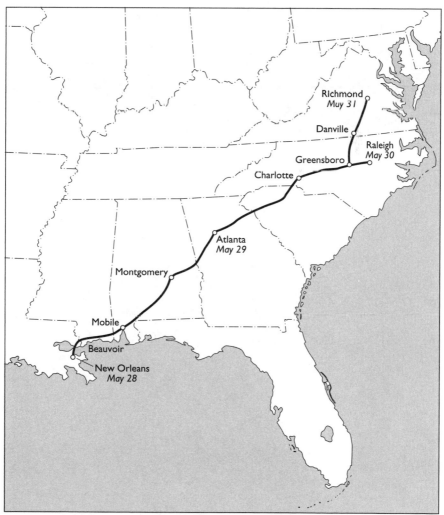

The route of the Jefferson Davis funeral train. The Confederate president was laid in state and processional parades were held in New Orleans, Montgomery, Atlanta, Raleigh, and Richmond during the dates of May 28–31, 1893.

The open grave of Jefferson Davis in Hollywood Cemetery. The Third National Flag of the Confederacy decorated the head, and the Battle Flag the foot. Valentine Richmond History Center

The funeral car carrying the remains of Jefferson Davis en route to the state capitol building in Raleigh, North Carolina, May, 30, 1893. The driver was James Jones, a local businessman and politician who had served Davis during the war as a free black. Four young girls dressed in white, including the daughter of Confederate General Robert Hoke, sit at each corner holding confederate flags. North Carolina Office of Archives and History

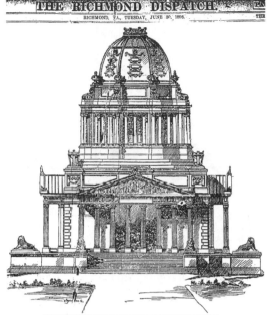

DESIGN ADOPTED FOR THE DAVIS MONUMENT, PERCY GRIFFIN, ARCHITECT.

In 1896, Jefferson Davis Monument Association approved this grand temple, designed by New York architect, Percy Griffin, as a memorial to the Confederate president. Although the cornerstone was laid, the project was abandoned when the association was unable to meet the high cost of construction. Richmond Dispatch

Davis Circle in Hollywood Cemetery, Richmond, Virginia. The family plot was part of the agreement by which Varina Davis agreed to permit her husband's burial in Richmond. Jefferson and Varina Davis lie in graves in front of the statue of the Confederate president. The statue to the left marks the grave of daughter Margaret, while the statue to the right marks the grave of daughter Winnie.

Model of the proposed triumphal arch as a memorial to Jefferson Davis by Louis Gude-brod. The design was opposed by Varina Davis because of its location at a busy intersection and her belief that an arch was inappropriate because her husband had led a losing cause. The arch was ultimately rejected because of its high cost of construction. Valentine Richmond History Center

The above statue and column design by Virginians Edward Valentine and William C. Noland succeeded where the others failed. It was unveiled on Davis's ninety-ninth birthday, June 3, 1907, and shows the floral tributes left that day. Valentine Richmond History Center

• 4 •

Jefferson Davis's Last Ride:
New Orleans to Richmond

*A*lthough the movement toward reconciliation between the formerly warring sections continued to move forward, the reburial of Jefferson Davis three and a half years after his death demonstrated that southerners increasingly were growing more overtly proud of the Confederacy while still manifesting their loyalty to a united country. The establishment of the United Confederate Veterans and the construction of Confederate monuments and dedication of statues to southern soldiers and military leaders went along with simultaneous veterans' reunions, expressions of national loyalty in the southern press, and recognition of the same among northern editors.

Jefferson Davis died on December 6, 1889. Southerners who had fought under him during the war of 1861–1865 and their children were determined to see that he did not go quietly into the night. For six days, the nation's press was consumed with every detail of his life and death. New Orleans temporarily became the South's most populous town as hundreds of thousands of mourners entered the city to pay homage to the dead Confederate president. Southerners, joined by a small number of northerners and Union veterans, dipped into their pockets to ensure that the deceased leader's family was financially secure. Yet one thing remained unsettled: the location of his permanent resting place.

The issue of a permanent burial site was one of the first items taken up on the day Davis died by the committee called by Mayor Shakespeare to plan funeral arrangements. Although Varina had placed the family's affairs in the hands of Judge Fenner and Davis's nephew Edgar H. Farrar, both of whom were familiar with the family situation, she had not discussed with them whether she had received final wishes from her husband regarding the place of permanent burial. Though Farrar and Judge Fenner had been requested to act as they saw fit, they did not know whether the place of burial would be in New Orleans or elsewhere.[1] Discussion at that time held that the permanent burial site would most likely be on Davis's Brierfield plantation below Vicksburg on the Mississippi River where his brother Joseph was buried. Yet funeral ceremonies of the size demanded for the only president of the Confederacy necessitated burial, at least temporarily, in New Orleans.

Regardless of the theorizing by the committee, any decision on a final site would have to be left to the entire family, and Winnie was still in France with an indefinite return date. That, however, did not stop the efforts by one southern city after another as they bombarded the widow with telegrams requesting possession of her husband's remains. Pleas came from six of the eleven former Confederate states and from the border state of Kentucky, which claimed Davis as its own by reason of his birth.

The debate between the former states of the Confederacy had been foreseen by the ex-Confederate leader himself. Some time before his death, Varina approached him concerning where he would prefer to be buried. He answered that he did not care. He would just as soon be buried under one of the live oaks on his Beauvoir plantation in Mississippi. But, he added, "you must take the responsibility of deciding this question, I cannot—I foresee a great deal of feeling about it will arise when I am dead." Mrs. Davis did not broach the issue again before his death.[2]

The states of the former Confederacy, however, appeared to have no qualms about presenting the delicate topic to his still-grieving widow. Within twenty-four hours of her husband's death, a headline in the *New York Times* proclaimed, "Richmond Wants the Body."[3] Before the sun had set on the day of his death and while the grieving widow was still exhausted and weak from weeks of treating her dying husband, one city after another had implored her to allow Davis's remains to lie in their soil. Resolutions from state and city governments and veterans' associations as well as telegrams from leading individuals offered enticements such as the erection of monuments dedicated to her husband.

Louisville, Kentucky, played on Davis's sentimental attachments to the state. It was claimed that during a visit two years earlier to dedicate a church built on the site of his birthplace, he "several times expressed the hope that he might be buried in his native State."[4] This, coupled with a belief that his family favored Kentucky, led the state to believe that their offer would be accepted. Accordingly, the Confederate Association of Kentucky telegraphed Davis's widow with an offer of a lot in Cave Hill Cemetery, a location that had close ties to her husband's past. Thirty years earlier, it had been set aside for his friend and former father-in-law Zachary Taylor but remained unused when the dying U.S. ex-president decided that he desired instead to be buried on his farm near the city. The site was Davis's for the asking.[5] As an added inducement, should the offer be accepted, Varina was promised an elaborate burial ceremony to which "all the Southern military organizations will be invited to attend, and the surviving members of Mr. Davis's Cabinet and the Senators and Representatives of the Confederacy will be cordially invited to attend the services."[6] Unrealistically optimistic, a committee was selected to proceed to New Orleans in hopes of conveying Davis's body back to Louisville. The city deceived itself into believing that it had an inside track by listening to questionable secondhand hearsay evidence. A Captain Leathers reported seeing "a telegram from a lady in Nashville, who stated that it was Mr. Davis's desire to be buried in Kentucky, the State of his birth. We made this tender [to Varina Davis] in the telegram, and it is reasonable to think that, as Mr. Davis expressed this wish, our affectionate offer may be accepted."[7]

Memphis, Tennessee, played on sentimental family ties in its appeal. Its Confederate Historical Association urged that Davis be buried in Elmwood Cemetery beside his two sons. The organization wired Varina "beg[ging] the boon of bringing his honored remains here for burial and [we] assure you and the country that his grave shall be kept green throughout the coming ages. We urge this, as he was a member of our association, made his first home here after the war, and was dear to the hearts of the community."[8]

Montgomery, in its appeal, played on Davis's historical ties to the city, pointing out that it was the first capital of the Confederacy, and it was here that he was sworn in as its president. Governor Lowry telegraphed Varina that "bells are tolling, public buildings draped in mourning, and [an] immense meeting to be held at 4 P.M., with the view of dispatching [a] committee to claim [the] remains of the great dead for interment in Mississippi." As an added inducement, she was promised that her husband would be buried under the Confederate monument on Capitol Hill, which he had helped dedicate during his 1886 visit to the city and on which would be placed a life-size bronze statue of him.[9]

The cities of Macon and Atlanta, Georgia, vied with each other to possess Davis's remains. During his 1886 Southern Tour and his weeklong visit to Macon in 1887, the Confederate president was almost overwhelmed by the enthusiasm of their populaces, receiving the most robust ovations since the war. Macon promised Varina "the most conspicuous burial lot" in Riverside Cemetery, overlooking the Ocmulgee River and the city. The grave site "will be ornamented with fountains and lakelets and the entire redoubt or fort with flowers, as directed by yourself, and a splendid monument will be erected if you accept." Varina was invited to visit Macon and "remain as the city's guests." An escort would be sent for the body.[10]

Atlanta was unique in that it had offered Davis a burial site during the February before his death. The city also had two powerful advocates in Henry

W. Grady, leader of the "New South" movement and editor of the *Atlanta Constitution* (one of the region's leading newspapers), and Georgia Governor John Gordon. A site in Westview Cemetery, "itself a battlefield on which his soldiers fought and fell," was offered, as was a statue of the Confederate president. Grady sent sculptor Frazee to New Orleans to secure a death mask in preparation for the Davis statue. Mayor John T. Glenn and Sidney Root separately sent telegrams promising that the remains of the Davises' deceased children would be brought to Atlanta to be buried alongside their father.[11]

In Mississippi, both Jackson and Vicksburg petitioned for Davis's remains. Mayor R. F. Beck of the latter city wired Varina on December 7 that in response to the wishes of the people expressed in a mass meeting, he was to offer a site within the corporate limits "for the remains of your illustrious husband."[12] On December 8, B. F. Jones, secretary of the Mississippi division of Association of the Army of Northern Virginia, wrote to Varina expressing the claim that the resting place of "our beloved chieftain" should be in the "sacred soil of his beloved state," promising to craft a monument to the "cause he presented and to Mississippi."[13]

Jackson, the state's capital, based its claim partially on questionable second-hand information. As expressed in the city newspaper the *Commercial Appeal*,

> There is ground for the opinion that Mr. Davis's wishes were to be buried in Jackson, the capital of this State. On his last visit there he was warmly urged to repeat the visit as soon as he could conveniently do so. He told a prominent lady of that city, so we are informed, that he doubted whether he would ever be able to visit Jackson again, but that he hoped it would be his final resting place.[14]

New Orleans had no wish to surrender Davis's remains. On December 7, William Preston Johnston, chairman of the Executive Committee on funeral arrangements, received a telegram from Gus. E. Breaux, president of the Metairie Cemetery Association, requesting that "Jefferson Davis be laid to rest within the city where he fell asleep." Toward that end, he offered "the mound to the left of the entrance to the cemetery and immediately opposite to and corresponding with that where rest the heroes of the Army of Tennessee."[15] A movement was started the same day by the *New Orleans Picayune* to erect a monument in one of the city's parks by dollar subscriptions from all over the South, the monument "to entomb the remains and to be equal to that of Abraham Lincoln in Springfield or that which may cover Grant at Riverside Park."[16]

The *New Orleans Times-Democrat* disagreed, offering what it believed to be a site that would have more appeal. In an editorial, "Where Shall He Rest?," it argued that the general sentiment of the southern people would probably approve the selection of Richmond, Virginia, the capital of the Confederacy, as the most suitable place for the tomb of its only president. Following that city, the paper speculated that the next most suitable place in southern minds would be Lexington, Virginia. Robert E. Lee and Stonewall Jackson were there, and the "quiet little village among the mountains is regarded by the people of the South as a peculiarly sacred spot, for that reason. . . . It would be most appropriate if the three greatest leaders of the Confederate cause were laid to rest together in the heart of the everlasting hills that overlook the scenes of the great war with which their names and their fame are so intimately identified."[17]

Richmond, like the other cities and towns throughout the South, was draped in mourning, with the sounds of cannons firing repeated salutes to its deceased former leader. The former Confederate capital, however, viewing itself as the natural resting place for Davis's remains, lost no time in impressing its desires on the new widow. The days, weeks, and months following his death were filled with intense activity, all aimed at claiming the body for Richmond.

Jefferson Davis died at 12:45 A.M. in the Fenner home in New Orleans. Before noon, Virginia Governor Fitzhugh Lee, a thousand miles away in Richmond, busily prepared two telegrams. The first was a comforting message of condolence to Mrs. Davis. The second, however, to Judge Fenner, went straight to the point: "I voice the unanimous desire of our citizens in asking that the last resting place of . . . Jefferson Davis be in Richmond. As the capital of the Confederacy, here he lived; here then, let him sleep, watched over by the city which for as many years, was the object of his loving solicitude."[18]

The movement was joined immediately by virtually every influential citizen and organization in the city, including a cross section of the city's social, economic, and political elite. The state legislature, then in session, appointed a committee to prepare suitable resolutions. The Confederate veterans of Lee Camp met that evening, and the chamber of commerce met the following day to prepare requests that the Davis family permit the former president's remains to be buried in Richmond.[19] Mayor J. Taylor Ellyson and the city council took similar action, requesting that the city might become the permanent custodian of the remains. His widow was offered her choice of any of the public grounds in the city for his burial site.[20]

On Saturday, December 21, a mass meeting was held at the Mozart Academy of Music to unify the various efforts. The result was the establishment of the Jefferson Davis Monument Association (JDMA), created for the dual purpose of building a monument to Davis and securing his body for Richmond. Mayor Ellyson, a Confederate veteran who had served in the Richmond Howitzers during the war, was elected president and would guide the board and act as its leader during most of its history. The board of directors, also southern veterans of the war, included N. V. Randolph, Peyton Wise,

John Ellett, George L. Christian, and W. D. Chesterman. This membership remained constant, working individually and together to complete the task. For the next three and a half years, the committee's charge to build a monument remained secondary, while it placed its emphasis on the reinterment of the remains in Richmond.

In late December, Ellyson forwarded the city council's request for the right to rebury the Confederate president in the soil of Richmond. Varina replied on December 21, 1889, in a letter from her Beauvoir home that she would be unable to reach a decision for approximately twelve months because she also had to consider similar requests from other southern cities.[21] The Virginia city, although anxious for a final determination in its favor, waited patiently before approaching her again. The JDMA did not meet again until June 13 of the following year, when it sought the cooperation of the Richmond Chamber of Commerce to join it in urging Mrs. Davis to have her husband buried in the city. In response, the chamber sent a committee of six men, headed by Ellyson, to visit Varina in New York, where she had decided to remain following a visit to prospective publishers of her deceased husband's memoirs and because the hot climate of the Mississippi coast was bad for her health. She informed the committee that she could not in fairness make a decision until after she had met with representatives from Jackson, Mississippi, who were due to arrive the following day.[22]

With no firm answer in hand, Ellyson and his committee returned to Richmond. The following days were anxious ones, as it was believed that the Davis family was split on the location of the reinterment. Mrs. Davis and her daughter Winnie were said to favor the former Confederate capital, while others were thought to be in favor of Jackson, located in Mrs. Davis's home state of Mississippi.[23] In order to enhance its prospects, the city of Richmond gave its assurance to Davis's widow that she could select the site of her husband's grave and monument, including, if she wished, the former "White House of the Confederacy," where Winnie was born, son Joseph had died, and the Davis family had lived during the war years.[24]

Correspondence between Ellyson and Varina Davis show that the two families were developing a friendly relationship that went beyond discussions of business matters. Whether this entered into Varina's decision to choose Richmond cannot be determined. However, Varina was cooling to requests from her home state. In a letter not made public until after her death, she said that while overtures had been made to her by several states after her husband's death and delegations had visited her, she waited for Mississippi to make clear its claim. In the end, she believed that Mississippi had not handled the matter with the necessary dignity and consideration. She had also taken offense at criticism from the state for her decision to live in the North.[25]

When Ellyson, accompanied by a committee from the Richmond Chamber of Commerce, approached her once again in June 1891 in her New York hotel, she was ready to be persuaded. Several weeks later, General Joseph R. Anderson, who had headed the committee, received a letter from Varina advising him that she had decided to accept the invitation extended to her "by the people of Richmond to inter the body of Mr. Davis" in Richmond.[26]

The long-awaited decision was announced in the press in the form of a public letter, dated July 12, 1891, from Varina to the "Veterans and the People of the Southern States." In it, she revealed that her first choice was the Davis plantation in Mississippi. However, fears that the waters of the Gulf of Mexico would someday rise above the land caused her to turn to Richmond, which "at short intervals throughout the last eighteen months . . . has renewed her tender insistence that he [Davis] should rest among the heroic dead of all the States who fell in defense of the Confederacy." She asked that the other states relinquish their plans "for the sake of gratifying the majority of the veterans who have written countless letters to me from each of the before-mentioned States to urge Richmond as the proper place." The letter was signed "Your countrywoman, Varina Jefferson Davis."[27]

On October 31, 1891, Mrs. Davis, accompanied by Winnie, visited Richmond to choose a site for the grave and the monument. The issue absorbed the city, and the Davises were the center of attention, attending crowded receptions daily. On the evening of November 5, a committee of the JDMA called on Mrs. Davis at the home of General and Mrs. Anderson to discuss the various sites. After the interview, Mrs. Davis said that she preferred that her husband's remains be buried in Hollywood Cemetery. As far as the monument was concerned, her preference was for it to be located on the grounds of the Soldiers' Home, but she would leave that decision to the committee.[28]

Varina's decision in favor of Hollywood Cemetery disappointed some who believed that the old Davis mansion (the Confederate White House) should be the preferred location. This she rejected, however, because her husband had often expressed his aversion to any public, noisy thoroughfare as a place of burial and had desired a quiet and secluded place for himself where his whole family might be near him. In a later reply to a suggestion that he be buried in a crypt under the Confederate White House, she responded that the former president himself had "expressed objections to a crypt on the occasion of seeing the Duke of Wellington's crypt in St. Paul's" church in London.[29] It was for those reasons that Hollywood was selected over other sites. Mrs. Davis also expressed her desire and was given assurances that additional burial spaces would be provided for her and other members of the family and that the remains of her children who had died and been buried elsewhere would be moved to the Davis section of Hollywood.[30]

The site she selected was one of the most beautiful in the picturesque cemetery. The Davis Circle, as it came to be known, was elliptical in shape and overlooked the rapids of the James River some distance below. The graves of presidents James Monroe and John Tyler were located nearby, and the cemetery served as the final resting place of twelve thousand Confederate veterans as well as generals George E. Pickett, James Ewel Brown "Jeb" Stuart, and A. P. Hill. Downtown Richmond and the Confederate capitol building could be seen in the distance. From a symbolic standpoint, the site was ideal for the burial of the man who had served as the Confederacy's only president.

Varina's decision was not accepted without criticism and some bitterness by Richmond's rivals. In April 1892, a Colonel Johnson wrote separately to her and Ellyson to complain that the Virginia delegation had pressured her to make a decision in favor of Richmond. Varina wrote that the "grating and weary debate" was useless, as she had made her decision. On the contrary, Varina wrote that the Virginians had waited patiently on her in New York for seventeen days without remonstrance and that they had waited seventeen months before they made a formal application to her. "You may rely," she wrote to Ellyson, "on my disabusing the minds of our people . . . of any idea that anything was done by Virginia which was not kind, generous and reverent to [Jefferson Davis's] memory and to me."[31]

With Mrs. Davis's approval of Richmond's request and the site of the reburial selected, planning for the second funeral of Jefferson Davis made steady progress. On February 2, 1893, the board of directors of the JDMA met and adopted a resolution that the remains of former president Davis be transferred from New Orleans to Richmond, with the reburial taking place in Hollywood Cemetery on May 30, Hollywood Memorial Day, a date normally observed for the decoration of Confederate graves. Ellyson, at the head of a committee of five, visited New York, where he sought and received Varina's agreement to the board's plans.[32] While there, she reiterated her desire that the remains of her children who had died elsewhere also be interred in the Davis family plot in Hollywood.[33] A son, Joseph, popularly called "Little Joe," who had died as the result of a fall from the balcony of the Confederate White House during the war, was already buried in the Richmond cemetery. His grave would have to be moved to the family plot. One child was buried in Washington, D.C., and two in Memphis. In addition, the deceased daughter of the Davises' daughter Margaret Hayes was also buried in Memphis and would have to be transferred.[34]

The following month, Ellyson traveled to New Orleans to meet with generals John Gordon and John Glynn, national and Louisiana commanders, respectively, of the United Confederate Veterans associations, to make further arrangements for the removal. While in Louisiana, he had three conferences with Glynn and others during which it was decided that the ceremonies at New Orleans would be the responsibility of the Louisiana Division of the United Confederate Veterans and the State Guard, both under the command of General Glynn. In addition, the Confederate Veterans of New Orleans, who had guarded the Davis tomb night and day for three years, were granted the right to have charge of the conveyance of the remains to Richmond, where they would relinquish them to Lee Camp, which was in charge of the civic and military displays there. It was further agreed that the route of travel would be selected by the monument association in Richmond and that all the details of the parade and reinterment would be in the hands of Lee Camp.[35]

As Ellyson traveled between Virginia and Louisiana, the plans for the route of the funeral train grew as state after state expressed a desire to participate. He found a lively interest among the cities and towns through which the funeral train would pass. Even though he arrived in Montgomery at the early hour of 6:00 A.M., he found the governor of the state and the mayor of the city on hand at the train station for a half-hour conference. They expressed the desire that the train bearing Davis's remains stop for several hours in the city in which he was inaugurated president. Georgia's interest in paying tribute to the Civil War leader was similarly expressed by Governor William J. Northen, who boarded the train at a station outside Atlanta for a lengthy conference. Elias Carr, governor of North Carolina, expressed the same wishes for his state in a letter dated March 30, 1893.[36] Since the original route through that latter state called for bypassing Raleigh, the state's capital, Carr asked that the association revise the route so as to allow Davis to lie in state in Raleigh. Since Varina was willing that the train should stop in Montgomery, Atlanta, and Charlotte or Raleigh, the change was made. The JDMA further realized that to do justice to those cities, permitting them to have ceremonies consistent with the dignity of the occasion, the date of the reburial had to be delayed. The new date for Davis's reburial was set for May 31, 1893.[37]

With the desires of the principal participants expressed either in writing or in person, the schedule for the long-awaited funeral procession and reinterment could be set. This was done at the JDMA's board of directors meeting in Richmond on April 19. The body of the Confederate president would be removed from its temporary grave in Metairie Cemetery on Sunday, May 27, to lie in state in the city of his death until the following day. After leaving New Orleans at 7:30 P.M., on May 28, it would make a brief stop of a few minutes at Beauvoir, the Davis home on the Gulf coast, followed by a stop of five hours for ceremonies in Montgomery on May 29. The funeral train would then proceed to Atlanta, where the remains would lie in state later the same day. On May 30, it would make brief stops at Greenville, South Carolina, and Greensboro, North Carolina; then, following three hours in Raleigh, it would arrive at Richmond at 9:00 P.M. to lie in state until his burial on May 31.[38] The multihour stops in the state capitals of Alabama, Georgia, and North Carolina would permit the people of those cities to view Davis's coffin as it was paraded through the streets and lie in state in their capitol buildings before permanent burial in Richmond. Davis would be honored by the governors of those states and South Carolina. These men would serve as escorts of honor on the train as it passed through their jurisdictions.[39]

The Davis Monument committee soon came to regret its approval of the Raleigh segment of the route and voted to request Governor Carr to allow them to omit his state's capital and to have the North Carolina ceremonies in Greensboro instead. Carr disagreed, and it stayed on the schedule.[40] This refusal would force the train to backtrack from Raleigh to Greensboro, through which it had already passed, before moving into Virginia, thereby leaving the train little leeway in the amount of time permitted per stop.

Within the following two weeks, Macon, Georgia, and Columbia, South Carolina, made unsuccessful applications to the board for the train to stop in their cities. The JDMA offered special regrets to the governor of South Carolina, but it explained to him that whereas the other governors wrote their applications weeks earlier, he had failed to do so until arrangements had been completed. On May 5, the association agreed to the date of June 1, 1893, for the reburial of the Davis children in the family plot in Hollywood.[41] While the funeral procession was to be the most elaborate in southern history, the association planned for comparatively simple graveside ceremonies for the deceased Confederate president since it was decided that the original funeral services of December 11, 1889, should not be repeated.[42]

Southerners grew increasingly anxious as the departure date neared for what was expected to be one of the most elaborate and ceremonious funeral processions in American history. As with the original funeral, newspapers throughout the South and many in the North reported every move. Some sent their best reporters along on the train. The *Boston Globe* sent A. Maurice Low, whose writing presented readers in Massachusetts with vivid word pictures of every aspect of the trip. The JDMA included among its official delegation G. Watson James, an assistant secretary of the organization and an editor of the *Richmond Dispatch*, to represent that body and to write a complete record of the transfer. Other reporters on the train included John S. Irby of the *Richmond Times* and George W. Blake of the *New York World*.[43] Railroads took advantage of the funeral procession through the South by advertising reduced individual and group rates to Richmond and to cities along the route at which the funeral train would stop. Cities, towns, and hamlets prepared appropriate decorations, ceremonies, and salutes, even if the train was only to speed through their jurisdiction nonstop during the night.

Mayor Ellyson arrived in New York on May 25 to accompany the Davises to New Orleans, where they would participate in ceremonies there and along the route of the funeral train. Varina, however, chose to remain in New York and to participate only in the reburial in Richmond. Although she publicly stated that she was too frail for the trip, a letter written the following day to her friend Ann E. Grant in Richmond reveals that her inability to face the emotional drain played as much a factor as health in her decision. "I do not wish to remain [in Richmond] any longer than I can help," she wrote, "for I cannot talk to the outside world just now. It does not devolve upon many women to twice bury a husband and four children and I am overcome by memories of the past."[44] En route to New Orleans, Ellyson and Winnie were joined by the remainder of the committee from the JDMA in Danville, Virginia.

During the coming week, the procession of the funeral train to Richmond and the reburial in Hollywood Cemetery fascinated the South and much of the country. The New Orleans segment, however, was distinctly more low key and with less public participation than anywhere along the route. *Boston Globe* reporter Low and others attached this to dissatisfaction over being forced to surrender the remains that it had faithfully guarded for three and a half years. "New Orleans is not at all pleased with her prominence in the proceedings, and for that reason, perhaps, displays less excitement than other places throughout the South."[45]

Low touched on another aspect of the proceedings that caused concern among those in the North who believed that the demonstrations associated with the Davis reinterment illustrated that southerners were unrepentant and were still disloyal to the national government. The Boston journalist did this in two interviews with prominent Louisiana citizens held four days apart. To state supreme court Justice Fenner, in whose home Davis had died, and attorney W. S. Parkerson, he asked, "What is the meaning, the real significance of the popular demonstrations attending the transfer of the remains from New Orleans to Richmond," why is Davis still a popular idol to southerners, and "why more so than any of the other great fighters who were projected on the state at that time?" Fenner replied that Davis was the leader of the Confederacy—the embodiment and spirit of the idea. Touching on the symbol of the dead southern president as a martyr, he said, "No matter what others might do, he was always true and stanch to the cause which he considered right. He was the only man who had to bear the brunt after all others made their peace, whom the North proscribed and visited with obloquy." But at the same time, he argued that southerners now "are devoted to the past of the Confederacy, but [are also] devoted to the future of the Union." The demonstrations attending the removal of the remains, Fenner explained, were purely sentimental, without any political sentiment attached to it. Parkerson expressed similar feelings, holding that the present demonstrations for Davis were "merely the sentimental regard of the people to the memory of the man who . . . embodied all the ideas which they held to be right and conceived to be just." Because Davis had been their president and their leader, that "made him the greatest figure of the Confederacy."[46]

The Richmond delegation arrived in New Orleans on the morning of December 27. While Ellyson met with General Glynn, who took him to the cemetery and explained the arrangements he had made for Davis in the city, others took Winnie to the St. Charles Hotel, where she was reunited with her sister Margaret and brother-in-law Addison Hayes. During the day, numerous friends visited the Davis sisters, among them relatives, veterans, and others, some of whom would be returning with the train to Richmond for the final burial services. These included General George W. Jones of Iowa, Judge and Mrs. Fenner, J. U. Payne, former Confederate Governor Francis R. Lubbock of Texas, William Preston Johnston, and Robert Brown, the last having been one of the Davis family's most trusted servants.

Brown, because of his status as a former slave of the Davis family, attracted special attention on his arrival in New Orleans. It is probable that he was included as a member of the funeral escort and invited to participate in the reburial services at Varina's request, as he was invited by the JDMA, which paid his travel expenses.[47] While on his way to visit Ellyson and Winnie at their hotel, a *Picayune* reporter asked him to come to the newspaper's office, where he was interviewed and sketched by an artist.

Brown told the reporter that he had been sold to Davis during the first month of his administration in 1861 and remained with him from that time on. He was with him at the time of his capture in Georgia in 1865 and afterward took the Davis children to their grandmother in Canada. After a decade in New Orleans with the Fenner family, he rejoined the Davises at Memphis and remained with them until Jefferson Davis died at Beauvoir in 1889. He then moved to St. Elmo, near Mobile, Alabama, where he was living when Ellyson contacted him to join the family for the funeral procession.[48] Brown's firm loyalty to the Davis family provoked one observer to comment, "He is not altogether reconstructed, and is not a very firm believer in the glories of reconstruction."[49]

Davis's remains were removed from the mausoleum of the Army of Northern Virginia on the afternoon of May 27, 1893, where they had lain for three and a half years under the constant day and night guard of Confederate veterans. Varina ordered that the removal of the body be done privately at a time when there would be no crowds in order to avoid the stares of onlookers. There would be no music or ceremonies. According to plan, Davis's remains would be taken to Memorial Hall, where he would lie in state until five in the afternoon of the next day. Then, following brief ceremonies, a procession would take him to the train for transfer to Richmond.

The first steps in the removal of Jefferson Davis's remains from his burial chamber in Metairie to his final resting place in Hollywood Cemetery began before 7:00 A.M. while much of the city was still sleeping. The removal ceremony was witnessed by E. H. Farrar, representing the Davis family; Frank Johnson, the undertaker who had charge of the original funeral and would escort the remains to Richmond; Paul Scholz of Metairie Cemetery; and representatives of the Army of Northern Virginia. Glynn and Ellyson arrived late but were there for the closing scene. The slab covering Davis's vault, which was made of black marble with white lettering, was opened, allowing undertaker Johnson and his assistants to gently remove the "crumbling black plush casket" that they placed on a nearby table to open. In a few moments, they had opened the lid, which "had succumbed to the corroding dampness."[50] The body was originally buried in a copper casket, with a plate-glass top, that was enclosed inside the coffin. According to the witnesses, Davis's "remains were naturally somewhat decomposed, and the mold of the damp grave had touched the body with its hunger, but . . . the remains were in a fair state of preservation and the face could be easily recognized."[51] After identification of the body as that of Davis, the copper case was removed from the original coffin and placed inside a new casket made of hand-carved antique oak, which was of a design normally used only on state occasions.[52] At the suggestion of Mayor Ellyson, the top of the new coffin included a replica of the heavy ornamental brass plate from the old coffin on which was engraved

JEFFERSON DAVIS
At Rest
Dec. 6, 1889

Ellyson issued a formal written order for the delivery of the old casket into the custody of Camp No. 1 of the United Confederate Veterans. The empty coffin from which Davis's remains had been removed was returned to the Army of Northern Virginia to be placed back in the vault. Before this was done, however, it was filled with the faded flowers that had been placed on the bier three years earlier and that had been saved for the family. The casket was then carefully restored to the vault in the tomb, and the mouth of the grave was resealed with the black marble slab that had marked the spot for over three years. Ellyson watched as the empty tomb was resealed, then left the cemetery. Davis's vault would remain empty and guarded as though his remains were still there. The only evidence that marked the spot was a facsimile of his signature, with the dates of his birth and death: "June 3, 1808, Dec. 6, 1889." A reporter later asked Mayor Ellyson if he had seen the remains. "I never look upon the face of a dead friend," was the reply.[53]

Although the transfer had taken place during the early morning, the escort from the Army of Northern Virginia did not arrive to remove remains to Memorial Hall until mid-afternoon. In the meantime, Davis's coffin remained waiting in the lower corridor of the tomb under the guard of the Confederate veterans of the Army of Northern Virginia. At precisely 3:00 P.M., a detail of cavalrymen in gray coats and slouch hats arrived at the tomb. A small number of people who were visiting the cemetery stood around and watched as Johnson's black hearse was driven up the mound to the head of the flight of steps. The escort dismounted, then formed in double lines on either side of the entrance, and the eight pallbearers descended into the vault. When they returned, the few bystanders bared their heads while the casket was placed in the closed hearse. The curtains were drawn, and the cortege began the march into the city. Four men rode in front, four on each side, and four took up the rear. At the gate, they passed the Richmond delegation in a carriage that took its place at the end of the procession.[54]

The air was humid, the heat was intense, and the horses kicked up dust as the cortege moved along Canal, Washington, and Camp streets toward Memorial Hall. As the removal was intended to be done without publicity, there were no crowds along the streets. The few persons along the way bared their heads as the procession passed. A few blocks before the hall was reached, a body of gray-clad Confederate veterans on foot joined the parade as dark clouds appeared and a light rain began to fall. As the cortege turned at the base of the statue of Henry Clay, the cloud thundered forth an artillery salute. The procession marched on unmindful. Everywhere hats were lifted, and everywhere American flags were at half-mast.[55] The procession from tomb to Memorial Hall had taken two hours. By that time, it was 5:00 P.M. The entire process from the tomb to the place of lying in state had taken place in complete silence without music or ceremonies.

Local veterans' camps had been waiting outside the hall for an hour. These were joined by a large crowd of New Orleans citizens. The escort formed on both sides of the street and removed their hats as the coffin was carried into the hall, which, like the air outside, was oppressively hot. The coffin was placed on a low oaken stand at the upper end of the hall. Two uniformed veterans were placed at the head of the bier as guards of honor. Generals Stephen D. Lee and George Jones of Iowa stood nearby. The veterans saluted and spread over the coffin the flag of the First Mississippi Regiment, which Davis had commanded during the Mexican War. The banner was in a poor condition, the red and blue entirely faded away and the entire flag reduced to a mellow yellowish tint, with holes where the stars had been. Memorial Hall served as a museum of the war, and Confederate flags, some with bullet holes and tears from battle, lined the walls. Other than the trophies of war, the decorations were kept simple for the lying in state. The hall remained open all night to visitors with a steady stream passing the coffin until midnight, when the building was left empty except for the guards.[56]

The following day, despite the continuation of the hot, humid weather of the day before, was different. The people of New Orleans, who had seemed indifferent earlier, showed more interest and turned out in large numbers. The sounds of drums and fifes filled the air as military bands marched to their places of rendezvous. Memorial Hall was never empty, as a large number of people continued to file by Davis's coffin. The funeral train was scheduled to leave at 7:00 P.M., and as the day progressed, activities around the hall became more animated. The streets became alive with veterans in gray clothes and slouch hats, numbers of whom were minus limbs lost in the war.[57]

The ceremonies for the transfer of Davis's remains from New Orleans to Richmond began at 5:00 P.M. Memorial Hall was crowded to suffocation. A "solid phalanx of gray-haired veterans" stood at attention in front of the coffin. The Richmond committee appeared on the platform in Confederate uniforms, while Davis's two daughters, dressed in black, sat near the coffin. Louisiana Governor Foster delivered a short address in which he announced the transfer of the body from Louisiana to Virginia. This was followed by a reading of Varina's order directing the transfer of the body from the Army of Northern Virginia to Mayor Ellyson, who in turn read an order appointing General Glynn to assume charge of the remains during the trip from New Orleans to Richmond. The ceremony closed with the crowd joining the Reverend A. Gordon Bakewell in a recitation of the Lord's Prayer.

The procession was then formed. It consisted of the militia, the two Davis daughters and other relatives, Confederate and Mexican War veterans, civic associations, state and city officials, members of the judiciary and bar, and elderly veterans from the Soldiers' Home. The coffin was placed on a funeral car pulled by six black horses. This was the same carriage used during Davis's burial in Metairie in 1889.[58] Thousands of persons lined Canal Street. At one point, the press of the crowd was such that the procession could barely make its way through. Confederate flags were made obvious by their absences. There were no Stars and Bars flags among the funeral cortege, but small, crossed U.S. flags adorned both sides of the roof of the funeral carriage. When the parade reached the Louisville & Nashville station, a crowd of thousands more awaited.[59]

The funeral train was a special provided for the occasion by the Richmond & Danville Railroad system. It was pulled by one of the largest and fastest engines in the South. To guard against any mishap, three engines with their boilers full of steam stood ready along the route to take over as needed.

Headed by locomotive number 69, the train was draped in mourning colors of black and white from the engine to the back of the last car. The funeral car was a specially designed observation car of unusual width, with the sides and ends made almost entirely of glass so that the casket would be visible as the train passed through the cities and countryside of the southern states. All the seats had been removed, except a few for the immediate escort to the remains, and a substantial bier erected in the center of the car. The funeral car was heavily draped in mourning, with the glass plates left unobstructed so that people who gathered at the various stations would be rewarded with a momentary glance at the raised bier carrying Davis.[60]

The sounds of a band playing the funeral dirge were heard as the procession moved toward the train, and the crowd, including several thousand Confederate veterans, became quiet. The caisson bearing Davis's remains came to a halt beside the glassed-in observation car, and the pallbearers gently carried the casket up the steps of a specially built black platform and passed it through an opening made by removing one of the car's windows. The crowds watched through the wide windows as the casket was carefully placed on a sable-covered catafalque in the center. Floral offerings from all over the South were placed at the head of the casket, and a guard of honor selected from the state escorts was placed to guard over it.[61]

The Davis family members and the funeral escort boarded the train, Winnie, Margaret, and her husband occupying the last Pullman. Ellyson and the Richmond delegation, as well as the Mississippi group, were also provided with separate cars. Others onboard included the veteran escort sent from Virginia, representatives of the governor of Louisiana, funeral director Johnson and his wife, and reporters from northern and southern newspapers. The plan devised by the JDMA called for the governor of each state through which the train traveled to board and act as honorary escort as the train passed though his jurisdiction.[62] The train would thus stop at some point as it entered each state to take on that state's governor.

The train pulled out of the station at 7:50 P.M., fifty minutes past schedule. Crowds watched at every street corner on both sides of the track until the city limits were passed. As soon as open country was reached, the thirty-five-man military escort laid aside arms and uniforms except for their gray coats so they would be ready to take their turn standing guard over the casket. The escort included men of all ranks, with colonels standing guard the same as a private soldier. The journey from New Orleans to Richmond would continue to see a series of demonstrations honoring in large and small ways the former president of the Confederacy.[63]

Regardless of time of day or night, there were little groups of men and women at every crossroad and flag station, and when occasionally the train stopped for orders, there was a rush for the funeral car and sometimes an attempt made to get inside.[64] While some demonstrations were spontaneous or locally organized, others were orchestrated to ensure large turnouts. This was particularly the case involving Confederate veterans. General John B. Gordon, who was to serve as grand marshal of the Richmond reburial procession, issued the following order in his capacity as national commander of the United Confederate Veterans associations:

> Commanders of the UCV [United Confedrate Veterans] in the states along the route   will assemble as many veterans as they possibly can, in bodies with their respective camps where practicable, and see that all unite with the local camps, committees and authorities in the cities and towns through which the funeral cortege will pass in showing every possible mark of respect and making the ceremonies everywhere along the route of the most imposing character and in every way worthy of the occasion and the man. The major-generals in adjoining states in the eastern department to those already named will join the funeral train with the veterans of their divisions at points most convenient to their respective camps. The general commanding will join the funeral procession at Atlanta, Ga.
>
> Persons who reside along the route of the funeral procession are especially requested to drape their houses or doorways. Black and white will, of course, be most appropriate for the decorations.[65]

The first scheduled stop after leaving Louisiana was at Beauvoir, where Davis had spent twelve years of his life. Children had strewn white rhododendron flowers along the track for a distance of three hundred yards, and the station platform was decorated with evergreens and Spanish moss. Three large wreaths made from wildflowers picked by Davis's niece hung in front of the station, and as the train stopped, they were carried into the funeral car. General and Mrs. Joseph B. Davis, accompanied by their daughter, boarded the train and looked at the decorations surrounding the bier. After ten minutes, the train moved on.[66] After leaving Beauvoir, a brief stop was made at Scranton, where a special car bearing Mississippi Governor Jones and his staff was added to the Davis train.

Shortly after midnight, the train pulled into Mobile, where locomotive number 69 was replaced by number 75 for the trip to Montgomery. Two hundred Confederate veterans stood on the platform while a battery of the Alabama State Artillery fired a twenty-gun salute. At least one thousand people took what view they could of the casket through the windows of the funeral car, although none was allowed inside because of the difficulty of accommodating such a large number. After approximately twenty minutes, the train resumed its journey.[67]

The train picked up speed, reaching sixty-two miles per hour in order to make up lost time. Journalist Low of the *Boston Globe* reported catching momentary glimpses of men and women along the tracks who had apparently waited some time to catch a glimpse of the coffin as it sped past.[68] A brief stop was made around 6:00 A.M. at Greenville, Alabama, where, despite the early hour, a large number of persons waited at the station. By this time, the oak casket had become almost indiscernible under the mass of flowers of every variety heaped on and around it. As the train moved on toward the Alabama capital, Low noted that "at every little white-washed cabin, with its chimney on the outside, at every crossing and clearing were men and women on the watch."[69]

The Davis train drew into the long, rambling station in Montgomery just as the sun was rising. There were at least fifteen thousand persons at the depot when the train arrived to the roar of an artillery salute that wakened its passengers from their sleep. The rain had been coming down in torrents for more than an hour, but it drove no one to seek shelter. Simultaneous with the arrival, the Montgomery True Blues and the Montgomery Grays marched down alongside the train, one on each side, and then halted and presented arms. Governor T. G. Jones, his staff, and a delegation of prominent citizens boarded to greet the passengers and view the coffin. One of the delegation was Letitia Tyler, granddaughter of President John Tyler, the only former American president to serve in any official capacity in the Confederate government. Miss Tyler had raised the first Confederate flag over the capitol building while Jefferson Davis was taking the oath of office. Also present to meet the train was Theus Raoul, who, as a young girl, fired the first gun salute to the new Confederate flag.[70] After breakfast, the Davis daughters drove to the capitol building to see where their father had been sworn in as president. As they passed the columns into the building, the rain suddenly stopped and the sun shone through the clouds.

Meanwhile, Governor Jones had ordered that the procession would begin at precisely 8:30 A.M. regardless of the weather. There began "such bustle and commotion in the streets of Montgomery as have not been witness there in 30 years" as squads of men and cavalry hurried to their posts. Then the sound of a bugle rang out, the minute guns boomed again, the "sabers of the cavalrymen drawn up at the depot flashed out, the infantry presented arms, and there came lumbering to the train a huge caisson drawn by six horses." The funeral wagon, instead of being draped in the traditional black color of mourning, was covered with lilac cloth while the horses were clothed in the same color. The roof of the car was topped with a gilt crown, with bunches of cattails at the corners. Shields with the word "Davis" were on each side of the vehicle. *Globe* writer Low observed that "nothing like it had been seen outside of a circus parade."[71]

The New Orleans escort carried the coffin from the train to the caisson, and instantly the crowd quieted and the men removed their hats. Then, as the funeral car moved down Commerce Street, "the first note of that most mournful of funeral hymns, the dead march in 'Saul,' began to play."[72] The only other sounds were church bells and the firing of minute guns. Every window, balcony, and sidewalk was filled. Governor Jones, with his uniformed staff, led the way, followed by a unit of mounted police, then the caisson bearing Davis's remains, by which a body of Confederate veterans marched in fours. These in turn were followed by the Louisiana escort, behind which came a long line of infantry, a body of artillery men, a squad of cavalry, and fifty cadets from Auburn. The route down Commerce and Dexter streets to the capitol building was deep in mud from the heavy rains.

The procession came to a halt at the capitol building, the historic birthplace of the Confederacy. The Alabama veterans formed in two lines at the entrance, and three crippled officers, two carrying the torn battle flags of the 64th Alabama and 32nd Georgia regiments, advanced and laid their flags on the casket. Davis was then carried up the steps from which he had made his inaugural address in 1861 and over the spot where he had been sworn in as president and was laid in state in the supreme court chambers. A large Stars and Bars flag hung over a painted portrait of Davis, which was entwined in white roses. A bust of the former Confederate president, crowned with laurel, stood on the fireplace near the head of the coffin. On the wall over the desk of the justices were the words "He Suffered for Us" written in evergreens. The chamber was "redolent with the perfume of Southern flowers" which had been cut and placed around the room the previous day for the occasion.[73] Large U.S. flags were displayed on both sides of the door leading into the library. Beneath the flags, the words "Monterey" and "Buena Vista," associated with Davis's service in the war with Mexico, were written in gold letters on broad bands of lilac silk. The front of the justices' desk bore a quotation of Davis festooned with flowers:

> That the Union may promote the general welfare, it is needful that the truth, the whole truth, should be known, so that crimination and recrimination may forever cease, and then, on the basis of fraternity and faithful regard for the rights of the States, there may be written on the arch of the Union—*Esto perpetus*.[74]

There were neither speeches nor formal ceremonies of any kind attending the lying in state. For the next two hours, a steady stream, estimated at five thousand persons, filed two abreast past the coffin between two lines of Montgomery True Blues standing at "present," with bayonets fixed on their rifles. The veterans passed first with their heads bared, then several hundred ladies, each with a white flower to deposit at the base of the casket as they passed. Next came a large number of young girls. Then came the military and finally the public. The crowd was so dense that several women fainted and were carried away with some difficulty. The sentries were repeatedly obliged to cross bayonets to keep the crowds back. Finally, it became necessary to double the guard, which had all it could do to keep the people back. There was concern that people might be pushed onto the points of the bayonets.[75]

African Americans joined the white population in visiting the remains of the Confederate president. An elderly black man, identified in the press only as Uncle Jack, and his wife, who had made the trip upriver from their plantation cabin, stood with tears in their eyes. He had been at Davis's inauguration with his master in 1861 and was reportedly saddened by the fact that both were now dead.[76]

Just before 11:00 A.M., the order was given to remove the body to the depot. As the coffin was lifted from the bier, everyone present rushed forward to pick up a flower as a souvenir. The procession returned to the train by the same route it had taken, while church bells tolled and minute guns continued to fire. As they would do at every stop, Davis's daughters appeared on the rear platform to greet the crowd and say their farewells. The train pulled out at 11:30 A.M. Cannons fired, and the soldiers, who had drawn up in long lines on both sides of the train, came to present arms while the train passed through the gates of the city on its way to Atlanta.

The funeral train left Montgomery forty-five minutes late and again attained a speed of more than sixty miles per hour. Low continued his fascination with the wayside observances. He noticed that at station after station, people stood silent and expectant. A few miles out of the Alabama capital, an African American woman rushed out of her cabin with a child at each side and frantically waved her handkerchief. The train briefly stopped at Chehaw, where the pleading of the people caused the guard to relent and allow them to pass through the funeral car. About ten miles farther, men with rifles and shotguns stood in line and fired salutes as the train hurried by. During a brief stop at Opelika, a large crowd met the train. Low noticed that, whether on purpose or by chance, the African Americans lined one side of the track and whites the other. A large green arch had been erected on the platform with the words "He is not dead" inscribed on it. There was curiosity to see Winnie Davis, and the "Daughter of the Confederacy" stepped on the platform and bowed to the crowd. A high-pitched rebel yell was given as she and her sister were introduced. A delegation carrying a battered Confederate battle flag presented the more popular Winnie with a wreath of flowers for the funeral car.[77]

As the train entered Georgia at West Point, it passed under a magnificent floral arch that spanned the track. Again, thousands were at the station, while the town's soldiers fired salute after salute and young women "fairly showered" flowers into the car windows. Governor Northen and his staff, dressed in Confederate gray laced with yellow, came on board as part of the escort and the train moved on.[78]

The train passed through La Grange, the home of Ben Hill, at 2:30 P.M. Even though it did not slow its speed, fire bells rang; the stores, schools, and factories closed; and everyone was at the depot. The local cavalry, mounted and with hats at salute, was drawn up near the tracks. A solid line of women and children lined the road for 250 yards. In back of them the men stood in line, and to the left of these stood another row of about two hundred young women dressed in gray homespun jackets with red and white ribbons on their breasts. Beyond them, factory workers watched the train pass.[79] At Newnan, the train only slowed while flowers were thrown on the tracks and in the windows, and cannons and muskets fired salutes. At Moreland, a stop was made just long enough to enable a man to hand Winnie a floral piece with the inscription "He lives in the hearts of the people." She read it and replied, "That is the way I want him to live."[80]

Atlanta was reached at 3:00 P.M., promptly on schedule. The Georgia capital was different than any other stop along the trip. While the emotion for Davis and the ceremonies were at least equaled, if not surpassed, the Georgia state capital was unrivaled in unintended black humor and embarrassments for the Davis reinterment procession. There were indications of this even before the train arrived in Atlanta. Even though Davis had been dead for a full three and a half years, the city would not permit a funeral procession without the issuance of a new death certificate. Accordingly, a new one was made out, showing that, indeed, Jefferson Davis, "occupation: ex-president," was dead as of December 6, 1889.[81]

Atlanta was different in other ways. The enthusiasm and emotions were more visible than in other southern cities. The crowds began to gather an hour before the arrival of the train. All through the day, various railroads had been bringing in long trains to see the last visit of Jefferson Davis. It was estimated that twenty-five thousand visitors were in Atlanta for the procession and lying in state. By the time the train pulled into the depot, five thousand people crowded the streets and bridges to see the casket and to view the popular "Miss Winnie."

A thousand people crowded by the guards to watch the pallbearers carry the coffin from the train through two lines of soldiers at present arms to an artillery caisson restructured to serve as a funeral car for Davis's remains. A profusion of flowers had been a feature of the ex-president's 1886 visit to Atlanta, and this tradition continued as part of the celebration of his visit in death. White flowers, arranged on the four sides of the car, read "Our Warrior Statesman," "A patriot always," "Great in War, Greater in Peace," and "Representative of the Lost Cause."[82]

Several minutes passed in making the transfer and getting the procession formed. The pallbearers carried Davis's coffin up an elegant black stairway attached to the side of the caisson and placed it on the bier, which was now banked in flowers of every kind. As soon as the casket was secure in its mounted position, the funeral car, led by six gray horses, slowly began to move. A rather bizarre plan that failed to materialize called for the caisson to be followed by fifty ex-slaves. It was believed that this would "show the respect that the veterans still have for the faithful old Southern darkies of the ante-bellum days."[83]

The procession was of such length that it required an hour or more to pass any given point. General Clement A. Evans, commander of Georgia Confederate Veterans' Association and acting as grand marshal, led the parade on horseback, accompanied by his aides and the mounted police. Then came the various military companies: the Gate City Guard, the Atlanta Artillery, the Fourth Battalion Georgia Volunteers, the Hibernian Rifles, and the Police Battalion. The caisson, with the casket standing several feet above the carriage for all to see, followed with the pallbearers and funeral escort. A line of more than two thousand Confederate veterans, some with missing arms and legs and walking on crutches and others showing the effects of age, followed behind their wartime leader on the long march to the state capitol. They were joined by several members of the Grand Army of the Republic, there at the invitation of their former enemies. The *Atlanta Constitution* commented favorably the following day, "Their presence attested the fact that the war was over, and emphasized . . . that Americans were brothers and the flag of the union was the flag of fraternity."[84] The veterans were followed by a long line of two hundred or more carriages in which rode senators Gordon and Colquitt, governors Northen and Jones and their staffs, members of the Davis family, the mayor and city council, prominent officials from the local and state levels, and general citizens.

The procession arrived at the Capitol Street entrance to the capitol at a few minutes past 5:00 P.M. The casket was removed from its perch on the caisson and carried into the capitol building by twelve Confederate veterans who gently placed it on a flower-covered bier only a few feet from the Ben Hill statue that Davis had helped dedicate during his 1886 Southern Tour. The sides of the thirty-foot-long catafalque on which the bier rested was, like the bier itself and the caisson, covered with a wide variety of freshly cut flowers, the perfume of which filled the chamber. Of the many floral offerings near the coffin, one was a pillow of immortelles on which was formed a red, white, and blue Confederate flag. An attached card read "The Flag, the Cause, the President; Like the Flowers All Dead, All 'Immortal.'"[85]

As the casket was being placed on the bier, the Gate City Guard came to present arms. A young bugler of the Atlanta Artillery stepped to the head of the bier and played "Taps" using the same instrument used at Metairie Cemetery in 1889 for the original funeral of Jefferson Davis. In an emotional response, a veteran broke the silence with his audible sobbing.

An estimated forty thousand persons filed by the bier in two lines over the next two hours. The uniformed military units were the first to pass, carrying their weapons at trail arms. These were followed by the veterans, some old and infirm, others minus an arm or a leg, and many limping. A number were overcome with emotion. The first veteran to pass the casket placed his hand on it and let it glide gently along the edge in loving touch while his face was bent downward to hide his grief. As the procession passed, the feeling became more intense. G. W. Howard brought the battle flag of the Nineteenth South Carolina regiment that he had carried during the war. For a time, he stood holding the banner over the heads of the passing veterans. One threw his arms around it and then with one hand held it to his heart and with the other touched the casket. Another old veteran with one arm missing leaned over and pressed his lips against the polished cover of the coffin, then, in an unsuccessful effort to hide his tears, put his hand to his mouth and pretended to cough. Most veterans, however, were content with being allowed to touch the casket.[86]

As soon as the veterans passed through, the general public began to enter, and in scenes reminiscent of the old soldiers, some expressed their feelings toward the deceased Confederate president. A woman in "widow's weeds, simply and poorly clad" reached out and patted the casket lovingly. Wiping her eyes with a black-bordered handkerchief, she told one of the guards, "My husband was with him, you know." Said another, as she stooped to kiss the side of the casket, "My brothers loved him."[87]

As in Montgomery, a small number of African Americans remembered Davis fondly. Among these, an elderly black man and his wife carried a bunch of flowers. He placed them on the catafalque after asking permission, then, as he was leaving, commented, "Young marster died for him, and he died brave."[88]

At one point, the pressure to see Davis's coffin became so great that the guards at the Washington Street entrance were swept aside by the crowd. Order was finally restored when a squad of policemen armed with Winchester rifles arrived on the scene. At 7:00 P.M., Superintendent Dobson of the Richmond & Danville Railroad announced that it was 8:00 and for the coffin to be returned to the train. When the veterans complained that it was only 7:00, he told them that the railroad company was using Washington time, which he incorrectly argued was an hour later than Atlanta time. The veterans gave no further argument and prepared to remove Davis's remains to the funeral train. The casket was placed on the caisson and taken under escort of the Gate City

Guards to Union Depot and placed again in the funeral car. The removal of the casket from the state capitol's rotunda led to a frantic rush for the flowers in the just-vacated chamber. The guards, who were supposed to protect them, allowed the pilfering to continue until none were left.[89]

The Davis daughters, who had not attended their father's lying in state, had spent the day meeting visitors at the Kimball Hotel and touring Atlanta with General Gordon, Ellyson, and others. They were at the hotel when the casket was returned to the train, and they were summoned back. On reaching the train, the sisters stood on the rear platform. Men and women eager to meet them crowded around as the two women leaned over the railing to shake every hand extended to them. A small newsboy edged his way through the crowd and asked them to purchase a paper. Margaret handed him a coin and took the newspaper, only to have Winnie hand it back, insisting that he sell it again. Just before the train moved off, a member of the Atlanta Artillery handed Winnie a bugle and asked her to lay her hands on it. She took it, then handed it to her sister. Handing it back, Winnie told him, "When it calls for your men to charge, I know that they will always respond." When the train began to pull away from the station, someone cried out "goodbye," to which the younger daughter replied, "I cannot say goodbye to the southern people." She and her sister remained on the train's platform and waved as the train departed. Minute guns were fired, and "Taps" was played, using the same bugle that was blown in 1889 at Metairie and that would be sounded again in Richmond for the same purpose.[90]

Confusion in time zones between Georgia and Alabama resulted in thirty members of the funeral train being left behind in Atlanta. Members of the Texas, Louisiana, and Mississippi delegations, as well as a number of the Atlanta escort, thought that the train was to leave at 8:00 P.M. Central time, when it was leaving according to Eastern time. Superintendent J. A. Dobson held the train for forty-five minutes after the scheduled departure time, then, with the concurrence of Mayor Ellyson, ordered the train to leave. Ten minutes later, those who missed the train began to arrive. General Gordon, who was to serve as the grand marshal in Richmond, was the first to reach the depot after the train had gone. Generals S. W. Ferguson and Stephen D. Lee were being entertained by the South Carolina Club along with other members of the escort, and all missed the train. An attempt to secure a special to catch the funeral train failed, and the party had to spend the night in Atlanta and take a regular train to Greensboro, North Carolina, where it would meet the special on its return from the ceremonies in Raleigh.[91]

The funeral train reached Gainesville at 10:40 P.M. As it pulled into the station, a great shout arose from the estimated six hundred people, and church bells began to chime. The small Georgia town was the home of General James

Longstreet, who had lost favor with southerners following his departure from the Democratic for the Republican Party. The former Confederate general and president had reunited during the latter's Southern Tour of 1886. Longstreet had planned to attend Davis's lying in state in Atlanta but was prevented by illness from doing so. The brief stop in Gainesville was to allow him to visit the family and pay his respects. However, only his daughter, a young girl of about seventeen years of age, came aboard the train to meet the Davis daughters, explaining that her father was unable to come because of illness. After five minutes, the train moved on toward South Carolina.[92]

As the train made its way through Georgia and the Carolinas, the wayside tributes continued. Soon after leaving Atlanta, an elderly gray-haired man was observed watching with a young girl of around five years of age who held in her hand a Confederate flag edged in black.[93] Occasionally, bonfires were seen lighted along the tracks, revealing crowds of people watching as the train sped past. Church bells were tolled, while here and there cannon fire rang out. Repeatedly, three-volley rifle salutes were heard, while out of the darkness a command would be given and a report would disclose the presence of still another group waiting to honor the Confederate president. Low, who was skeptical when he arrived in New Orleans several days before the reinterment movement began, had become convinced that the South's love for Jefferson Davis was genuine. The Boston correspondent noted that "on all sides, in the little hamlets and in the large cities, at cross-roads and State capitols, the same manifestations of respect have been shown, the same reverential regard and respect for the dead, and the same sympathy and affection for the living descendants of the old chieftain." "Something more than mere curiosity," he wrote, "induced these people to brave the discomforts and personal inconveniences to which they were subjected so as to be on hand at the appointed time." They were, he felt, animated by the same spirit as during the war, "when their leader spoke, and they followed."[94]

Low noted that other than these salutes and a piercing "rebel yell" as the train passed a small station without stopping in South Carolina, the receptions were generally silent. There was scarcely an African American or white person at work in the fields who did not bare his or her head and stand quietly as the train passed.[95]

At 12:46 A.M., the train made an unscheduled stop at Seneca, South Carolina, and floral offerings were placed on the catafalque and casket, which by this time were barely discernible under the flowers that had been placed on them and around them. The veterans were out in force, included Joe Watson, who had been on guard at the Davis Mansion when Winnie was born there. The military companies fired three salutes, and the train departed.[96]

The train reached Greenville, South Carolina, a short time after 2:00 A.M. and despite the early hour was greeted by a crowd of two thousand persons, including Confederate veterans from surrounding counties. Despite the fact that speeches had been studiously avoided at all earlier stops, Colonel James A. Hoyt, in command of a body of local veterans, presented a formal address expressing the admiration and love of the people of South Carolina for Jefferson Davis. He then presented a floral offering from the women of Greenville, a Confederate battle flag worked in flowers, a sword, and a palmetto wreath. Governor Benjamin Tillman then boarded the train to serve as honorary escort through his state and to continue on to participate in the reinterment in Richmond. The train then departed through a corridor of soldiers standing at "present," while others fired a three-volley salute and minute guns fired.[97]

The train arrived in Charlotte, still at an early hour, to pick up the North Carolina delegation to the funeral in Richmond, the most notable of whom was former Confederate General Robert F. Hoke, the governor choosing to wait until Raleigh to board the train. The railroad station was thronged with people as the town's population turned out en masse.

As it drew into the station, a Naval Reserve Corps battery fired a twenty-one-gun presidential salute, three rifle volleys were fired, and double ranks of infantry stood at present arms. A body of Confederate veterans was drawn up in line with its battle flag furled and draped in crepe.[98]

Another demonstration was made during a brief stop in Salisbury, only a short distance from Charlotte. Minute guns were fired, and schoolchildren were released to meet the train. A Major Withers, who had been adjutant general for John Hunt Morgan, came aboard with the battle flag of his command. A large crowd clustered around the funeral car and begged for flowers that had fallen to the floor. Some were handed out by the guard of honor and eagerly clutched by the few who received them. By this time, the flowers, which had been offered at every station, had grown to the point that they formed a pile four feet out from the head of the coffin and along the sides and had to be rearranged to allow passage. The train then departed, again to the salute of artillery.[99]

The funeral train arrived in Greensboro two hours behind schedule. Finally, at 9:30, it drew into the station, where the passengers dined on a breakfast described by a passenger as an "oasis . . . in a wide sandy desert of meals to be remembered, but not with pleasure."[100] While the train was in the city, banks and stores were closed, and flags flew at half-mast. A notice on the door of one saloon read, "Closed in honor to our patriot, the illustrious dead, Hon. Jefferson Davis."[101] A crowd of people swarmed over the platform in an attempt to pass through the funeral car. But because of experience with relic hunters who had earlier carried away flowers at every opportunity and had even attempted to chip souvenir splinters from the coffin, the car was closed to all strangers, who had to be content with peering through the windows. Winnie accepted flowers from the town's mayor and spent ten minutes before departure shaking hands with all who reached her.[102]

Durham, which had already gained a reputation as a famous tobacco town, presented the funeral train with one of the prettiest demonstrations along the entire route. Six thousand people gathered at the depot. Some 250 veterans and the Durham Light Infantry were drawn up in line. The tracks were strewn with flowers, and onlookers bared their heads. As the train stopped, veterans fired a funeral salute, and five hundred children from the public schools filed through the funeral car, each one dropping a flower on the coffin. As in most places, the first question asked was, "Where is the President's coffin?" and the next was, "Where is Miss Winnie?" The stop lasted only a brief ten minutes.[103]

Raleigh was reached several minutes after 1:00 P.M., approximately two and a half hours late. The Tar Heel capital turned out to be one of the most impressive of the journey despite the smaller population than earlier cities. There had been anxiety about the weather because of the previous day's rain, but the skies cleared, and the weather was warm and sunny. Excursion trains ran all morning, swelling the effective population of viewers to as many as twenty thousand. Businesses closed, church bells rang, flags flew at half-mast, and the city was decorated in funeral colors. The liberal display of large and small Confederate flags appeared to give more emphasis to Davis's ties to the Confederacy than had been done in Montgomery and Atlanta.

Approximately a thousand were on hand when the train arrived at the station, while others lined the funeral route and waited at the state capitol building for the arrival of the funeral procession. People pushed toward the cars to see Winnie and the coffin through the train windows. Mayor Badger and state Adjutant General F. H. Cameron took official charge of the coffin, which was passed through the windows of the train to the shoulders of eight veterans who carried it to the funeral car waiting at the Martin street entrance.[104]

Raleigh authorities had taken great care to create a funeral carriage to surpass any other that had carried the coffin up to this point. The essence of the design placed Davis's remains inside a fourteen-foot-high cloth-covered black domed "temple," trimmed in white, with eight columns through which the casket could be observed by people along the route. The dome itself was topped by a casket-shaped tower. The casket rested on a bearskin-covered platform that rose three feet from the carriage floor and was covered by the bullet-torn battle flag of the Fifth North Carolina Regiment. The Confederate theme was further augmented by four young daughters of southern veterans (including General Robert Hoke of the North Carolina delegation to

Richmond) who, dressed in white dresses with black sashes, sat in each of the
four corners of the carriage holding four different flags of the Confederacy.

The driver, attired in a black suit and Prince Albert coat, was the object
of special attention. James J. Jones was a free black man who served the Davis
family during the war and who continued a close relationship afterward. Born
in 1831 in Raleigh, he hired himself out as a gentleman's servant and waiter.
He served Davis in the Confederate White House during the war and was
with the president when Union troops captured him in Georgia in 1865. After the war, he became a successful businessman in his hometown as well as a
Republican politician serving as a delegate to a state freedman's convention
and as a Raleigh city alderman. He nevertheless remained close to the Davis
family, and when he learned that his former employer would lie in state in the
capitol, he asked for and was granted the right to drive the funeral carriage.
Like Robert Brown, who had also been in Davis's service during the war, he
joined the funeral train and was given a role in the reinterment ceremonies in
Richmond.[105]

The procession began at precisely 1:20 P.M. The police took the lead, followed by three companies of troops bearing the state, national, and Confederate flags. The funeral car came next, pulled by six black horses, each led by a
veteran in Confederate uniform. The remainder of the procession included
veteran escorts from the train, students and teachers from local schools and col-
leges, and a variety of societies and associations. Church bells tolled, and people crowded the streets, windows, and other vantage points to view the parade
as it slowly passed, all on foot except for the train escorts, who were driven in
carriages. Those along the parade route watched in silence, the only sounds being the mournful dirge played by the band, the roll of muffled drums, and the
tolling of church bells.[106]

An estimated ten thousand people, including Governor Carr and his staff,
were on hand at Capitol Square as the head of the procession entered the north
gate, with the remainder separating into segments that entered different gates
and converged in the center. The funeral carriage came to a halt, and Davis's
coffin was removed. Before moving inside, however, a seventy-five-member
choir made up of members of local churches stood on the portico of the capitol and sang Pleyel's hymn, "How Sleep the Brave." Episcopal chaplain M. M.
Marshall offered a prayer; then, to the sound of the choir singing another
hymn, the coffin was gently lifted and carried into the capitol building, where
it was placed in the rotunda.[107]

While this was taking place, the choir moved upstairs and took a position
at the rotunda rail just above the casket and continued to sing. Before the public was admitted, a guard of honor was placed around the coffin, and the four
young girls who had ridden on the funeral caisson took up positions, one on

each corner of the catafalque, where they remained holding their flags toward the coffin during the lying in state. The coffin lay on a high black bier, elaborately decorated with Spanish bayonet, palmetto, roses, lilies, and other flowers. At its head was a large floral Confederate flag formed from clematis, crimson roses, and jasmine, and above it the words "North Carolina" were spelled out in flowers. The hallway, doorway, arches, and pillars of the rotunda were draped in mourning.[108]

With the official ceremonies concluded, the public began to pass by the coffin. During the next hour and a half, a steady stream of as many as five thousand people poured through the building, including a large number of African Americans. Hundreds of persons took flowers from the catafalque and carried them away as souvenirs. The crowd was so dense at times that several women fainted. Old soldiers by the hundreds pressed through. Some persons expressed disappointment that Davis's face was not exposed, disregarding the fact that he had been dead for three and a half years. All were kept moving by a double guard of veterans and the military.[109]

Because of the late arrival of the train in Raleigh, the lying in state was shortened to less than two hours. Around 3:00 P.M., preparations were made to return to the depot, leaving many persons still in line who had not yet had time to see even a glimpse of Davis's coffin. During the move, the choir formed again to sing an ode and a chant. The crowd at the depot was described as immense. Many stood around the funeral car and, seeing the mound of flowers, begged the guards for souvenirs, a few of which were handed out. The earlier decision to refuse admittance to the car was applied inconsistently, and a line of mostly women was allowed to file past the coffin. It was 3:40 P.M. when the train, with the governor's car having been added during the stop, finally pulled out of the station heading north toward its final destination of Richmond while an estimated 2,500 watched.[110]

The original route called for the Davis train to move directly north through Keysville, Virginia, to Richmond. However, the people of Danville, Virginia, where Davis had moved the Confederate government following the fall of Richmond, pleaded urgently to have it stop in their town. Railroad officials contacted Ellyson, who consented to the change after being assured that the train could stop there and still arrive in Richmond in sufficient time for the reinterment ceremonies.[111] The rerouting brought the train back to Durham and Greensboro, where crowds gathered again, bells tolled, and fresh flowers were brought aboard. The brief stop at the latter station was the good fortune of the thirty men who had been accidentally left behind in Atlanta and who were now able to rejoin the train and resume the journey to Richmond. At Reidsville, the last stopping point in North Carolina, between two thousand and three thousand people were assembled. Confederate veterans stood with a faded Stars and Bars flag, while the Third Regiment of State Troops presented arms, fired three volleys, and marched up to inspect the funeral car.[112]

While the train was entering Virginia moving north toward Richmond, Varina Davis was aboard another train coming from New York City to Richmond, where she would reunite with her daughters and son-in-law on the morning of the funeral. Joining her on the train were her niece, Clara Davis, and Robert and John Taylor Wood, grandsons of Zachary Taylor and nephews of her husband's first wife. As the train pulled into Union Station, she was met by a crowd of people, including a committee of prominent citizens and members of the grand camp of Confederate Veterans of Virginia. She appeared to be feeble as she made her way through the crowd, walking with the aid of a cane and supporting herself on the arm of a Major Brander. She was taken to the Exchange Hotel, where she retired immediately to her apartment to rest and await the arrival of her children.[113]

The funeral train reached Danville at 9:00 P.M., two hours beyond the scheduled time of arrival. As it rolled into the station, a choir sang "Nearer, My God, to Thee." An estimated six thousand people were assembled, some coming from as far away as fifty miles in the country. The crowd was so dense and determined to see the funeral car and "the Daughter of the Confederacy" that soldiers were forced to pressure them back with their rifles in order to permit the escort to reach the dining room and for the trainmen to attend to their duties. Two cars were added to the train, one for Virginia Governor McKinney and his staff and the other for the Richmond Light Infantry Blues, a Richmond militia unit that had come from the Virginia capital to serve as an honorary escort.[114]

When the train left Danville, the Davis sisters, Mayor Ellyson, and General Glynn visited the funeral car to look at the floral tributes. By this time, the flowers were heaped on all sides and piled so high that they reached the ceiling and the coffin was completely covered. Fully half the car was covered. Winnie Davis became so overcome with emotion at the scene that she rushed from the car in tears, unable to speak.[115]

The Davis train arrived in Richmond at 3:05 A.M., approximately one and a half hours behind schedule and only two days after the anniversary of the transfer of the Confederate capital from Alabama to Virginia. Regardless of the arrival at a time when most of the city was sleeping, the Confederate veterans' camps planned a grand entrance and procession of the remains to the Virginia state capitol building, where it would lie in state. A large crowd of men, women, and children, many of whom had gone without sleep that night, waited at the station. Also on hand were the First Virginia Infantry Regiment and the Robert E. Lee and George E. Pickett camps of Confederate veterans, a drum corps, and a detachment of artillery. On the first sight of the train, the cannon fired a salute of thirteen guns, the first shot of which served as an alert to those who wished to go to the depot.[116]

The first to leave the train were the flowers that had been placed on board at virtually every stop from New Orleans through Danville. These were placed in several carriages. Then the coffin was removed through the windows of the funeral car for the final time and placed on a hearse drawn by four white horses and flanked by veterans for the journey to the state capitol building to lie in state. The Richmond Light Blues, which had gone to Danville with the governor to accompany the remains back to Richmond, led the procession, followed by the Lee and Pickett camps of the United Confederate Veterans and the veteran escorts from Louisiana, Mississippi, Georgia, and North Carolina.

The movement to the state capitol was as impressive as it was unusual as it moved though the darkness of the predawn between the spectators who lined the street. There was barely a sound except for the wailing notes of the dead march on fife and drum and the steady tramp of the veterans marching in fours behind the bier. On reaching the capitol building, where another crowd waited to witness the arrival of the remains, the military units opened ranks and stood at present arms while the veterans marched through until the doors of the building were reached. There a halt was made, and the casket was carried to the door of the senate chamber in the rotunda and placed on a catafalque under a guard of honor from Lee Camp.[117]

The flowers from the funeral train were removed from the carriages and placed around the catafalque, adding to those already contributed by Virginians, until nearly half the area of the rotunda was filled with flowers and floral tributes. The bier presented a very somber appearance. The whole room was shrouded in black velvet and crepe. The doors were surmounted by a circular shield, wreathed in flowers and bearing the Confederate colors. The doors of the capitol through which the visitors would enter were draped in mourning.[118]

Just as the sun rose, artillery and musket fire awakened the people of Richmond from their sleep, and the city became astir with activity. Starting at five in the morning and lasting until the funeral cortege began its procession to the cemetery, the Richmond Howitzers were under orders to fire their cannon at regular fifteen-minute intervals. The streets became filled with military units from every branch marching and countermarching in every direction, while men, women, and children in large numbers were seen leaving their homes moving toward the capitol to view the casket and pay homage to Davis. People began entering the rotunda to view the coffin as daylight broke. As was the case in Raleigh, a rumor had been started that Davis's face would be exposed to public view. A spokesman for the JDMA, which was overseeing the reburial exercises, disabused the public of that notion in a statement to the press.[119]

The original schedule called for Davis's remains to lie in state in the rotunda until 3:00 P.M., when they would be carried in a procession to Hollywood Cemetery for burial. During those hours, an estimated twenty-five thousand persons filed by the bier. Beginning when the escort that brought the coffin left the building, the crowd surged through the western entrance and out the eastern door as rapidly as possible under the circumstances. Men, women, and children struggled to secure an advantageous position in the line, which was ten or twelve abreast at the door and which narrowed to couples at the exit. Many tried to linger at the catafalque. The crush was greatest between 11:00 A.M. and 1:00 P.M., during which time the throng was so great on the capitol grounds between the Washington Monument and the entrance to the building where Davis lay that it was almost impossible for anyone to move. The guards detailed from the local infantry and cavalry organizations had great difficulty in restraining the people, who were startled every fifteen minutes as the Richmond Howitzers fired one of their cannons located on the south slope of the capitol grounds.[120]

During the hours of 9:00 to 11:00 A.M., six thousand children from the city's public schools passed by the bier. Dressed in white, each carried a bouquet of moss roses, honeysuckle, or some other flower picked freshly from gardens around Richmond. Unlike the adults, they passed orderly in a double line, each child placing his or her flowers on the coffin until it was almost hidden from view.[121]

It was estimated that between seventy-five thousand and one hundred thousand people were present in Richmond for the ceremonies. Crowds began to congregate along the parade route as early as four hours before time for the procession to begin. By 3:00 P.M., people had massed as closely as possible along Grace, Franklin, and Laurel streets, and lines from there to the cemetery were three or four deep. Thousands more waited in the cemetery. The windows and every other vantage point were crowded with people attempting to get a good view. Virtually every house was decorated in black and white. National, Confederate, and state flags, the latter predominating, either floated in the breeze or were worked into the funeral colors.[122]

As elsewhere, plans called for Davis's remains to pass over a bed of flowers. Women and young girls, mostly dressed in white and carrying baskets of flowers, were stationed at regular intervals. As the funeral caisson passed, one of them walked in front of the horses spreading flowers in the path until her basket was empty, then the task was taken up by another.[123]

The route called for Davis in death to pass by sites he had known in life: the Confederate Congress; his office in the old custom house; the site of the First Presbyterian Church, where he made his last speech in Richmond; the Washington Monument, where he took the oath of office as president of the permanent Confederate States; and St. Paul's Church, in which he worshipped and where he received the telegram from Lee announcing the necessity of evacuating the city. An arch had been built the previous day for him to pass under as he left the capitol grounds for the last time.

At 3:30 P.M., the body of Jefferson Davis was carried from the capitol building and placed on an artillery caisson on which a platform covered in black velvet had been constructed. It was pulled by six white horses covered in black netting that reached nearly to the ground. Each horse was guided by an artilleryman dressed in gray, while six active pallbearers dressed in Confederate uniforms flanked the caisson. After the procession was formed, the entire line came to a "front" and uncovered as the funeral caisson and carriages containing the Davis family and the honorary pallbearers passed.

The procession was a long one, numbering some four thousand to five thousand participants, consisting of civilians, Confederate veterans, and uniformed militia units of infantry, mounted cavalry, and artillery. A large number of Confederate camps brought their bands, which played dirges and the funeral marches during the procession. The overall tone of the procession was one of respectful silence. Not even the playing of "Dixie" and "Carry Me Back," the former of which normally brought an outburst from all southern veterans and the latter from Virginians, elicited anything but silence from the marchers and spectators.[124]

The procession was headed by General John Gordon with a staff of fifty mounted Confederate officers, including twelve of general rank, among them Robert Hoke and Joseph Wheeler, and others of lesser ranks who served during the war. At least fourteen other wartime southern generals participated in various aspects of the parade, including Jubal Early, Dabney Maury, Stephen D. Lee, Thomas Rosser, Fitzhugh Lee, Henry Heth, and Edward C. Walthall. Following immediately behind the chief marshal's contingent were the infantry, the artillery with three batteries of thirteen cannons, and four troops of cavalry.

The military organizations were followed by the catafalque, the active pallbearers, and a long line of carriages in which the honorary pallbearers and distinguished guests were seated. As in the original funeral in 1889, the position of honorary pallbearer was assigned to southern governors, in this instance those of Tennessee, North and South Carolina, West Virginia, Maryland, and Alabama. Next came the carriages containing the Davis family; relatives; the funeral train veteran escorts from Louisiana, Mississippi, Georgia, and North and South Carolina; and an assortment of others with close ties to the deceased Confederate president. Noteworthy among the latter were ex-Texas Governor Lubbock; Jefferson Davis's lifelong friend George W. Jones of Iowa, whose two sons had served in the Confederate army; and three of Davis's wartime African American servants, James Jones of Raleigh, Robert Brown of Alabama, and

Frederick McGinnis of Baltimore. The latter had accompanied Varina Davis to Montreal following the war and was with her when she joined her husband in prison at Fort Monroe.[125] A rumor had spread that a band of aged slaves would follow the caisson bearing Davis's remains. This was rebutted by *The Freeman*, an African American newspaper of Indianapolis, Indiana, that commented that "the very thought of such an exhibition is enough to make the shades of Nat Turner, John Brown, and Lincoln revisit the glimpses of the moon and commit hari kari on the whole Negro contingent."[126]

The veterans followed, forming by far the largest contingent of the procession. Their number was estimated at between 2,500 and 3,000 persons. They were divided into three brigades, each led by a mounted officer. All wore gray, and many were in the same uniforms they had worn during the conflict. Their numbers led one correspondent to comment, "Never since the war have so many Confederate soldiers been seen in one body in Richmond. . . . Except for the absence of muskets and swords, it was as if the Confederate armies were on the march once more."[127] Some carried battle flags from the war. Perhaps the most significant of these were veterans from Charleston, South Carolina, who carried the first Confederate flag to fly over Fort Sumter following its capitulation. Others held aloft the battle flag of General Corse's brigade and the headquarters flag of General John Hunt Morgan.[128]

When the funeral cortege reached Hollywood an estimated twenty thousand to twenty-five thousand persons had crowded in to seek the best vantage point for watching the services. Men, women, and children thronged every hill overlooking the route, the edge of the main plateau, and every elevation. As the bands played funeral marches and dirges, the procession snaked its way along the winding avenues toward the Davis section on the edge of the plateau overlooking the rapids of the James River.

The massing of the troops and veterans in their designated sections was accomplished quickly, given the hilly nature of the land. The First Virginia Regiment and the Richmond Light Infantry Blues were stationed along the avenue nearest the river, while the veterans formed in ranks six to eight deep along Davis Avenue. The cavalry and artillery took positions to the west of the circle. The cannons had already been placed and were unlimbered for the final salute.

On arriving at the burial site, the carriages carrying the delegations from Louisiana, Texas, Mississippi, North and South Carolina, and Georgia descended from their carriages and formed on the circle surrounding the grave. Varina Davis, her daughters, and her son-in-law remained in their carriages during the troop movement and religious ceremony. When the veterans passed by the carriage in which Winnie Davis sat, one drum and bugle corps after another began to play the dead march. But when the Maryland men came by playing "Nearer My God to Thee," she burst into tears and hid her face in her handkerchief.[129]

When the military movement was complete, the grave site was surrounded by three solid walls of men. The pallbearers removed the coffin from the caisson and placed it on the ground beside the open grave, the interior of which was constructed of brick and was of an unusual depth. Large Confederate flags hung from the ends, dropping from ground level into the depth of the grave, the third national flag at the head and the battle flag the foot. The sides were lined with stripes of red and white, the Confederate colors.[130] All pretense of giving Davis the funeral of a U.S. soldier was forgotten, and he would be placed in a grave that symbolized him for eternity as he had lived: unreconstructed and in his mind still the leader of the Confederacy.

Beyond the group of men and women surrounding the grave, a dense mass of thousands of onlookers strained to see the services. The family of the deceased, the pallbearers, the escort of honor, the officers, and the officiating clergy took their places, and the religious services began. It had been decided not to repeat the funeral services of 1889, and the ceremony was kept simple. The Stonewall Band of Staunton, Virginia, played funeral music composed especially for the occasion by Professor Jacob Rinehart. Reverend William Munford read a selection of Scripture. Reverend W. W. Landrum read the hymn "How Firm a Foundation," which was also sung by those assembled around the grave. At the close of the hymn, Reverend Moses D. Hoge read a prayer, and Reverend O. S. Barten of Norfolk pronounced the benediction, and the casket was lowered into the ground. At this point, Davis's widow and her two daughters descended from their carriage and took their place beside the grave, accompanied by Virginia Governor McKinney, Richmond Mayor Ellyson, and Margaret's husband Addison. Varina bowed her head in apparent silent prayer, and the three women cried quietly as they looked down at the coffin.[131] After several minutes, they then returned to their carriage. As they left the grave, a bugle signaled the closing moments of the ceremonies. "Taps" was played, followed by three volleys from the First Virginia infantry and a twenty-one-gun presidential salute by the Richmond Howitzers, and the Davis reburial was completed. Finally, after a three-and-a-half-year odyssey during which his body lay aboveground in a state of unrest, Jefferson Davis was at peace.

The crowd began to disperse, some heading for their homes or preparing to leave Richmond. The military had one more duty. This was Memorial Day, set aside annually for the decoration of Confederate graves. The militia, women's groups, and veterans moved on to the Gettysburg Hill section of the cemetery to decorate the graves of the sixteen thousand Confederate soldiers who were buried there. While this was taking place, Davis's grave was decorated with the wagon loads of flowers that had been collected the previous four days as the funeral train passed from New Orleans to Richmond. They would remain for approximately one day and then be collected again by the staff of the Valentine Museum of Richmond, which promised to embalm or press every flower and floral arrangement for posterity.[132]

The only thing left to complete the agreement that brought Davis's remains to Richmond was the reinterment of his deceased descendants in the family plot in Hollywood. Varina and her family delayed their return to New York by one day, until June 3, in order to be present. The removal of the children had taken place prior to the arrival of her husband's remains and had awaited the completion of his reburial for their reinterment. Their son Samuel had been buried in Washington, D.C., where he died in 1854. Joseph, or "Little Joe" as he was popularly known, died in Richmond during the war. He was already buried in Hollywood but had to be transferred to the family plot. Two sons and a grandson by their daughter Margaret had died in Memphis, Tennessee. City authorities would not permit the removal of Jefferson Davis Jr. until October, so only son William and grandson Jefferson Davis Hayes were now in Richmond for reburial.[133]

The Davises, accompanied by Mayor Ellyson, drove to the cemetery on the morning of June 1 and spent several minutes at Little Joe's grave, then moved on to Davis Circle, where they remained in their carriage because of the large crowd gathered there. The reburial took place the following morning at 11:00, in the rain and without ceremonies of any kind, with only the family and Mayor Ellyson present. By afternoon, all five graves were covered with flowers.[134]

Southern response to the reinterment of Jefferson Davis illustrates his continuous rise in the esteem of white southerners who had rejected him following the failure of the Confederacy in 1865. Public opinion, as represented by his treatment in regional newspapers, showed little change either upward or downward since his death three and a half years earlier. Newspapers of the states of the old Confederacy used glowing terms to describe Davis, the progress of the funeral train to Richmond, and the final interment. He was "as knightly as [King] Arthur"; his body "one of our chief treasures"; his remains were "holy dust"; he was "our exemplar—our hero."[135] To some, he was now the equal of the military leaders Robert E. Lee and Stonewall Jackson. To others, he surpassed them as the single most important wartime leader. According to the *Durham (N.C.) Globe*, Davis was the South's "most honored son, the grandest and greatest man, greater even than the great Jackson or the greater Lee," a man " who, like Napoleon, died [defeated but] with triumphs."[136] Similarly, the *Raleigh (N.C.) State Chronicle* saw him as the "central figure" of the Confederacy.[137]

Northern opinion on Davis continued to mellow. Reconciliation had come a long way. Although the Grand Army of the Republic still took a negative view, a significant number of Union veterans willingly joined in the original funeral and later reburial ceremonies for Davis, joint reunions of Confederate and Union veterans were becoming common, and northerners were vacationing and settling in southern states in increasing numbers. Confederate military leaders such as Lee and Jackson had already won widespread acceptance among northerners. Jefferson Davis, however, was an exception. As the president of the Confederacy, he was seen as the leader of the rebellion, and his refusal to take the oath of allegiance to the Union marked him as an unreconstructed rebel who refused to admit that secession was wrong.

Critical reaction in the North ranged from mild forgiveness, primarily from Democratic newspapers, to extreme hostility, largely from Republican newspapers, the latter of which were agitated by the return to the White House of Democrat Grover Cleveland in 1893. Added to the political concern of Republicans were two other issues: the loyalty versus disloyalty of southerners to the Union and southern revisionism of Civil War history as expressed in the enthusiasm for Jefferson Davis and the Confederacy.

The *St. Louis Post Dispatch* saw the events surrounding the transfer of the remains of the Confederate president as a good sign for the country. "This week," it explained, "the United States will show the world this last of the series of exemplary and most honorable spectacles—the remains of the leader of the rebellion, the incarnation of all that rebellion meant, borne in triumph through the nation, the center of a vast outspoken sorrow and respect, which not the bitterest Union partisan would hinder, if he could. And this with the war not thirty years past, with hundreds of thousands of its soldiers still living and millions of those who bore its burdens."[138] "Uncle Dudley," writing editorially for the *Boston Globe*, praised and criticized Davis and the South in the same breath: "Their love of country," he wrote, " no longer can be doubted. . . . The South cannot be sorry for Appomattox. She ought not be ashamed of Sumter. . . . It was wrong for the North to denounce him as the arch traitor. It is wrong for the South to commemorate him as the arch-Patriot. He was neither." "He did not bring on the war," but he bore the brunt of the criticism because he was the president of the Confederacy, and it was, Dudley reasoned, the lot of the executive rather than the military man to bear the brunt of the criticism for the failure of the country. This was particularly true if that leader was caught "fleeing from his surrendered capital."[139]

Attacks on Davis and the South could be expected from northern Republican newspapers, although even there the criticism was sometimes moderate in nature. The *Wichita (Kans.) Eagle* of June 9, 1893, simply noted that there may have been "some feeling of regret that the secession experiment failed mingled with the expression of honor, but not much, and it is safe to say that there is not a particle of desire to try the experiment over again." However, some Republican newspapers saw the southern idolization of Jefferson Davis as a means to attack the Democratic Cleveland administration, which "owed its election to the South." Tying the Democratic Party to the Confederacy or "waving the bloody shirt of treason and rebellion" had been a favorite tactic against Republican opponents since the election of 1866. The *Bangor (Maine) Whig and Courier* regularly tied the Cleveland administration to the South and the Confederacy for political purposes. During the four days in which the funeral train sped toward Richmond, the paper linked together Cleveland, who was a "creature of the South," and "the odious rebel" Jefferson Davis on the emotional issues of pensions for Union veterans and for opting for a fishing trip over decorating the graves of Union soldiers on Memorial Day.[140]

The northern press also felt the need to attack Davis out of fear that the adulation showered on him by southerners would lead to further revisionism in the history of the war, as they saw it. In a speech delivered on Memorial Day at the tomb of Ulysses Grant, former Ohio Governor Joseph Foraker, who was noted for his acid tongue, spoke out on what he feared would be a result of the current demonstrations in favor of Jefferson Davis. He rebuked the sentimentality toward Davis, which he described as an effort to pervert history and give the rising generation and the outside world the wrong impression of the Civil War. The southern revision of the history of the war would dilute the cause of the Union and cause future generations to believe that it did not matter whether the combatants wore the blue or the gray. "It will stand in history," Foraker stated as a matter of fact, "that in that great struggle the side of the Union was the right side, and the other side was the wrong side. Not a little right, nor half-way right; not a little wrong nor half-way wrong, but absolutely and everlastingly right, and absolutely and everlastingly wrong."[141]

The emotional reaction of southerners to the Davis funeral procession caused concern for the reality of the South's loyalty to the Union. Those who held such fears peppered their editorials with quotes from the southern press. Southern support for the Union was "reluctant and forced"; "No man in the South, if he speaks the truth today, admits that the North was in the right"; "The issue that this is a nation from which no State can secede was not settled and established by the war"; and "the sin [of causing the war] lies at the door of Abraham Lincoln and his associates."[142] According to the *Whig and Courier,* "The gentlemen who are so fond of saying that the war is over, that the questions leading to it are settled and that the South accepts the result in good faith should paste these extracts up somewhere so they can consult them freely. If they can discover any difference between the actual sentiment of the South today as expressed here and in 1861 possibly they will point it out."[143] However, even the most rabidly anti–Davis newspaper grudgingly acknowledged that "there is a certain class" of newspaper in the North guilty of "parading a lot of editorial cant about the alleged patriotism of the South."[144]

The *St. Louis Post-Dispatch*, representative of those newspapers that accepted southern loyalty, wrote that "The Confederate flag will fly everywhere [during the Davis funeral procession through the South] only as a symbol of a memory" that could "no more come to life than the great leader dead in the coffin beneath it."[145] With few exceptions, the southern press agreed. The *Birmingham (Ala.) Age-Herald* argued that "there are none [more faithful to the Union] than the men who paid tribute to Davis at the Confederacy's first capital yesterday." The *Nashville (Tenn.) American* wrote similarly that southerners "fought under Jefferson Davis for the Confederacy not more willingly than will they and their descendants fight now for the maintenance of the Union."[146]

At the same time that southern newspapers expressed loyalty jointly for Davis and the Union, they were derisive of northern criticism. The *Raleigh State Chronicle* voiced the sentiments that were expressed over and over again in the regional press when it wrote,[147] "We have not concerned ourselves in the slightest degree what any person at the North might think or say in regard to the manifestations of respect which the Southern people have just made for Jefferson Davis." Now that Davis was resting permanently in the soil of Richmond, Southerners could concentrate on their last tribute to him, the creation of a monument befitting the memory of the only president of the Confederacy.

NOTES

1. *Charleston (S.C.) News and Courier,* December 7, 1889.

2. Ishbel Ross, *First Lady of the South: The Life of Mrs. Jefferson Davis* (New York: Harper & Brothers, 1958), 380.

3. *New York Times,* December 6, 1889.

4. *Cincinnati Enquirer,* December 8, 1889.

5. *Washington Post,* December 9, 1889; *Buffalo (N.Y.) Courier,* December 8, 1889.

6. *Cincinnati Enquirer,* December 8, 1889.

7. *New Orleans Times-Democrat,* December 11, 1889.

8. *Cincinnati Enquirer,* December 7, 1889;

9. J. William Jones, *The Davis Memorial Volume; or Our Dead President, Jefferson Davis, and the World's Tribute to His Memory* (Richmond, Va.: B. F. Johnson & Company, 1890), 481, 484; *Cincinnati Enquirer,* December 7, 1889.

10. Jones, *The Davis Memorial Volume,* 484–85.

11. Jones, *The Davis Memorial Volume,* 2:482, 484–85.

12. Jones, *The Davis Memorial Volume,* 2:505.

13. *New Orleans Times-Democrat,* December 9, 1889.

14. Reprinted in the *New Orleans Times-Democrat,* December 10, 1889.

15. Jones, *The Davis Memorial Volume*, 508.

16. *New York Times*, December 8, 1889.

17. *New Orleans Times-Democrat*, December 9, 1889.

18. *New York Times*, December 7, 1889.

19. *New York Times*, December 8, 1889.

20. Jefferson Davis Monument Association, *Minutes*, January, 1890, Eleanor S. Brockenborough Library, Museum of the Confederacy, Richmond, Virginia (hereafter cited as JDMA, *Minutes*).

21. *Richmond Dispatch*, December 27, 1889.

22. *New York Times*, June 24, 1891.

23. *New York Times*, June 24, 1891.

24. *New York Times*, November 6, 1891.

25. Ross, *First Lady of the South*, 384–85.

26. JDMA, *Minutes*, June 13, 1891.

27. *New York Times*, July 14, 1891; Ross, *First Lady of the South*, 381.

28. *New York Times*, November 6, 1891; JDMA, *Minutes*, November 3, 1891.

29. *New York Times*, November 6, 1891; Varina Davis to William L. White, July 14, 1892, Jefferson Davis Family Collection, Box 25, Eleanor S. Brockenborough Library, Museum of the Confederacy, Richmond, Virginia.

30. *New York Times*, November 16, 1891; JDMA, *Minutes*, November 3, 1891.

31. Varina Davis to J. Taylor Ellyson, May 1 and May 3, 1892, Jefferson Davis Family Collection, Box 25, Eleanor S. Brockenborough Library, Museum of the Confederacy, Richmond, Virginia (hereafter cited as Davis Family Collection).

32. JDMA, *Minutes*, February 2, 1893; *Washington Evening Star*, May 19, 1893, clipping in J. Taylor Ellyson scrapbook, Eleanor S. Brockenborough Library, Museum of the Confederacy, Richmond, Virginia. This contains primarily a large number of newspaper clippings, many without source or date, relating to the reinterment of Jefferson Davis and the Jefferson Davis Monument, as well as a small number of letters and other items (hereafter cited as the Ellyson scrapbook).

33. JDMA, *Minutes*, February 1893.

34. *New York Times*, February 18, 1893.

35. *New York Times*, March 23, 26, 1893; JDMA, *Minutes*, June 16, April 3, 1893; *Raleigh (N.C.) News and Observer*, March 31, 1893.

36. *Raleigh (N.C.) News and Observer*, March 31, 1893.

37. JDMA, *Minutes*, April 3, 1893.

38. JDMA, *Minutes*, April 19, 1893.

39. *Atlanta Constitution*, May 28, 1893.

40. JDMA, *Minutes*, April 19, 1893; *Raleigh (N.C.) News and Observer*, April 21, 1893.

41. JDMA, *Minutes*, May 5, 1893.

42. *Raleigh (N.C.) News and Observer*, May 21, 1893.

43. Unidentified newspaper clipping, Ellyson scrapbook.

44. Varina Davis to Ann E. Grant, May 26, 1893, Davis Family Collection.

45. *Boston Globe*, May 26, 1893.

46. *Boston Globe*, May 26, 28, 1893.

47. Robert Brown to JDMA Invitation Committee, reprinted in unidentified newspaper clipping in Ellyson scrapbook.

48. Unidentified newspaper clipping in Ellyson scrapbook.

49. Michael Ballard, "Davis' Last Ride to Richmond," *Civil War Times Illustrated* 32 (1993): 34.

50. *Boston Globe*, May 28, 1893; *New Orleans Times-Democrat*, May 28, 1893.

51. *New Orleans Picayune*, May 28, 1893.

52. *New Orleans Picayune*, May 28, 1893.

53. Unidentified newspaper clipping in Ellyson scrapbook.

54. Unidentified newspaper clipping in Ellyson scrapbook.

55. Unidentified newspaper clipping in Ellyson scrapbook; *Boston Globe*, May 28, 1893.

56. *New Orleans Times-Democrat*, May 28, 1893.

57. *Boston Globe*, May 29, 1893.

58. *Richmond Dispatch*, May 27, 1893.

59. *Boston Globe*, May 29, 1893.

60. *Atlanta Constitution*, May 27, 1893; *Raleigh (N.C.) News and Observer*, May 28, 1893.

61. Edison H. Thomas, "The Great Chieftain's Last Ride," in *Story of the Jefferson Davis Funeral Train*, reprinted from the February 1955 issue of the *L & N Magazine*.

62. Unidentified newspaper clipping in Ellyson scrapbook.

63. *Raleigh (N.C.) News and Observer*, May 30, 1893; *Newark Evening News*, May 29, 1893.

64. *Boston Globe*, May 29, 1893.

65. *Richmond Dispatch*, May 27, 1893.

66. *Richmond Dispatch*, May 30, 1893; *New York Times*, May 30, 1893; *Raleigh (N.C.) News and Observer*, May 30, 1893.

67. *New York Times*, May 30, 1893; *Richmond Dispatch*, May 30, 1893; *Raleigh (N.C.) News and Observer*, May 30, 1893; *Boston Globe*, May 30, 1893.

68. *Boston Globe*, May 30, 1893.

69. *Richmond Dispatch*, May 30, 1893.

70. Ballard, "Davis' Last Ride," 36; *Boston Globe*, May 30, 1893; *Raleigh (N.C.) State Chronicle*, May 30, 1893.

71. *Boston Globe*, May 30, 1893.

72. *Boston Globe*, May 30, 1893.

73. *Boston Globe*, May 30, 1893; *New York Times*, May 30, 1893.

74. *Boston Globe*, May 30, 1893.

75. *New York Times*, May 30, 1893.

76. *Atlanta Constitution*, May 30, 1893.

77. *Atlanta Constitution*, May 30, 1893; *Boston Globe*, May 30, 1893; *Atlanta Constitution*, May 30, 1893.

78. *Atlanta Constitution*, May 30, 1893.

79. *Wilmington (N.C.) Messenger*, May 30, 1893; *New York Times*, May 30, 1893.

80. *Boston Globe*, May 30, 1893.

81. *Atlanta Constitution*, May 30, 1893.

82. *Atlanta Constitution*, May 30, 1893.

83. *Atlanta Constitution*, as reported by the *Boston Globe*, May 27, 1893.

84. *Atlanta Constitution*, May 30, 1893.

85. *Atlanta Constitution*, May 30, 1893.

86. *Atlanta Constitution*, May 30, 1893.

87. *Atlanta Constitution*, May 30, 1893.

88. *Atlanta Constitution*, May 30, 1893.

89. *Atlanta Constitution*, May 30, 1893.

90. *Atlanta Constitution*, May 30, 1893; *Richmond Dispatch*, May 30, 1893.

91. *Atlanta Constitution*, May 30, 1893.

92. *Atlanta Constitution*, May 30, 1893; *Raleigh (N.C.) News and Observer*, May 31, 1893; Ballard, "Davis' Last Ride," 38.

93. *Boston Globe*, May 31, 1893.

94. *Boston Globe*, May 31, 1893.

95. *Boston Globe*, May 31, 1893.

96. *Atlanta Constitution*, May 31, 1893.

97. *Raleigh (N.C.) News and Observer*, May 31, 1893.

98. *Atlanta Constitution*, May 31, 1893.

99. *Wilmington (N.C.) Messenger*, May 31, 1893.

100. *Boston Globe*, May 31, 1893; *Raleigh (N.C.) News and Observer*, May 31, 1893.

101. *Boston Globe*, May 31, 1893.

102. *Boston Globe*, May 31, 1893.

103. *Boston Globe*, May 31, 1893; *Wilmington (N.C.) Messenger*, May 31, 1893; *Raleigh (N.C.) News and Observer*, May 31, 1893.

104. *Raleigh (N.C.) State Chronicle*, May 31, 1893.

105. *Atlanta Constitution*, May 29, 1893; *Raleigh (N.C.) Evening Visitor*, May 30, 1893.

106. *Richmond Dispatch*, May 31, 1893; *Wilmington (N.C.) Messenger*, May 31, 1893; *Raleigh North Carolinian*, June 2, 1893.

107. *Raleigh (N.C.) News and Observer*, May 31, 1893; *Raleigh (N.C.) State Chronicle*, May 30, 1893.

108. *Raleigh (N.C.) News and Observer*, May 31, 1893.

109. *Raleigh (N.C.) News and Observer*, May 31, 1893.

110. *Atlanta Constitution*, May 31, 1893; *Raleigh (N.C.) State Chronicle*, May 31, 1893; *Wilmington (N.C.) Messenger*, May 31, 1893.

111. *Richmond Dispatch*, May 26, 1893.

112. *Wilmington (N.C.) Messenger*, May 31, 1893.

113. *Newark Evening News*, May 31, 1893; *New York Times*, May 31, 1893; *Richmond Dispatch*, May 31, 1893.

114. *Richmond Dispatch*, May 31, 1893.

115. *Richmond Dispatch*, May 31, 1893.

116. *Richmond Dispatch*, May 31, 1893, May 31, 1893; *Wilmington (N.C.) Messenger*, June 1, 1893.

117. *Wilmington (N.C.) Messenger*, June 1, 1893; Ballard, "Davis' Last Ride," 39.

118. *Richmond Dispatch*, May 30, June 1, 1893.

119. *Richmond Dispatch*, May 27, 30, June 1, 1893

120. *Richmond Dispatch*, June 1, 1893.

121. *Richmond Dispatch*, June 1, 1893; *Washington Post*, June 1, 1893.

122. *Richmond Dispatch*, June 1, 1893; *Washington Post*, June 1, 1893.

123. *Richmond Dispatch*, June 1, 1893; *Washington Post*, June 1, 1893.

124. *Richmond Dispatch*, June 1, 1893.

125. *Richmond Dispatch*, May 31, 1893.

126. *Indianapolis Freeman*, June 3, 1893.

127. *Wilmington (N.C.) Messenger*, June 1, 1893.

128. *Washington Post*, June 1, 1893.

129. *Wilmington (N.C.) Messenger*, June 1, 1893.

130. *Wilmington (N.C.) Messenger*, June 1, 1893; *New York Times*, June 1, 1893.

131. *Richmond Dispatch*, June 1, 1893; *Atlanta Constitution*, June 1, 1893; *Washington Post*, June 1, 1893.

132. *Raleigh (N.C.) News and Observer*, June 3, 1893.

133. JDMA, *Minutes*, May 5, 1893; *Raleigh (N.C.) News and Observer*, June 3, 1893.

134. *Richmond Dispatch*, June 2–3, 1893.

135. Sampling of southern editorial opinion republished in the *Washington Post*, June 2, 1893.

136. Reprinted in the *Bangor (Maine) Whig and Courier*, June 6, 1893.

137. *Raleigh (N.C.) State Chronicle*, May 30, 1893.

138. *St. Louis Post-Dispatch*, May 28, 1893.

139. *Boston Globe*, May 28, 1893.

140. *Bangor (Maine) Whig and Courier*, May 31 and June 1 and 3, 1893.

141. *Newark Evening News*, May 31, 1893.

142. Excerpts from selected southern newspapers reprinted in the *Bangor (Maine) Whig and Courier*, May 31, 1893, and June 12, 1893.

143. *Bangor (Maine) Whig and Courier*, June 12, 1893.

144. *Bangor (Maine) Whig and Courier*, June 12, 1893.

145. *St. Louis Post-Dispatch*, May 28, 1893.

146. Selected abstracts of editorials reprinted in the *Washington Post*, June 2, 1893.

147. *Raleigh (N.C.) State Chronicle*, June 2, 1893.

· 5 ·

Recognition in Stone:
The Jefferson Davis Monument

$\mathcal{T}$he Southern Tour of 1886–1887 and the two funerals of 1889 and 1893 guaranteed Jefferson Davis, at least among white southerners, a place alongside of Robert E. Lee and Stonewall Jackson as one of the three great men of the Confederacy, if not the greatest. But unlike the two military leaders, no artist as yet had sculpted his likeness in stone for posterity. Jackson already stood tall on a pedestal fifty feet above the tomb of the Army of Northern Virginia in New Orleans, while Lee's likeness rested on the stone embodiment of his horse Traveler on what is now Monument Avenue in Richmond. The unveiling of the latter statue had attracted the largest crowd to gather in the Virginia capital up to that time. The issue of a monument to Davis had been broached within twenty-four hours of his death by authorities in several southern cities, at least some of whom used it as a lure to persuade his widow to place his remains in their city. This was also the task of the Jefferson Davis Monument Association (JDMA), which saw as its primary goal not a monument as indicated in its name but to obtain his body for burial in Richmond. The monument could and would come later.

At the time of his death, several cities offered to construct monuments to Davis, although this was generally predicated on receiving his remains for burial. Plans to build monuments in honor of Jefferson Davis as well as efforts to obtain the necessary funds to construct them were initiated by a number of cities and organizations within days of his death, some while his body still lay in state in New Orleans. In his home state of Mississippi, a state-level JDMA issued an address to Mississippians urging the formation of cooperatives in every city, town, and county in order to collect funds and to meet to urge the state legislature to provide $100,000 for the erection of a monument.[1] Other cities, such as Atlanta, sought to construct monuments of a more local character.

131

The significance of Richmond's proposal differed from those proposed by the other cities seeking Davis's remains for burial. Virginia, as the former capital of the Confederacy, sought not a local monument but rather one that stood out as a truly Confederate "national" monument in which all the states of the former southern nation could participate. Richmond, however, was not the first with the purpose of a Confederate "national" monument in mind.

In response to a call by the *Nashville (Tenn.) American* for a broad-based monument to Davis, representatives of twenty different newspapers in nine southern states came together in New Orleans the day following Davis's funeral and organized the Southern Press Davis Monument Association, which was abbreviated in usage as the Southern Press Association. Membership was left open to any other newspaper that wished to join. It would act in cooperation with the committee of the United Confederate Veterans (UCV), which had been formed by General Gordon for the same purpose. Funds were to be collected by each newspaper individually and funneled to the treasurer of the veterans' organization.[2] Over time, both of these organizations would hand over the leadership role to, and work jointly with, the JDMA of Richmond.

While the Southern Press Association was in the process of organization, authorities in Richmond moved quickly to consolidate support within the city, county, and state governments and in the social, military, and business communities to overwhelm its competition. The first concern, after offering condolences to the widow, was to secure his body for reburial in Richmond. Within days, resolutions to that effect were passed and sent to the widow by the mayor, city council, governor, state legislature, the Lee Camp of the UCV, and the Richmond Chamber of Commerce. A mass meeting was held at the Mozart Academy of Music on the evening of December 21 to emphasize these requests. The building was filled with citizens, veterans, and active military organizations as Richmond Mayor J. Taylor Ellyson called the meeting to order. A committee was formed to work toward securing Davis's body. Headed by Governor Fitzhugh Lee, it included a cross section of the political, economic, social, and military leadership of the area. Before the meeting adjourned, it also created the as-yet-unnamed Jefferson Davis Monument Association, whose membership would remain constant during much of the coming efforts to secure the right to become the permanent burial site and to build a monument to the deceased Confederate leader.[3]

The committee was made up entirely of Confederate veterans. It's president, J. Taylor Ellyson, was in his third term as mayor and had earlier served in both houses of the Virginia legislature. A son of the founder of the *Richmond Dispatch* newspaper, he had served in the First Richmond Howitzers during the war. He was well placed to accomplish the committee's objectives, having known the Davis family for several years. Once the decision was made in favor of Richmond, he developed a close personal relationship with Varina and would serve as her personal adviser in matters connected with the transfer of the remains for burial in Hollywood Cemetery.[4]

On January 4, 1890, the officers chosen at the Mozart Academy held an organizational meeting in Ellyson's office. They took as their name the Jefferson Davis Monument Association. A charter was drawn up and submitted to the General Assembly of Virginia, which gave its official approval the following month. In the meantime, Ellyson, accompanied by two committee members, personally delivered the city's request to Varina for her husband's remains. However, she informed the committee, it would be another twelve months before she could make a decision since she still had under consideration the requests from Jackson, Montgomery, Atlanta, and New Orleans.[5]

On June 13, 1891, the memorial association met with the Richmond Chamber of Commerce, which asked the committee to move on two fronts: funding for the monument and the remains of the Confederate president. In regard to the former, it passed a resolution urging Ellyson to "at once formulate and . . . execute a plan for collecting funds for the purpose of building a monument." These were to be kept by the JDMA if Richmond was chosen as the site and to turn it over to the "appropriate parties" if it was determined to build it elsewhere. The chamber then appointed a committee headed by former Confederate General Joseph R. Anderson to meet again with Davis's widow on the subject of her husband's remains.[6]

The committee traveled to New York City, where, on June 23, it met with Varina and her two daughters, the older daughter Margaret there on a visit from Colorado to her mother. By this date, the choice of burial sites had been narrowed down to Richmond and Jackson. There was speculation that the widow and her younger daughter favored the Virginia city, while others in the family were inclined toward the Mississippi capital. Regardless of which city they preferred, Varina informed the committee that she could not make a decision before conferring with a delegation from Jackson that was to meet with her the next day. She assured them, however, that after hearing the Mississippians, she would make her decision at the earliest possible time.[7] Three weeks later, as promised, she sent a letter addressed to General Anderson as head of the committee informing them that she had decided in favor of Richmond as the site of her husband's permanent grave. With that announcement, the question of a monument became a point of increased emphasis within the committee, although the coming months were taken up largely with the transfer of Davis's remains to Richmond and their reburial in Hollywood Cemetery.[8]

Richmond's Monument Avenue had already begun to take shape with the dedication of the Lee monument three years earlier. The process for creating memorials to its Confederate heroes remained constant: all began with the idea of a monument, the formation of a committee, the attempt to raise funds, the seeking and securing of a site, the commissioning of a design and a sculptor, the production of the monument, and finally the dedication.[9] The first and second steps had been accomplished. Once the committee had been formed, every step after that, with the exception of selecting a site, depended on securing funds. This would prove far more troublesome than expected and eventually proved beyond the ability of the original members of the committee to accomplish.

On October 31, 1891, Varina and Winnie Davis arrived in Richmond to look over possible sites for the grave and monument. After several meetings with the committee and others, she decided on Hollywood for the former. The following week, when the subject of a site for the monument came up during a meeting at General Anderson's home, she indicated that her preference was the grounds of the Soldiers' Home in Richmond but that she would leave the final decision up to the monument association.[10] This too became a point of controversy that would not be resolved until the current committee was replaced.

During the months of September through December 1891, the several organizations interested in erecting a "national" monument in honor of the president of the Confederacy moved to form a united front with a common purpose. In September, JDMA President Ellyson wrote to Major S. A. Cunningham of the Southern Press Association and General Gordon of the UCV in regard to collections made at various meetings held throughout the South on June 18 to obtain funds for a Davis monument. The correspondence eventually resulted in a meeting held in Washington, D.C., on December 21 between representatives of the Richmond monument and Southern Press associations in which they agreed to work together in their efforts to obtain funds to build the monument to Davis. According to the agreement, funds collected by the press association would be turned over to the treasurer of the Richmond group.[11] Cunningham was hired by the monument association as its agent to hire men to travel in various regions of the South to secure contributions. He proved ineffective at his job and was later removed from the position.

Following the union of the JDMA and the Southern Press Association, the Richmond group approached the UCV with the intention of further consolidation. When the Virginia organization learned that the veterans planned to discuss a monument to Jefferson Davis during their grand camp in New Orleans on April 8 and 9, 1892, it voted to send Ellyson to its meeting.[12] On his arrival, the Richmond mayor addressed the group in favor of a resolution calling for a veterans' committee to solicit funds for a monument to the Confederate president. In a lengthy speech, he argued in favor of the creation of the committee and said that the monument, when constructed, should be in Richmond. He pleaded that to all southerners, Davis was a great soldier, a profound statesman, and a grand leader of men but that to Virginians, he was more. "He was our honored fellow-citizen and cherished friend, and we felt and feel today that there was no American more steadfast or loyal to the principles of free government than Jefferson Davis."[13] Then, in an effort to downplay Richmond's aggressive role in attempting to secure the remains and the monument for itself and to encourage South-wide support for the JDMA's Davis memorial, he continued,

> The disposition of President Davis's remains was left with Mrs. Davis. We deferred to her wishes, and it was not until a final resting place for the remains that we inaugurated an active movement for the erection of a monument to his memory. It should be something more than a local monument, more than a mere tribute from the people of Richmond, and we hope that it will be erected by all the lovers of the Confederacy throughout the South, so it may be in every sense the Confederate monument.
>
> We have organized with that end in view, and we want the endorsement and hearty co-operation of the United Confederate Veterans, and we should like to present some reasons whey we should have the endorsement of this grand reunion of Confederate camps.[14]

Then, in a warning that was more accurate than even he realized, he reasoned that "as time passes there will be found more and more difficulties in the way of completing this purpose." Any measures toward that end needed to be carried into action immediately. "This movement should have been started immediately after his death, and the time passing only increases the difficulties in our way, and every year it will become more and more difficult to secure the money for such a monument as Mr. Davis deserves."[15]

The proposal passed unanimously, resulting in the formation of the Davis Monument Committee of the UCV. In May, General Gordon appointed fifteen men, one from each southern state, the border states of Kentucky and Missouri, the Indian Territory (present-day Oklahoma), and the cities of Chicago, Illinois, and Washington, D.C. Ellyson was appointed to serve on the committee as Virginia's representative. Former Confederate Lieutenant General William L. Cabell was made chairman.

The committee, with Cabell presiding, met in conference with members of the JDMA at the Exchange Hotel in Richmond on September 17, 1892. W. L. Calhoun of Atlanta, Georgia, was appointed treasurer; then, speaking on the location of the monument, he pointed out that since Davis's widow wanted it in Richmond, that issue was settled and need not be discussed. Ellyson spoke in favor of placing the Richmond association in a subordinate position to the

general UCV committee, as that would make it easier to secure the cooperation of the southern people at large in raising money. His suggestion was not
accepted, the joint meeting resolving that the veterans' committee and the
Richmond association should act together on the project.[16]

Despite Ellyson's earlier warning in New Orleans on the expectation of
increasing difficulty in raising funds, the general mood in the joint meeting was
one of optimism. Chairman Cabell thought that a million dollars should be
raised to build a monument that "should be a grand thing, indeed," with a
"shaft so high that the birds could not fly over it."[17] Norman V. Randolph of
the Richmond association, whose wife would later lead a more successful drive
for the memorial, proposed that the cost of the monument should be set at
$250,000, a little less than the equestrian statue of George Washington in
Richmond's Capitol Square. This still overly optimistic amount was approved.
Cabell, still dissatisfied, argued unsuccessfully that at least a half million should
be raised. It was estimated that all together, the treasurers of the various committees had only $10,000 on hand from the fund drives up to that time. It was
further resolved that the UCV committee and the Richmond association
would act in unison on the monument project.[18]

Before the joint committee meeting came to an end late that night, it
agreed to appoint committees of five men, one in each southern state and the
Indian Territory, to supervise work toward the monument in their territory, including the collection of funds that they were to transfer quarterly to the treasurer of the JDMA in Richmond.[19]

When the committee, which had worked until nearly midnight on the
seventeenth, met again on the following Tuesday (September 20), it issued a
proclamation addressed "To the People of the South" soliciting their support
for the "patriotic and pious work" of building an "everlasting memorial" to
Jefferson Davis, "the patriotic . . . statesman who commanded and typified the
most heroic soldier which the world ever saw." Playing on their patriotism for
the Lost Cause, the committee's petition challenged "the men and women
who fought for the Confederacy and their descendants . . . [to] quarry this
monument out of their heart's blood, if need be."[20] The document, which was
circulated throughout the South, went on to explain the committee system for
collecting funds and how and to whom to contribute. This address to the people of the South noted for the first time in print that the competition between
the three groups that were working toward a similar objective was at an end.
From this time forward, the UCV, the Southern Press Association, and the
JDMA acknowledged that they were working in unison for the same common
objective.

The September 20 meeting concluded with a discussion of possible locations for the Davis monument. A number of sites were suggested, and the ad-

vantages and disadvantages of each were presented until, at length, the committee agreed on Monroe Park, located in one of the most fashionable sections
of Richmond.[21]

The plans made by the joint committee of the UCV and the JDMA in
September 1892 fell by the wayside, largely forgotten or ignored during the
next three years. While the depression of 1893–1897 affected efforts to raise
money for the monument, progress (or the lack thereof) appears also to have
been the result of the lack of initiative and ability of the UCV and the JDMA
to bring the project to fruition. Records of the Richmond organization
show only infrequent meetings and concern with other issues. Between its
creation in January 1890 and September 1895, the memorial association met
only sixteen times, averaging approximately three meetings per year, which
included broad gaps followed by infrequent spurts of activity. During one of
its rare periods of intense activity, from February 2 to June 4, 1893, the association concerned itself solely with planning and carrying out the primary
reason for its existence—the transfer of the remains of Jefferson Davis from
New Orleans and their reburial in Richmond. There was little discussion of
the monument.[22]

Questions that appeared to have been settled during the September 1892
meetings between the UCV and the JDMA lingered without action. On June
22, 1893, Ellyson, acting on behalf of the association, wrote a letter to General
Gordon asking for the cooperation of the veterans' organization in raising
funds. On September 13, 1895, the Richmond group voted to petition the city
council for permission to erect the monument in Monroe Park. The fact that
these two issues had apparently been settled in 1892 indicates that little or
nothing had been done in active cooperation between the two groups. In
1894, members of the Richmond association attended the UCV's grand camp
in Birmingham, Alabama, in order to repeat the point made by Ellyson in 1892
that prompt action was needed to raise money for the monument. As of that
date, only $12,000 had been collected of the quarter-million goal set in 1892.[23]

Seeking help wherever it could find it, the JDMA, through Ellyson, appealed to the newly formed United Daughters of the Confederacy (UDC) requesting that they devote the coming year to raising funds for the Davis monument. The women's group took up the call with enthusiasm, writing that they
pledged themselves to do the work "not only for the next twelve months, but for
the rest of their lives."[24] The Richmond association did not realize it at the time,
but it had taken the first step in turning over the entire project to the women's
group.

On September 17, 1895, the monument association's officers met in the
mayor's office to discuss reactivation of the moribund plan passed during the
meeting of the joint committee of Confederate veterans and the Richmond

group in 1892. According to that agreement, the two organizations accepted cooperation in the monument's erection: a $250,000 limit on costs, Monroe Park as the location, and the final selection of the plan for the memorial. As the veterans' organization was required to have a say only in final decisions relating to the monument, the Richmond group decided that it could and would proceed to carry out the preliminary work on location, design, and cost on its own. Accordingly, a seven-man committee set to work on securing a design and selecting a specific location within Monroe Park.[25] The date set for laying the cornerstone was July 3, 1896.

The lack of adequate response by the Davis Monument Committee of the UCV to its efforts to move forward with the memorial was disappointing. Of letters sent to the members of that committee asking approval of the steps thus taken to secure a design, only five replies were received. Since the letters informed their readers that a nonresponse would be regarded as an affirmative answer, the plan stood approved. If no replies were received by November 10, that would also signify approval by the veterans' committee of the plan adopted by the Richmond association for the selection of the design for the Davis monument.[26]

The September 17 meeting between the UCV and the JDMA had decreed that the Richmond association should commence erecting the monument "as soon as sufficient money is in hand to justify it."[27] Although the $12,000 in hand was insufficient to build the memorial, the Virginians, in March 1896, announced a nationwide competition for designs, perhaps in hopes that the contest would act as a spur for donations. The subcommittee on designs announced that the completed monument should cost between $100,000 and $200,000 on completion. Submitters were required to provide models of their designs as well as estimates of the total costs, including construction of their monuments. In order to encourage artists to compete, prizes of $100, $300, and $1,000 were announced for the top three architectural designs.[28]

Twenty-seven designs were submitted, with the winners announced on June 29, 1896, only four days before the scheduled erection of the cornerstone. Pictures of the top three were published in the *Richmond Dispatch* of June 30, with detailed information about the designs and costs of each. First place went to Percy Griffin of New York City, with second- and third-place prizes awarded to local Richmond architects Edgerton Rogers and William C. Noland.

Griffin's winning design placed a large sculpture of Davis within a magnificent temple of Greek design. This concept of a temple or shrine as the most suitable monument for the president of the Confederacy was broached three years earlier in several southern newspapers during ceremonies surrounding the transfer of his remains from New Orleans to Richmond. As reported in the *Raleigh State Chronicle,*

Sentiment is crystallizing in favor of a shrine rather than some towering monumental structure. The suggestion has been made that the shrine be of a simple Greek temple, with a certain number of columns in front, and following the rule, double and one over the sides. In this temple it is urged that there should be a recumbent figure of Mr. Davis lighted from the top, and in bas-relief in the architrave, frieze, cornice, and pediment of the temple should be sculptured the principal events in the history of the Confederacy.[29]

Griffin's massive temple was on a grander scale than these earlier concepts, with a statue of Davis standing beneath the dome, the entire structure being identical on all four sides. The projected cost was approximately $210,000.[30]

The cornerstone was laid in Monroe Park four days later, on July 3, 1896, the final day of the annual encampment of the UCV, the date chosen with an eye toward attracting the greatest possible audience. Varina Davis and her daughters were among those attending, as were many of the living southern generals and other military leaders of the Civil War. The day was devoted to a massive display of devotion to the Confederacy. One hundred and fifty thousand people lined the streets with others waiting in the park. There was no pretense of reconciliation or loyalty to the Union in any aspect. Every house along the route was colorfully decorated, and everywhere the Confederate colors floated in the breeze. The procession to Monroe Park was the biggest seen in Richmond since the end of the war.

The speaker of the day was General Stephen D. Lee, who was a second choice to General Gordon, who declined for health reasons despite unseemly pressure on him to accept the role by JDMA President Ellyson. Gordon assumed the less demanding position of grand marshal. It took three hours for the end of the parade to reach the park. Eighty thousand men, including 15,000 veterans, some wearing their old wartime uniforms and carrying the old battle flags of their regiments, marched in the procession, the latter grouped according to state. Every state of the Confederacy was represented, as was the Indian Territory, West Virginia, Maryland, Kentucky, and Missouri. Unlike the funeral procession, the veterans were lively and enthusiastic, calling out the old "rebel yell" all along the route. The frequent playing of "Dixie" and other wartime songs elicited loud cheers.[31]

The park was filled before the procession reached it. The crowds cheered as Varina Davis and her daughters and son-in-law took their seats on the stand, followed by other dignitaries, including Gordon, Lee, Simon Bolivar Buckner, Joseph "Joe" Wheeler, Dabney H. Maury, William Cabell, T. L. Rosser, Harry Heth, and other general officers of the Confederacy. It took an hour for the military to get stationed in the park, and the veterans never stopped arriving during the whole afternoon.

The ceremony at the park began even before the long line of veterans reached the site. Once the invited guests were seated on the grandstand, a bugle call signaled the start of the exercises, which commenced with the laying of the cornerstone into which was inserted a copper box filled with numerous objects representative of the Confederacy and period, including books, newspapers, autographs, pictures, and other items. With the stone laid, General Lee spoke to the crowd, hymns were sung, and at a given signal the Richmond Howitzers fired a thirteen-gun salute, and the ceremonies were over.[32]

Despite the overwhelming outpouring of affection for Davis, his monument was in trouble. The temple project was a failure from the beginning. Having commissioned a memorial that cost $200,000 more than it had in the bank, the Richmond association had to admit at least temporary defeat. Accordingly, in January 1897, it notified Griffin that it could not justify beginning work on the monument at that time because of insufficient funds in the treasury and that it was better to postpone the beginning of work until it could raise more.[33] That, in essence, signaled the death of the temple as a design and was the beginning of the death throes of the JDMA as presently constituted. Since its origin in 1890 and even with the consolidation with the Southern Davis Monument Press Association and the UCV, the Richmond organization had succeeded only in the transfer of the Confederate president to Richmond for reburial.

In 1899, the UCV admitted its inability to build the monument to Davis. When the UDC met in Richmond in November of that year, the veterans asked the women's organization to accept the responsibility for the task that they had been unable to complete. After deliberating on the subject, the UDC accepted the charge, and the veterans deposited $20,590 dollars in the State Bank of Richmond, all the money collected to date.[34]

The UDC took over the project as a memorial not only to Davis but to the entire Confederacy. The broadening of the stated object of the association, that is, to build a monument to the Confederate president, was certain to broaden its appeal to southerners. "A monument to Mr. Davis," they reasoned in their literature pleading for contributions, "is a monument to the Southern Confederacy, and to every soldier who fought under its banner. It is a vindication of the truths and principles represented by Mr. Davis as our chosen Executive; and it is a duty for us to tell this to the world." Contributions were "a loving tribute to the noble cause" that was "so dear to Southern hearts."[35]

No restrictions were placed on the women's group other than that the monument had to be located in Richmond. The association under the UDC consisted of subcommittees in every southern state as well as the District of Columbia, Kentucky, Missouri, Maryland, and West Virginia. A representative from each, totaling twenty-four members, constituted the executive board, which could and would come together to decide on major issues. The board of directors, or central committee, continued to govern the association from Richmond.[36]

The former male board of directors of the association resigned when the UDC took over but remained on as an advisory committee, serving to ease the transition from a male to a female organization and to provide assistance in the future. The fact that several members of the board were the wives of former directors was a significant factor in adding to the sense of continuity. This was particularly true in the new chairman, Jan Randolph, whose husband had been a director and now served on the advisory board.

The JDMA immediately sought support through union with the Southern Memorial Association, a confederated organization of southern women who for years had dedicated themselves to building local Confederate monuments and to decorating the graves of Confederate soldiers. In joining the drive to erect the memorial to Jefferson Davis, they agreed to temporarily lay aside all work on local monuments in order to devote all their energy to the Richmond monument. They were thenceforth, for the duration of the project, added to the membership of the JDMA.[37]

The UDC gave priority to erecting the monument. In taking on the project, they noted that there were other activities that called for their attention: the disabled veterans who had no country to pension them, veterans' widows and orphans, and unmarked graves. But they wished to act quickly to construct the memorial while the veterans, whose "ranks are fast thinning out," were still alive to see it.[38] The UDC pledged that "they expect to complete the task begun long years ago. Mr. Davis was not only the chief executive and chosen leader of the Confederacy, he was our martyr, he suffered in his own person the ignominy and shame our enemies would have made us suffer. This was thirty-five years ago, and his monument is yet to be built. The women of the South have solemnly sworn to wipe out this disgrace at once." Then they pleaded, "Will you help us? Lord God of Hosts, be with us yet. Lest we forget. Lest we forget."[39]

The UDC brought renewed enthusiasm and an increased sense of urgency to the drive for a monument. Appeals went out to the young and old to join in the quest for funds. Aware that their own national organization and its chapters had already contributed, they nonetheless pleaded for "sending a free-will offering, no matter how small" and suggested that "an open subscription be taken up in every city and town. Let the children, as well as the grown people, be asked to give."[40] They proposed that every chapter should use June 3, Jefferson Davis's birthday, as the occasion for a fund-raising "entertainment." They asked that each UCV camp pledge to raise ten dollars or as much as possible. Although it was against the constitution of the veterans' association to levy money from members for any reason, General Gordon nonetheless issued a general order urging every veterans' camp to contribute at least one dollar for each member, the money to be forwarded to the monument committee.[41] Monument association chairmen in the various southern states were urged to collect promised but unpaid moneys.

Chairman Randolph wrote in her fund-raising letter that by carrying out these activities at once, the monument association would double the amount in hand within the year. Although her estimate was overly optimistic, the memorial drive under the UDC raised more than $12,000, more than the veterans had raised in the past three years. In November 1900, the new total was $32,672.[42]

Although this was insufficient to build a monument on the scale of the temple design, it was enough to begin plans for a scaled-down model. Consequently, the monument association met for three days in mid–November 1901 and laid out new plans for the erection of the Davis memorial. The form was shifted from a temple design to an arch. The location was shifted from Monroe Park to Broad Street, where that road met Twelfth. It would be constructed of southern granite, preferably from Virginia, and be unveiled on Davis's birthday, June 3, 1903. The minimum cost was set at $50,000, with the hope of raising $75,000 by 1904. Rather than advertise nationally for designs as in 1896, the individual state directors of the two women's organizations were asked to select one artist each, and these alone would enter into competition for the winning design. The models, with estimates of cost, thus submitted were to be placed in the rotunda of the Virginia state capitol on May 26, 1902, for inspection and selection.[43] The new plan for the Davis monument received the approval of the national UDC during its annual convention in November 1901.

Despite the approval of the national organization, the plan generated immediate opposition. The New York City chapter complained to Mrs. S. T. McCullough, who had succeeded Mrs. Randolph as chairman of the Central Committee, that "we . . . feel that this arch, although already endorsed by the convention, will be a great mistake." Not only was an arch, which signified victory, wrong, but the location was also wrong and the $75,000 price tag too high. Instead, the New York chapter argued, "a very handsome monument can be erected for $50,000" and placed "immediately in front of the Confederate White House."[44]

Criticism also came from dissatisfied members within the monument association itself. In late May, a Mrs. Kimbrough of Mississippi, who claimed to be speaking for one of the directors of the association, wrote to the editors of the *New Orleans Picayune* charging that "the building of a triumphant arch to our defeated President is a misappropriation of funds created by the people of the South." She added a further complaint that the Richmond group was planning to use the money for the monument "to decorate a certain section of Richmond."[45]

It was Varina Davis's discontent with the proposed monument, however, that was the most difficult for the UDC to overcome. She objected to it in both form and location. Her opposition became public when, rather than voice her concerns directly to officials of the women's organizations, she wrote a letter to the editor of the *New Orleans Picayune* to express her concerns. She was, she said, "very averse to the arch and to the erection of any monument to Mr. Davis on the site indicated." An arch signified victory by many and would incite ridicule if erected to a man whose cause, though nobly fought, had lost. While a triumphal arch might be erected to the valor of the Confederate soldiers or to the heroism of southern women, it was not suitable for her husband.[46]

She and her daughter found the proposed location even more objectionable than the arch itself. "I cannot approve of building a monument to President Davis in the place proposed," she wrote to the *Picayune*. They found "most inappropriate" the intersection of Broad and Twelfth, which was lined with shops and frequented by noisy, busy crowds.[47]

As the date for selection of a design for the arch neared and models began to arrive in Richmond, the JDMA felt that it was too late to change the form of the memorial, the hostility of Varina and the interstate quarrels notwithstanding. The controversy caused apprehension among some of the submitters, one of whom complained, "We have spent our time and our money, and it would be a great breach of faith that would injure the society irreparably if the matter were left in abeyance. It would forever damn the credit of the organization if such a course were taken after it has gone this far."[48]

Since changing the form of the monument at such a late date would be a breach of faith with the sculptors and architects who had brought their designs to Richmond, the UDC felt that they could meet Varina and her daughter Margaret only halfway. The monument association's board of directors met with its male advisory board for three days in an attempt to solve the quandary in which they found themselves.[49] As the competition date approached, members of the association began to make trips around the city to inspect alternate locations for the arch. As a result, the association arrived at a compromise solution. The memorial would remain in the form of an arch but would be built in Monroe Park, its originally intended location.[50]

On June 3, directors from the monument and memorial associations from throughout the South met in the rotunda of the state capitol building to decide on the winning design. The winner was twenty-eight-year-old Louis A. Gudebrod, who had earlier been a finalist in the contest to build a memorial to James Ewell Brown "Jeb" Stuart in Richmond. The New York sculptor took as his inspiration the Arch of Titus in Rome. His projected arch measured sixty-five feet high and seventy feet wide; the archway measured twenty-five feet wide, and forty feet high, and twenty-four feet deep. It was to be embellished by inscriptions honoring Davis, the Great Seal of the Confederacy, and thirteen state seals.[51] His projected cost was $75,000, although he informed the committee that he could reduce this to $50,000 by removing the bronze statues at the ends which could be added later as the association might wish.[52]

The Gudebrod arch proved to be another misstep in the monument association's quest to build a memorial to the Confederate president. The drawback, as in the case of the 1896 temple design, was money. The agreed-on contract between sculptor and the monument association called for a scaled-down arch, with much of the ornamentation omitted, to be built for $50,000. Sculptures and any other features could be added at a later date as the association received additional contributions. However, when Gudebrod informed the association that a rise in the cost in materials meant that the arch could not be constructed for less than $62,000, the women balked, refusing to pay the new price. As a result, the sculptor and the association amicably agreed to cancel the contract, with Gudebrod being paid for his expenses up to that time.[53]

On April 15 of the following year (1903), the monument received a financial boost from a great Confederate bazaar put on jointly by the UDC and the Southern Memorial Association and held in the Masonic Temple in Richmond. Earnings were earmarked for the newly created Museum of the Confederacy, located in the former the Confederate White House, and the Jefferson Davis monument. Donations of all sizes and values, "anything that could be converted into money," were sought and received from every southern state, with free transportation provided for items less than a specified number of pounds. Appealing to southern sentiment, flyers advertising the bazaar informed donors that in "erecting a monument to our only President we are doing that in which everyone who has the slightest semblance of true Confederate sentiment would feel proud to be enlisted."[54] The bazaar was a success. In addition to its share of the profits, the Museum of the Confederacy added $4,500 of its share to the monument association to complete the memorial. As a result, the monument fund had grown by $12,000 over the previous year to $52,000.[55]

Thus far, the efforts of the old and new monument associations had resulted only in failure. But with the refusal of Gudebrod to sign a contract for the agreed-on amount and the monument association unwilling to spend more, the UDC changed tactics. In June, they met in secret session, determined to come up with a new plan before adjourning. Everything was up for grabs, including the design and the location. A small minority still favored the arch, but this had proven unpopular with the public and many members of the association itself. One member suggested returning to the temple design, while another favored a statue of Davis.[56] It was known that Davis's widow at one time wished to have an equestrian statue of her husband, but the committee felt that that was not appropriate for a civilian leader.

Without holding a competition among sculptors and architects in which they would submit designs as in the past, the UDC went directly to Edward V. Valentine, a Richmond sculptor who was normally opposed to entering competitions and was well known for his statue of the "recumbent Lee" in the chapel of Washington and Lee University. Valentine chose Richmond architect William C. Noland to work with him. The two men worked together, the former sculpting the statue and the latter designing the remainder of the monument. They agreed to produce the memorial at a cost of $60,000, to be completed by June 3, 1906.[57]

The work proceeded smoothly. Noland and Valentine drew up designs that were submitted to the monument association's Central Committee for comments and suggestions. The committee in turn heard from chapters who wished modifications, as in the case of Maryland, which was concerned that its state was not given equality with other states. Following the suggestions from the UDC and the Southern Monument Association, Noland and Valentine produced a design for the monument that was acceptable to all.[58]

A new site for the monument was sought and received from the Richmond city council, which granted a location on Cedar Avenue (later renamed Davis Avenue) and also appropriated $1,000 toward construction. But the monument conceived by Valentine and Noland demanded more space, and the city complied by cutting off the corners of adjacent property, compensating the owners. The location had a symbolic value beyond its proximity to the Lee Monument. It had been the site of a fort that formed part of the Confederate inner defense line surrounding Richmond.[59]

The dedication of the monument, originally scheduled for 1896, was delayed until June 3, 1907, in order to coincide with the annual reunion of Confederate veterans and the almost simultaneous dedications of the "Jeb" Stuart and Jefferson Davis monuments. The three activities taking place at the same time was certain to draw one of the biggest crowds in Richmond's history. The monument association did its best to produce a grand show. On April 16, 1907, there was a procession in which the children of Richmond joined with Confederate veterans to pull the eight-foot-tall bronze statue of Davis to the site of the monument that was nearing completion. With the statue placed on a decorated wagon, the three thousand children, with the girls dressed in white, pulled two seven-hundred-foot-long ropes along Monument Avenue. A fife and drum corps dressed in blue and white uniforms with scarlet capes led the procession through the crowded streets. They were followed by the veterans of Lee and Pickett camps, and then came the children with the statue. On arrival at the monument, the ropes were cut into small sections and taken away as souvenirs by the children and veterans.[60]

The dedication of the Davis monument was set for the last day of the Confederate reunion of May 29–June 3, 1907, which was the ninety-ninth anniversary of his birth. While many in the crowds were attracted to Richmond by the combination of events being held during the five-day period, the dedication of the monument to the Confederate president was the main attraction. An estimated eighty thousand persons arrived in the Virginia capital on special trains that mushroomed the crowds to the hundreds of thousands already there. The schedule of events called for a grand parade to the monument site, followed by addresses by Virginia Governor Claude A. Swanson, Richmond Mayor Carlton McCarthy, and the orator of the day, General Clement A. Evans of Atlanta, Georgia, concluding with the unveiling of the statue by Margaret Hayes, the only surviving member of Davis's immediate family, addresses by officers of the various women's associations, and the placing of flowers on the monument by the public.

Following two days of rain, the skies turned sunny and the weather pleasant for the dedication of the monument. A solid wall of people, estimated at more than two hundred thousand—five and in some places ten deep—lined the three-mile route from the capitol building to the monument. Others filled windows and stood on rooftops cheering as the parade passed. Homes were decorated, and Confederate flags appeared in profusion along the route. At 11:30 A.M., the parade formed, stretching, with no spaces between units, for a distance of twenty blocks through the city. As the procession began to move a half hour later, its length was such that it took more than two hours to pass the reviewing stand. A detachment of mounted police led the way, followed by military units, the veterans, and dignitaries in carriages. All along the route, flags were waved and people cheered as the seventy bands passed playing "Dixie," "Maryland, My Maryland," "The Bonnie Blue Flag," and other Civil War–era songs.[61]

Perennial Democratic presidential candidate William Jennings Bryan and his wife, who were the invited guests of the reunion, drew ovations from the crowd, but it was the surviving veterans (numbering some 1,200) and the generals, colonels, and other officers of the Confederacy, including Stephen D. Lee, Clement Evans, and Eppa Hunton, who rode at the head of military and veteran units and in carriages who drew the most attention. The widows of deceased Confederate military heroes also drew favorable comment, including those of "Stonewall" Jackson, A. P. Hill, "Jeb" Stuart, George E. Pickett, W. H. F. "Rooney" Lee, William Mahone, and Henry Heth. The veterans marched in divisions representing each of the states of the Confederacy; the border states of Missouri, Maryland, and Kentucky; and units from West Virginia, Oklahoma, New York City, and the Northwest and Pacific coast regions. Several units of full-blooded Indian veterans represented the Indian Territory. The veterans appeared rejuvenated during the march and gave out cheers and "rebel yells" as they passed.[62]

The area around the monument was already filled to overflowing with an estimated 125,000 persons when the head of the procession arrived. The speakers and other guests were led to the platform, while participants in the parade were left to find the best vantage point they could. Following speeches by Virginia Governor Claude Swanson and General Evans glorifying the Confederate president, the Confederacy, and the heroism of southern armies, the Davises' only living daughter, Margaret Hayes, stepped forward to remove the veil from the bronze statue of her father. As the canvas cover fell, it created a wind that sent Confederate flags on each side of the monument to flying straight out in the breeze. After a brief moment of silence, the crowd began to cheer, bands began to play, and the Richmond Howitzers fired a twenty-one-gun presidential salute. As each gun fired, it sent a bomb over the audience that, when it exploded, revealed a small Confederate battle flag that floated down into the audience.[63] Although the program was not over, the crowd could not be kept quiet for the remainder. The people who had formed around the monument sang songs and placed floral decorations on the monument.[64]

In its basic design, the monument consisted simply of a sixty-foot-tall central column topped by a Greek-style statue, partially surrounded by a semicircle of columns, with a statue of the Confederate president standing to the front. Yet taken in its individual parts, the monument represented an unapologetic tribute to and defense of the Confederacy, Jefferson Davis, and his political belief in the sovereign rights of the states. Atop the central column, the spirit of the South is represented by the classically carved female figure of Vindicatrix, to be later dubbed locally as "Miss Confederacy." Her base reads "Deo Vindici," the words of the Confederate national seal. Three bands surrounding the column on which she stands proclaim "Jure Civitatum" (for the rights of the states), "Pro Aris Et Focis" (for hearth and home), and "Jefferson Davis President of the Confederate States of America, 1861–1865."[65]

The states of the Confederacy, including the border states of Kentucky, Missouri, and Maryland (all three of which sent regiments to the war in support of the seceded states), found representation on the monument in the form of the thirteen columns and/or state seals. The Confederate army and navy were commemorated on the terminating piers that formed the end pieces of the semicircle of columns. The Stars and Bars flag decorated the stone urns that sat atop the two piers.

Davis's image, words, and actions were placed liberally around the monument. His eight-foot bronze statue stands with left hand on an open book and the other pointing toward the former Confederate capitol and the statue of Robert E. Lee, as if, in the words of a *Richmond News-Leader* reporter, "he were expounding the Southern Doctrine, and was on the point of pleading with his countrymen to stand by the things for which so many had laid down their lives."[66] The front of the five-foot-high pedestal on which his statue stands identifies him to future onlookers as the post–Civil War South wished them to see him. He was "Jefferson Davis, Exponent of Constitutional Principles, Defender of the Rights of the States." And to further identify him, they were informed on the right side of the pedestal that "As citizen, soldier, statesman, he enhanced the glory, the fame of the United States. When his allegiance to that government was terminated by his sovereign State, as President of the Confederacy, he exalted his country before the nations." And, on the left side, they were informed about the characteristic that endeared him most to southern whites of his day: "With constancy and courage unsurpassed he sustained the heavy burden laid upon him by the people. When their cause was lost, with dignity he met defeat, with fortitude he met imprisonment and suffering, with entire devotion he kept the faith."[67]

After eighteen years, Jefferson Davis had his monument. He was still the hero of the South, ranked in his own region alongside of Lee and Jackson by most and, above them, by some. His memory, the *Atlanta Constitution* editorialized, was "revered above all others."[68] In the same vein, the *Richmond Times Dispatch* wrote following the ceremony: "Such an outpouring of people has never before been seen at any gathering of veterans at any unveiling of monuments, at any burial of Confederate heroes." And in separating him from southern military leaders, a one-legged veteran said, "We each loved our own commander, but Jeff Davis belongs to the whole Confederacy.[69]

Yet Jefferson Davis no longer excited either the enthusiasm of the South or the hostility of the North in the degree that had existed in earlier years. The southern states had spoken with a common voice during his Southern Tour of 1886–1887 and on his death in 1889 and reburial in 1893, rising up to respond in unison to calls to honor him made by newspapers, mayors, governors, veterans' organizations, commercial leaders, and virtually anyone in authority. These events were "national" in scope. Now, as his monument rose in Richmond, the press's coverage of the event was far less than for the earlier events, and only Georgia responded to the order from the UCV's Commander in Chief, General Stephen D. Lee, requesting southern governors to call on the people to observe in silent tribute during the unveiling of the Davis monument.[70] His image received even more of a public diminution. Whereas the events of the 1890s had filled the region's press with either understanding or hostility, the erection of the monument generated little interest. Some, such as the *St. Louis Post-Dispatch*, gave it neither news nor editorial coverage, while others, including the *New York Times,* ignored it editorially and relegated news coverage to one brief article in the interior pages.

But at least among veterans and Confederate heritage groups, Davis had attained a status equal or superior to Stonewall Jackson and Robert E. Lee, the two icons among the South's military leaders. Beginning in 1916, his image was included alongside those two men as one of the trio of great Civil War leaders in the carving on Stone Mountain in Georgia, created by Gutzon Borglum and Augustus Lukeman, the former of which sculpted the more famous busts of Abraham Lincoln, George Washington, Thomas Jefferson, and Theodore Roosevelt on Mount Rushmore in South Dakota.

However, Davis's place in the sun as a Confederate hero was destined to decline yet again with the end of the Lost Cause movement, the death of the Confederate generation, the revision of Civil War and antebellum history by historians, and, in particular, from the civil rights movement as it moved from fighting legal discrimination in the courts and through state and federal legislation into an assault on the Confederacy itself and the place of African Americans in southern history.

NOTES

1. *Newark Evening News,* December 18, 1889.
2. *New Orleans Times-Democrat,* December 13, 1889; *Charleston (S.C.)News and Courier,* December 11, 1889.
3. *Richmond Dispatch,* May 28, 1893.
4. Clipping in J. Taylor Ellyson scrapbook, Eleanor S. Brockenborough Library, Museum of the Confederacy, Richmond, Virginia (no title or date) (hereafter cited as the Ellyson scrapbook).
5. *Richmond Dispatch,* May 28, 1893.
6. Jefferson Davis Monument Association, *Minutes,* June 13, 1891 (hereafter cited as JDMA, *Minutes*).
7. *New York Times,* June 24, 1891.
8. JDMA, *Minutes,* June 13, 1891; *New York Times,* July 14, 1891.
9. Sarah Shields Driggs, Richard Guy Wilson, and Robert P. Winthrop, *Richmond's Monument Avenue* (Chapel Hill: University of North Carolina Press, 2001), 37.
10. JDMA, *Minutes,* November 3, 1891.
11. JDMA, *Minutes,* September 11, 1891, December 23, 1891.
12. JDMA, *Minutes,* March 22, 1892.
13. Ellyson scrapbook, newspaper clipping (no title or date).
14. Ellyson scrapbook, newspaper clipping (no title or date).
15. *Richmond Dispatch,* May 28, 1893.
16. Ellyson scrapbook, newspaper clipping (no title or date).

17. *Richmond Dispatch*, September 18, 1892.

18. *Richmond Dispatch*, September 18, 1892; Ellyson scrapbook, newspaper clipping (no title or date).

19. JDMA, *Minutes* (undated, but c. September 20, 1892).

20. JDMA, *Minutes* (undated, but c. September 20, 1892).

21. JDMA, *Minutes* (undated, but c. September 20, 1892); *Richmond Dispatch*, September 21, 1892.

22. Analysis of minutes of the JDMA, January 1890 through September 1895.

23. Ellyson scrapbook, newspaper clippings (dated June 22, 1893, and April 17, 1894).

24. JDMA, *Minutes*, December 12, 1895.

25. JDMA, *Minutes*, September 27, 1895.

26. JDMA, *Minutes*, November 11, 1895.

27. JDMA, *Minutes*, September 17, 1892.

28. JDMA, *Minutes*, March 4, 1896; Driggs et al., *Richmond's Monument Avenue*, 64–65.

29. *Raleigh (N.C.) State Chronicle*, May 28, 1893.

30. *Richmond Dispatch*, June 30, 1896.

31. *Richmond Dispatch*, July 3, 1896; Ishbel Ross, *First Lady of the South: The Life of Mrs. Jefferson Davis* (New York: Harper & Brothers, 1958), 388.

32. *Richmond Dispatch*, July 3, 1896.

33. JDMA, *Minutes*, January 14, 1897.

34. Jefferson Davis Monument Association, United Daughters of the Confederacy, Central Committee, fund-raising form letter unsigned, c. 1900, in Ellyson scrapbook.

35. Jefferson Davis Monument Association, United Daughters of the Confederacy, Central Committee, fund-raising form letter, c. 1900, signed by Mrs. Edgar D. Taylor, treasurer.

36. Mrs. Norman V. Randolph, Chairman, Central Committee, Jefferson Davis Monument Committee, to the *Richmond Dispatch* (no title or date), in Ellyson scrapbook.

37. Jefferson Davis Monument Association, United Daughters of the Confederacy, Central Committee, fund-raising form letter, c. 1900, signed by Mrs. Edgar D. Taylor, treasurer, in Ellyson scrapbook.

38. Mrs. Norman V. Randolph, Chairman, Central Committee, Jefferson Davis Monument Association, undated fund-raising form letter, in Ellyson scrapbook.

39. Jefferson Davis Monument Association, United Daughters of the Confederacy, Central Committee, fund-raising form letter, unsigned, c. 1900, in Ellyson scrapbook.

40. Jefferson Davis Monument Association, United Daughters of the Confederacy, Central Committee, fund-raising form letter, c. 1900, signed by Mrs. Edgar D. Taylor, treasurer, in Ellyson scrapbook.

41. General John B. Gordon, General Commanding, Headquarters, United Confederate Veterans, New Orleans, October 11, 1901, General Orders No. 263, in Ellyson scrapbook.

42. General John B. Gordon, General Commanding, Headquarters, United Confederate Veterans, New Orleans, October 11, 1901, General Orders No. 263, in Ellyson scrapbook; Jefferson Davis Monument Association, United Daughters of the Confederacy, Central Committee, fund-raising form letter, unsigned, c. 1900, in Ellyson scrapbook.

43. JDMA, *Minutes*, November 13–15, 1901.

44. Ellyson scrapbook, newspaper clipping (no title or date).

45. *Richmond Times?*, c. May 31–June 1, 1892. Ellyson scrapbook, newspaper clipping.

46. *New York World*, April 8 (no year), in Ellyson scrapbook.

47. *New York World*, April 8 (no year), in Ellyson scrapbook; Ross, *First Lady of the South*, 394.

48. Ellyson scrapbook, newspaper clipping (no title or date).

49. Ellyson scrapbook, newspaper clipping (no title or date).

50. Ellyson scrapbook, newspaper clipping (no title or date).

51. Driggs et al., *Richmond's Monument Avenue*, 66.

52. Lewis A. Gudebrod to Board of Directors, Jefferson Davis Monument Association (no date).

53. Ellyson scrapbook, newspaper clipping (no title or date).

54. Flyer, "The Confederate Bazaar," April 1903, in Ellyson scrapbook.

55. Newspaper clipping, Charleston, South Carolina (no name), November 12, 1903, in Ellyson scrapbook.

56. Newspaper clipping, Charleston, South Carolina (no name), June 10, 1893 [*sic*], in Ellyson scrapbook.

57. JDMA, *Minutes* (no date), in Ellyson scrapbook.

58. Elizabeth W. Hall, Baltimore, Maryland, Chapter, United Daughters of the Confederacy, to Mrs. S. Thomas McCullough, President, Jefferson Davis Monument Association, June 21, 1904, in Ellyson scrapbook.

59. Driggs et al., *Richmond's Monument Avenue*, 67.

60. *Richmond Times-Dispatch*, April 19, 1907; "Jefferson Davis Monument," *Confederate Veteran* 15 (1907): 199.

61. *Richmond Times-Dispatch*, June 4, 1907; *Atlanta Constitution*, June 3, 1907.

62. *Richmond Times-Dispatch*, June 4, 1907; *Atlanta Constitution*, June 4, 1907; Lizzie George Henderson, report on the unveiling of the James Ewel Brown Stuart and Jefferson Davis monuments, *Confederate Veteran* 15 (1907): 348.

63. "The Richmond Reunion," *Confederate Veteran* 15 (1907): 349.

64. *Atlanta Constitution*, June 4, 1907; *Richmond Times-Dispatch*, June 3, 1907.

65. Driggs et al., *Richmond's Monument Avenue*, 71.

66. Driggs et al., *Richmond's Monument Avenue*, 71.

67. Driggs et al., *Richmond's Monument Avenue*, 71; "The Davis Monument," *Confederate Veteran* 15 (1907): 198.

68. *Atlanta Constitution*, June 4, 1907.

69. *Richmond Times-Dispatch*, June 4, 1907.

70. *Atlanta Constitution*, June 3, 1907.

Conclusion

$\mathcal{H}$ow does one view a national figure of the stature of Jefferson Davis over his lifetime and after? The former Confederate president rode a roller coaster of opinions in the eyes of his contemporaries and historians. Either one likes him, or one does not. There appears to be little middle ground. This characteristic continues to this day.

Various book titles indicate these variations, be they *Jefferson Davis, American* or *Jefferson Davis, Confederate President*. Davis died at the age of eighty-one years. For fifty-three of these, he was seen as a nationalist, one who was viewed favorably by a majority of Americans regardless of their state of origin. Building on a reputation gained as a military hero at the battles of Monterey and Buena Vista in the Mexican War, he became an exceptional and well-liked U.S. senator, secretary of war, and, in 1860, potential Democratic presidential nominee with intersectional support. Had he died at that moment, Jefferson Davis would be remembered positively in American history.

Unfortunately for Davis, the Civil War fixed his image in the minds of Americans then and now. He was a patriot or a traitor, an incompetent president or the only man who could have held the Confederate states together for the four years of the war, and a proponent of slavery or the man who was willing to end the practice in the interest of southern independence. At the war's conclusion, he was neither liked nor admired by Americans of any category—northerner, southerner, black, or white. Had Jefferson Davis died at that point, there is little likelihood that his image could or would have been resurrected—certainly he would not have gained the stature that southerners and some northerners accorded to Confederate generals Robert E. Lee and Thomas "Stonewall" Jackson. Yet shifting memories over a span of decades raised his status among southerners to the equal of those two military heroes.

153

A current school of historiography attempts to determine how time and memory affected both the occurrence of events and how those events and their participants were viewed at the time and are viewed now by people living in the present. Studies by such memory historians as David W. Blight, in his *Race and Reconciliation: The Civil War in American Memory*, and Bertram Wyatt-Brown, in his *The Shaping of Southern Culture: Honor, Grace, and War, 1760s–1880s*, take a geographically broad view of the effects of memory on history. The present study of Jefferson Davis's final years benefits by the findings of those regional studies but also demonstrates that Davis was in a class by himself, different from the great military heroes of the Confederacy. While Lee and Jackson came to be remembered even in the North as national heroes, Davis remained a sectional one. And as this author shows, southerners initially resurrected Jefferson Davis in their memory not as their former political leader but as the man who suffered for them and the South and whose continued defense of the constitutionality of secession, the war, and the Confederacy justified their own participation in it.

"Martyr," more than any other word, describes Davis's rise from the obscurity of 1865. An unnecessarily harsh two-year imprisonment in Fort Monroe by the victorious Union cemented his position in the late nineteenth-century southern mind. This was noted as early as 1886 by Connecticut's *Hartford Courant* as "the spirit which inspired the Southern people." In writing of Davis's introduction to the crowds in Montgomery during the Southern Tour, that newspaper quoted "a prominent Southern general" as telling his audience that although "we [Southerners] were well treated by the North, . . . and admitted into the circle of a new nationality . . ., it was different with Mr. Davis. Failure left him no future. . . . He had borne our burdens with grace, and it is but fitting that . . . the Southern people whom he represented, should pay a tribute to his devotion and sacrifice."[1] "He suffered for us" became a constant theme in the resurrected image of Jefferson Davis. His wartime presidential record was mentioned sparingly. Constant references to suffering for and in place of the southern people undoubtedly raised his estimation with white southerners. By the 1890s, Davis had reached par with Lee and Jackson, and in the eyes of some was even above them. He remained as one of the Confederate greats well into the twentieth century, with the erection of the Davis monument in Richmond, the incorporation of his features in the Stone Mountain carving alongside those two generals, and the naming of a transcontinental highway that stretched across the country into the state of Washington.

Yet, as both Blight and Wyatt-Brown point out, it is clear that Davis could not have regained his former status with southerners had it not been for the way in which ex-Confederates chose to lead the country to accept a southern-friendly interpretation of the war in which Confederates were not traitors and their military leaders were in fact national heroes.[2] The New South movement, which they created, dominated southern remembrance of the Confederacy from 1870 until World War I and after.

Without the nostalgia of white southerners for the Lost Cause that supplanted the defeatism of 1865, the Confederacy might have been a cause to forget rather than one to remember. For a few years, the returning veterans had little concern for remembering. There was, according to Blight, a crisis of confidence in the leadership ranks of the fallen Confederacy.[3] Davis, whose wartime presidency had been rejected in 1865, shared their suffering in his prison cell, thus giving southern whites of the postwar generation and their children reason to remember him. In 1866, the gathering nostalgia for the Confederacy acquired a name from Alfred Pollard's *The Lost Cause*. This movement, led for the first two decades after the war by what Blight terms the "diehards," set out to reverse negative interpretations of the war and the Confederacy written by their former enemies.[4] These men dedicated their lives to combating northern histories of the war and to presenting southern-friendly histories—the truth as they saw it.

The Lost Cause grew alongside a movement for reconciliation between the former enemies that developed in the 1870s and continued through the following decades: joint commemorations of Memorial Day, friendly reports written by northern travelers in the South, romanticized stories of the war written by veterans of both armies in which the horrors were forgotten, and joint reunions by former combatants who came to see each other as honorable men who had fought nobly helped reunite the country. Lost Cause adherents eventually accepted reconciliation while at the same time celebrating the Confederacy and its soldiers. Initially, however, the movement was in the hands of the die-hards, who included Jefferson Davis as one of their own. Both the die-hard and the reconciliationist factions of the Lost Cause movement, however, used Davis's memory to further their cause, thereby helping to bring him out of the obscurity of 1865.

Concerned that "Yankee" histories would distort the truth of the war, former Confederate military and political leaders dedicated themselves to retelling the war's history in their own version of the truth. This was done through books and articles in popular magazines and through such organized efforts as the Southern Historical Society (SHA), which published and documented Confederate history in its *SHA Papers*, and magazines such as the *Confederate Veteran* and *The Land We Love*. Since the end of the war, every organ of the Lost Cause declared itself a bulwark against prejudiced Yankee history.[5]

Davis and the SHA exalted and benefited from each other. The former president looked to the society and its publications as the guardians of truthful Confederate history. The society in turn wrote about and to Davis: "Nothing will give us more pleasure than to do everything in our power to put right on the record the able statesman, gallant soldier, pure patriot, and accomplished gentleman who presided over the Confederacy."[6] Although Davis did not create the Lost Cause, Blight credits him with providing the movement's "lifeblood."[7]

From his release from prison in 1867 to his death in 1889, the former president set the tone for the die-hards' historical interpretation. He placed responsibility for secession and the war entirely at the feet of the North. The South's action was merely to protect its natural rights against the "tremendous and sweeping usurpations," the "unlimited, despotic power" of the federal government. His fierce defense of states' rights and secession, his pleas for "Southern honor," and his mystical conception of the Confederacy gave ideological fuel to die-hards. Using Davis's rationale, the term "rebellion" became a misnomer. In 1874, he wrote, "Sovereigns cannot rebel." Davis provided the die-hards with endless expressions of solemn faith. "We may not hope to see the rebuilding of the temple as our Fathers designed it," Davis wrote to a friend in 1877, "but we can live on praying for that event and die with eyes fixed on the promised land."[8]

If Davis exercised as much influence on the Lost Cause movement as Blight credits him, the ex-southern president received as good as he gave. His resurrection could not have taken place without it. Although he was undoubtedly in the die-hard camp, he also faced the reality that the future was in reunification, and toward the end of his life, he accepted, if perhaps grudgingly, reconciliation with his former enemies.

During the final years of the 1880s, leadership in the Lost Cause movement shifted from the die-hards to a faction that endorsed both reconciliation with the North and devotion to Confederate memory. A primary leader among the reconciliationists was former Confederate General John B. Gordon of Georgia, who in 1889 brought together the numerous state, local, and unit veterans' organizations, that is, "the grassroots of the Lost Cause" movement, into the newly formed United Confederate Veterans.[9] It was particularly the reception of Davis by the veterans during his Southern Tour of 1886–1887 that first revealed to the South through its coverage in the southern press and to the former president himself that he had once again reached the top rung of southern leadership. Yet the primary memory of the man revealed during the tour and in numerous southern editorials then and afterward was less that of a former president than that of a hero of the Mexican War and a postwar martyr for the Confederacy. Gordon, in speech after speech, spoke of loyalty to the union in the same breath that he praised the memory of the Confederacy. While Davis was associated with the die-hards, he was by the end of his life also at home with the reconciliationists, as demonstrated by his close relations with northern publishers and the fiancé of his own daughter Winnie.

When Davis died in 1889, there is little doubt that his enhanced memory among white southerners had been influenced by the efforts of both the die-hards of the 1860s–1880s and the reconciliationists of the late 1880s and after. These men continued to stress Davis's memory not only for his stalwart defense of the Confederacy but also for his heroism in the war of 1846–1848 and for his postwar suffering at the hands of the federal government. The transition of southern memory of Davis away from this martyr/American military hero view to being primarily a Confederate hero was strongly influenced by the transfer of the Davis memorial from the all-male United Confederate Veterans, Southern Press Association, and Jefferson Davis Monument Association to their female counterparts, particularly the newly formed United Daughters of the Confederacy and the Confederated Southern Memorial Association in the late 1890s. From this time forward, Davis was to be remembered in history primarily as the political leader of the southern Confederacy. As evidenced by the monument erected to his memory in 1907, he was no longer Davis the martyr but Davis the hero of the Confederacy, on par with Robert E. Lee and Stonewall Jackson.

However, Davis never won the hearts of northerners as did the previously mentioned Confederate military leaders. As president, he had led the rebellion. After the war, he refused to seek a pardon, and he refused to admit that he, the Confederacy, secession, or states' rights were wrong. Whereas there was overwhelming agreement among white southerners in regard to Davis's positive image, opinions toward him in the North varied according to population groups. African Americans excoriated him for his role in defending slavery and in attempting to continue it by means of a proslavery Confederate government. Northern whites were divided. Many Democrats, most of whom had not given enthusiastic support for the war, never felt a strong antagonism toward Davis and were willing to forgive and forget. On the other hand, Republicans were loathe, largely for political reasons, to forgive. His image was used in the party's "Bloody Shirt" propaganda to attack the Democratic opposition in every election into the 1890s. Yet even Republican hostility tended to vanish as memories of the Civil War were pushed further into the background as the United States moved into the twentieth century. If anything, popular culture rejuvenated the image of the Confederacy as films such as *Gone with the Wind*, the publication of Civil War novels, and post–World War II reenactments tended to romanticize the Confederacy and southern soldiers.

Yet history does not stand still. Presentism, or the tendency to examine the past in light of the realities of the present, has resulted in a return of the negative image of immediate post–Civil War years of the Confederacy and its leaders. However, this time, even the military leaders were not to be spared condemnation. The vehicle for the return was the post–World War II civil rights movement, led by such organizations as the National Association for the Advancement of Colored People and the Southern Christian Leadership Conference. As these organizations won the necessary battles against legal discrimination by the 1980s, the emphasis shifted to an attack on slavery and the Confederacy as a vehicle for its perpetuation.

Davis, like the Confederate flag, became a symbol to be repudiated as demeaning to the African American population. The political and social culture of the 1990s and into the twenty-first century called increasingly for an end to symbols that held negative meanings for minorities of all kinds. As the Civil War moves further into the past, those individuals and organizations that honor the memory of the Confederacy grow—and will probably continue to grow—smaller in numbers and influence. It is not likely that the southern Confederacy will rise again as a positive image. Jefferson Davis's place in the sun has, with little doubt, sunk below the horizon.

NOTES

1. Reprinted in the *Atlanta Journal*, May 1, 1886.
2. David W. Blight, *Race and Reunion: The Civil War in American Memory* (Cambridge, Mass.: Belknap Press, 2002), 265.
3. Blight, *Race and Reunion*, 256.
4. Blight, *Race and Reunion*, 258–59.
5. Blight, *Race and Reunion*, 277.
6. William J. Cooper, *Jefferson Davis, American* (New York: Knopf, 2000), 621.
7. Blight, *Race and Reunion*, 260.
8. Blight, *Race and Reunion*, 259.
9. Blight, *Race and Reunion*, 259.

Bibliographic Essay

$\mathcal{T}$he story of Jefferson Davis's decline and resurrection in southern public opinion following the collapse of the Confederacy has yet to be treated in historical literature in other than piecemeal form. Further, his first and second funerals, his restoration among southerners as one of the Civil War greats, the drive by southerners to erect a permanent remembrance in stone, and the reaction by northerners and African Americans to these events have yet to be dealt with by historians to any significant degree. As a result, book-length literature relating specifically to this topic is nonexistent, and journal literature is sparse.

Davis's place in history has been determined primarily by his position as president of the Confederate States of America. Thus, the broad scope of the published literature concentrates on those years. As a result, only the first chapter of this volume, dealing with his rise to prominence and fall from grace, is literature rich. For those wishing to study Davis's life and his role in the Civil War, there are a number of superior critical bibliographies that may be consulted. *Leaders of the Civil War: A Biographical and Historiographical Dictionary* (Westport, Conn.: Greenwood Press, 1998), edited and written largely by Charles F. Ritter and Jon L. Wakelyn, surveys the post–Civil War literature on the major figures of the war. The sketch of Davis is harshly critical but representative of the views of many historians. Another useful critical survey of the literature that is conveniently arranged by person and subject is David J. Eicher's *Civil War in Books: An Analytical Bibliography* (Urbana, Ill.: University of Chicago Press, 1997). Also valuable for its broad coverage in bibliographic essay format is *The American Civil War: A Handbook of Literature and Research*, edited by Steven E. Woodworth (Westport, Conn.: Greenwood Press, 1996). Herman Hattaway and Richard E. Beringer's *Jefferson Davis,*

Confederate President (Lawrence: University Press of Kansas, 2002) is the most recent book to look at the literature on Davis and the Civil War. Although not technically a bibliographic essay, its frequent discussion of the works of other historians makes it useful for this purpose.

There are also several good book-length studies that treat the whole span of Davis's life. Two of the best recent biographies for this period are William J. Cooper Jr.'s Jefferson Davis, American (New York: Knopf, 2000), and Felicia Allen's Jefferson Davis, Unconquerable Heart (Columbia: University of Missouri Press, 1999). The former work touches only briefly on the immensely important Southern Tour of 1886–1887 and ends with his subject's death in 1889, with no mention of the funeral. Although the treatment of each of these events is brief, Allen provides sufficient coverage of Davis's Southern Tour, death, funerals, and reinterment to inform the reader. For an excellent popularly written brief account of Davis's life, readers should consult the July/August 1991 issue of Civil War Times Illustrated, the entirety of which is devoted to a biographical account by Mark Grimsley titled "We Will Vindicate the Right." Perhaps the best older biographical treatment of the southern president's life is the three-volume series by Hudson Strode, Jefferson Davis, American Patriot, 1808–1861 (New York: Harcourt Brace, 1925), Jefferson Davis, Confederate President (New York: Harcourt Brace, 1959), and Jefferson Davis, Tragic Hero, the Last Twenty-Five Years, 1864–1889 (1964; reprint, New York: Harcourt, 2000). The author treats his subject in a detail that is missing in the previously mentioned works.

As is the case with the book-length biographies, the vast majority of journal writings emphasize the war years. Readers interested in reading more on the causes of the deteriorating image of the Confederate president during the war will find the following to be useful. The initial optimism in the North is presented in Michael B. Ballard's "Yankee Editors on Jefferson Davis," Journal of Mississippi History (Vol. 43, November 1981). Similarly, the decline in sentiment as revealed in southern newspapers may be found in J. Cutler Andrews, "The Confederate Press and Public Morale," Journal of Southern History (Vol. 32, November 1966), and Harrison A. Trexler, "The Davis Administration and the Richmond Press, 1861–1865," Journal of Southern History (Vol. 16, May 1950). The effect of the loss of support among southern women is discussed in Drew Gilpin Faust, "Altars of Sacrifice: Confederate Women and the Narratives of War," Journal of Southern History (Vol. 76, March 1990). Grady McWhiney reports on anti-Davis sentiment in the North in the decades following the war in "Jefferson Davis—The Unforgiven," Journal of Mississippi History (Vol. 42, May 1980). William J. Cooper Jr. contradicts Davis's critics in providing a positive view in "A Reassessment of Jefferson Davis as War Leader: The Case from Atlanta to Nashville," Journal of Southern History (Vol. 36, May 1970). How Davis's serious lifelong illnesses negatively impacted his political career is presented in the two-part essay by Harris D. Riley Jr., "Jefferson Davis and His Health, Part I: June, 1808—December, 1860," *Journal of Mississippi History* (Vol. 49, August and November 1987). Frank E. Vandiver, in a positive essay on Davis as president, discusses his critics and the problems he faced in "Jefferson Davis—Leader without Legend," *Journal of Southern History* (Vol. 43, February 1977). For Davis's career following the war, readers may consult W. Stuart Towns, "'To Preserve the Traditions of Our Fathers': The Post-War Speaking Career of Jefferson Davis," *Journal of Mississippi History* (Vol. 52, May 1990).

Davis's Southern Tour, which assured his place on top of the hierarchy of Confederate heroes by the turn of the century, receives scant attention in the literature. Curiously, Varina Davis, in her two-volume biography of her husband, *Jefferson Davis, Ex-President of the Confederate States of America: A Memoir by His Wife* (New York: Belford, 1890), excludes any mention of the tour and treats his death only briefly. The best published treatment of this subject is contained in Hudson Strode, *Jefferson Davis, Tragic Hero, The Last Twenty-Five Years, 1864–1889* (1964; reprint, New York: Harcourt, 2000). Similarly, journal literature is scarce. The tour receives only minor attention in the previously mentioned essay by W. Stuart Towns, and Michael B. Ballard's "Cheers for Jefferson Davis," *Civil War Times Illustrated* (Vol. 16, May 1981), treats only the 1886 portion, giving no mention of the visit to Macon, Georgia, in 1887.

Jefferson Davis's death and funeral are not dealt with extensively in published literature. Ishbel Ross's *First Lady of the South: The Life of Mrs. Jefferson Davis* (New York: Harper & Brothers, 1958), although old, is a good resource for his widow's role in the events surrounding the death, burial, reinterment, and erection of a memorial to her husband. There is, however, a wealth of information in two books issued during the year of his death that were published with the intent of preserving his memory for future generations. The most useful of these is J. William Jones, *The Davis Memorial Volume; or Our Dead President, Jefferson Davis, and the World's Tribute to His Memory* (Richmond, Va.: B. F. Johnson & Company, 1890). This 672-page work is a treasure house of items collected during the period of Davis's death, including biographical writings, tributes, resolutions, newspaper accounts, telegrams sent and received, and miscellaneous other items relating to Davis, his final illness, death, and funeral. Essential to a study of the topic are the previously mentioned work and: *Life and Reminiscences of Jefferson Davis, by Distinguished Men of His Time* (Baltimore: R. H. Woodward & Company, 1890), a collection of biographical and other reminiscences of Davis written by leading southerners and ex-Confederates, collected specifically for this volume.

Journal literature on the Davis funeral is rare. Two of the best were produced for obscure publications of the funeral industry. The only essay to date to treat both the 1889 funeral and the 1893 reinterment is Todd W. Van Beck, "Jefferson Davis, 1808–1889," *American Funeral Director* (Vol. 122, December 1999), which provides a chronology of both events. An earlier article by Seabury Quinn, "The Burial of Jefferson Davis," *American Funeral Director* (Vol. 62, October 1939), is brief but useful. The best essay currently in print on the reinterment is Michael B. Ballard, "Davis' Last Ride to Richmond," *Civil War Times Illustrated* (Vol. 32, 1993). Charles Reagan Wilson's "The Death of Southern Heroes: Historic Funerals of the South," *Southern Cultures* (Vol. 1, 1994) has value, although the treatment of Davis's funeral is minimal.

Given the scant nature of secondary literature concerned with Davis's resurrection in popularity among southerners and the reaction of his former northern enemies to this rise in stature, researchers should turn to two sources written by eyewitnesses to these events, that is, newspaper reports and manuscript materials. These supply what the historical literature omits. The best and most readily available of these are the contemporary newspapers of the period. Many major northern and southern newspapers sent their best reporters to cover the Southern Tour, the funeral of 1889, and the reinterment procession across the South of 1893. Such correspondents as Frank A. Burr of the *New York World*, who rode the Davis train on the Southern Tour, and A. Maurice Low of the *Boston Globe*, who accompanied the funeral train to Richmond in 1893, provided their readers with vivid word pictures of the events as well as interviews with and comments by onlookers and participants. The newspapers of both sections provide, through their editorial pages and news articles, the best evidence of public opinion available for a period before professional polling existed. This value is extended greatly by the practice of printing numerous excerpts of editorials and articles from other newspapers across the country. Many of these newspapers may be found listed in the end notes of this book's chapters.

There is little written on the reinterment of Davis in Richmond and the erection of a Confederate "national" monument to him. *Richmond's Monument Avenue*, by Sarah Shields Driggs, Richard G. Wilson, and Robert P. Winthrop (Chapel Hill: University of North Carolina Press, 2001), devotes a chapter to detailing the history of the Davis monument, from its inception to completion. While this work is of great value, it was carelessly written, with numerous factual errors on virtually every page. Yet, used with care, this is the best publication on the topic.

Readers interested in the history of the quest for and erection of the monument to Davis in the former Confederate capital must of necessity turn to the newspapers of the period, primarily the *Richmond Dispatch*, and manuscript collections. Perhaps the best sources for the story of Richmond's drive for the reburial of the Confederate president and the erection of a statue are those located in the Eleanor S. Brockenborough Library of the Museum of the Confederacy in Richmond. One will find there the papers and scrapbooks of J. Taylor Ellyson, who led the drive for the reinterment and monument, and the records of the Jefferson Davis Monument Association. The scrapbooks include a small number of letters relating to the topic as well as a large number of newspaper clippings. Unfortunately, the latter suffer from a failure to include the sources and dates of many items. The minute books of the monument association are essential to the inner workings of the committee in bringing Davis's remains to Richmond and the erection of the monument.

Index

Brannon, E. E., 57

Breaux, Gus. E., 90

Breckenridge, John C., 11

Brierfield plantation, 3–4, 12, 20, 25, 50–51, 88

Brown, Robert, 98, 114, 119

Bryan, William Jennings, 146

Buchanan, James, 10

Buckner, Simon Bolivar, 70, 140

Burr, Frank A., 27, 28, 29, 31, 32, 34, 35

Burton, Henry S., 19

Butler, Benjamin, 2, 11

Cabell, William L., 135–36, 139

Calhoun, W. L., 135

Cameron, F. H., 113

Carr, Elias, 95, 96, 114

Cass, Lewis, 7

Cave Hill Cemetery, 88

Chaille, Stanford E., 51, 52, 53

Chalaron, J. A., 67

Charlotte, North Carolina, 95; funeral train at, 112

Chatham Academy, 37

Chatham Artillery, 36, 37

Chesterman, W. D., 92

Christian, George L., 92

Civil Rights Movement, 158

Clark, James G., 66

Clay, Henry, 7

Clay, Virginia, 30

Cleburne, Patrick, 15

Cleveland, Grover, 123, 124

Cobb, Mrs. Howell, 35

Cobb's Legion, 43

Colquitt, Alfred H., 42, 43, 108

Columbia, South Carolina, 79; denied visit by funeral train, 96

Comer, H. M., 36

Compromise of 1850, 7, 8

Confederate Association of Kentucky, 88

Confederate Cavalry Association, 60, 62

Confederate Historical Association (Memphis, Tennessee), 89

Confederate Veterans Association, 67

Conrad, Charles M., 60

Cooper, Miles, 53–54, 57, 72; visits Jefferson Davis's deathbed

Corse, Montgomery, 79

Craven, John, 19

Cunningham, S. A., 134

Davis, Clara (niece of Jefferson Davis), 116

Davis, Jefferson, 2–4, 7, 6–12, 13, 14, 15, 20, 25, 49–50, 50–53, 76, 79; acceptance of national reconciliation, 38, 45, 156; adviser to Franklin Pierce, 8–9; adviser to James Buchanan, 10; appearance in death of, 65, 73, 99; association with Zachary Taylor, 3, 6–7, 10; belief in states' rights, 2, 6–10, 13–15, 19–20; burial sites and, 61, 87–93; centralization of Confederate government by, 15; coffin of, description, 99; comments on, by African Americans, 57–58, 66, 69, 106; criticism of, 2, 14, 15–16, 18, 38–39, 55–57, 123–125, 153, 157–158; and Davis Land Company, 80–81; death mask of, 50–53, 66, 90; decline in public image, 149; early life, 2–5; early military service of, 4–6; election of 1860 and, 10–11; flight from Richmond and capture, 17; funeral of (1889), 60–78, 93, 119–21; health of, 2, 3, 8, 10; health impact of, on Jefferson Davis's presidency, 13–14, 20, 44–45, 51; image of, carved on Stone Mountain, Georgia, 149; imprisonment in Fort Monroe, 1–2, 18–19; lying in state (1889), 63–71; lying in state (1893), 100–101, 104–6, 108–10, 114–15, 117–19; Missouri Compromise, opposition to, 9; Nationalist Democrat, 2, 6–12; Northern opinion of, post-war, 122–25; opposition in Southern press, 15–16; personal relations of, with slaves, 2–4; post-war

About the Author

Donald E. Collins is a native of Miami, Florida. He attended Vanderbilt University and received the bachelor's degree in history from Florida State University and the master's and Ph.D. in history at the University of Georgia in 1975. His early specialization was the internment of Japanese Americans in western concentration camps during World War II. His book *Native American Aliens: Disloyalty and Renunciation of Citizenship by Japanese Americans during World War II* is widely regarded as one of the most important books in that field. His book *Libraries and Research* went through several editions and was used as a textbook in several universities. Since joining the Department of History at East Carolina University in 1992, he has done work on the Confederate national flags, Jefferson Davis, and the Civil War in eastern North Carolina. He contributed chapters to Steven Woodworth's *The Art of Command in the Civil War* and *The Human Tradition in the Civil War and Reconstruction*, as well as articles in historical encyclopedias and other works. He retired in July 2003 and is currently working on history of the Second North Carolina Union Volunteer Regiment. He lives in Greenville, North Carolina.

THE AMERICAN CRISIS SERIES

Books on the Civil War Era

Steven E. Woodworth, Associate Professor of History, Texas Christian University
Series Editor